# THE JEWS
# OF SUMMER

STANFORD STUDIES IN JEWISH HISTORY AND CULTURE
Edited by David Biale and Sarah Abrevaya Stein

# THE JEWS OF SUMMER

## SUMMER CAMP AND JEWISH CULTURE IN POSTWAR AMERICA

SANDRA FOX

STANFORD UNIVERSITY PRESS
Stanford, California

Stanford University Press
Stanford, California

Printed in the United States of America on acid-free, archival-quality paper

Library of Congress Cataloging-in-Publication Data
Names: Fox, Sandra, 1988- author.
Title: The Jews of summer : summer camp and Jewish culture in postwar America / Sandra Fox.
Other titles: Stanford studies in Jewish history and culture.
Description: Stanford, California : Stanford University Press, 2023. | Series: Stanford studies in Jewish history and culture | Includes bibliographical references and index.
Identifiers: LCCN 2022019302 (print) | LCCN 2022019303 (ebook) | ISBN 9781503632936 (cloth) | ISBN 9781503633889 (paperback) | ISBN 9781503633896 (ebook)
Subjects: LCSH: Jewish camps—United States—History—20th century. | Jewish youth—Recreation—United States—History—20th century. | Jews—United States—Social life and customs—20th century. | United States—Social life and customs—1945-1970. | United States—Social life and customs—1971-
Classification: LCC BM135 .F69 2023 (print) | LCC BM135 (ebook) | DDC 796.54/22—dc23/eng/20220608
LC record available at https://lccn.loc.gov/2022019302
LC ebook record available at https://lccn.loc.gov/2022019303

Typeset by Elliott Beard in Garamond Premier Pro 11/15
Cover design by Gia Giasullo
Cover photograph: Beth and Sharon, Camp Boiberik, 1973. Photographer unknown.

*To Grandma, with love*

# Contents

# Acknowledgments

IT IS NOT LOST ON me, a historian who thinks a lot about age, that working on this project carried me through a period psychologists call "emerging adulthood," anchoring me through a number of big life moments. Over that time, I have been honored to be in conversation with colleagues, mentors, and friends of many generations, absorbing their wisdom and sustained by their warmth and kindness. I am moved to have a formal opportunity to acknowledge them.

I began to undertake the research on which this book is based at New York University's Skirball Department of Hebrew and Judaic Studies, where I received support from the Graduate School of Arts and Sciences, the Goldstein-Goren Center for American Jewish History, the Taub Center for Israel Studies, and the Graduate Research Initiative. Additional research grants from the American Jewish Archives, the Association for Jewish Studies, and the Ben-Gurion Research Institute for the Study of Israel and Zionism helped make my research possible during my graduate work and in the year immediately after. Most significant, the Jim Joseph Postdoctoral Fellowship at Stanford University ensured that I had the time and resources to complete this book. I am forever grateful to all the committees and individuals who selected me and this project for these fellowships.

Many archivists and librarians patiently assisted me throughout the years, including Ilya Slavutskiy, Melanie Meyers, Sara Belasco, and many others at the Center for Jewish History. I am also thankful to Dana Herman at the American Jewish Archives, Ina Cohen and Rabbi Jerry Schwarzbard at the Jewish Theological Seminary, Shulamith Berger at the Yeshiva University Library, and the staff at the Tamiment Library at NYU. I wholeheartedly thank my editor, Margo Irvin, and the entire team at Stanford University Press for believing in this book and for shepherding it through the publishing process with the utmost professionalism.

Dozens of former campers supplied me with camp photographs, documents, and memories, and answered clarification questions I posed on alumni Facebook groups when archival documents did not suffice. I thank each of them for their openness and willingness to help. Their recollections and contributions bettered this book in every way.

While the pandemic got in the way of my spending much time in Palo Alto, I treasure the time I spent as a postdoctoral fellow within Stanford University's Concentration in Education and Jewish Studies and thank Ari Kelman for being such a staunch supporter of me and my work. I am so grateful to Jonathan Zimmerman, whose perspective as a historian of education and his generous feedback during the early phases of this project deeply shaped the final product. Ofer Shiff supported me through my first year after graduate school as a postdoctoral fellow at Ben-Gurion University and has remained a friend and mentor in the years since. I cannot thank him enough for his support and for all the meaningful conversations we had on trips back and forth to Sde Boker.

Having attended graduate school a mere eight city blocks away from my undergraduate institution, I have remained in regular contact with many of my professors from Eugene Lang College, the New School for Liberal Arts, whose style of learning and commitment to questioning is in the very DNA of this book. Val Vinokur, Jeremy Varon, and Oz Frankel have continued to offer me astounding professional guidance, mentorship, and friendship in the eleven years since my graduation, and I am eternally grateful to all three for their support and generosity.

I have been lucky to have a wider community of fellow historians, interlocutors, and readers of my work, including Shari Rabin, Elia Etkin, Beny Hary, Melissa Klapper, Geoffrey Levin, Shayna Weiss, Noah Efron, Matthew Berkman, Joshua Friedman, Rachel Kranson, Laura Levitt, Rachel Gross, Liora Halperin, Dekel Canetti, and Sasha Senderovitch. Thank you all for your support and friendship over the years. I am also grateful for my Yiddish family, including my fellow editors at *In geveb: A Journal of Yiddish Studies*; the listeners, supporters, and participants of *Vaybertaytsh: A Feminist Podcast in Yiddish*; and the many teachers and friends who made my Yiddish voice possible: Gennady Estraikh, Naftali Ejdelman, Yankl-Peretz Blum, Rivke Galpern, Miriam Trinh, and Eliezer Niborksi.

Of all my mentors and supporters, I am most thankful to Hasia Diner. Hasia always goes above and beyond the call of duty when it comes to supporting me. A brilliant historian and a thoughtful, honest, and exacting critic, she remains my most important reader, as well as my fiercest advocate. Her voice, wisdom, and commitment to scholarly integrity guided me through every stage of this project. I can only hope that the final product does justice to her belief in me as a scholar and as a human being.

My friends are my family, and it takes a lot of restraint not to list every one of them. I am beyond grateful for my relationships with Hannah Grossman and Reuben Karchem, who kept me sane and smiling through all the years of research and writing. Beginning as camp friends, we have been fortunate to be neighbors over the past several years, nurturing our childhood friendships into adulthood. Hannah's commitment and approaches to experiential Jewish education inspire me and undeniably shaped how I thought about the Jewish educators I wrote about in this book. I am proud to be her friend. I am overwhelmed by appreciation for another camp friend, Shifra Whiteman, who introduced me to the possibility of a Yiddish-speaking life when I was only a kid in her house in Queens. *A dank zeyer.* For all of the years in Brooklyn and Tel Aviv, my heart is filled with love for so many. Special thanks to Sarah Knapp, Hanna Sender, and Raviva Hanser for fifteen years of friendship in New York City, to Abi Goodman and Mayrav Weiss for making Tel Aviv feel more and more like home, and to Tammy Cohen and Eric Salitsky z"l for ten years of love and support in both cities. As I watch Eric's Jewish camp and youth movement communities come together to mourn his untimely death, I am reminded of the intense bonds of friendship these institutions cultivate, lasting years beyond childhood. May Eric's memory be a blessing to us all.

My father, Bruce, a professional editor, offered me free editing services at various stages of the process. Please refer any complaints about typos and errors to him. His belief and pride in me are unparalleled, and I thank him for being my biggest cheerleader. Thanks to my stepmother, Sara Watkin-Fox, for being such an important source of support in my life and for making sure I ended up at Camp Young Judaea Sprout Lake in 1998. My brother, Harry Watkin-Fox, was a bar mitzvah boy when I began this book; he is now a bright and promising college student. I hope that having this book in his dorm room will bring him a smile. I also thank Ron, Tammy, and the entire Unger clan in Rehovot and Jerusalem for welcoming me into their warm and beautiful family with open arms. Facing the adversity of a mother debilitated by illness, I was more than a little lucky to have my energetic, loving, and fabulous grandma, Barbara Roaman, who stepped up to mother a child, teenager, and young adult through her sixties, seventies, and eighties. At ninety-one years old today, she is my rock and greatest confidant. I dedicate this book to her.

For my mother, Lisa Roaman: I keep her memory close to my heart always, especially in big life moments such as these.

I met my husband, Amir Unger, at the very moment this project came into being, and our love for one another has carried me through every step of the way. A brilliant and creative mind, he has been an incomparable support system, sounding board, and source of ideas over the years. He even came up with the title of this book! Amir has never allowed the challenges that come our way stop us from building a beautiful life together, whether it be the six thousand miles between our hometowns, the precarity of the academic job market, or bureaucracy and borders during a pandemic. I cannot thank Amir enough for his love and support and for making this period of my life sweeter than I could have ever imagined.

# THE JEWS
# OF SUMMER

# INTRODUCTION

# The Jewish Camp

## Between Fantasy and Reality

IN THE LATE 1960S, A group of campers at Camp Hemshekh, a Yiddish cultural sleepaway camp in upstate New York, took a field trip to see a local theater production of *Fiddler on the Roof.* At Hemshekh, campers spoke Yiddish on a daily basis, immersed themselves in the literature and history of Ashkenazi Jewry, and commemorated the recent Holocaust through celebrating and emulating the Yiddish-speaking culture that thrived in the past. To one counselor named Jo, watching *Fiddler* that day evoked a surprising feeling, less like watching a fictionalized depiction of the past than "an expression" of life at Hemshekh, causing the campers to "feel very much like the 'chosen people.'" As the group watched the play, and "more importantly, watch(ed) the rest of the audience watch the play," they "felt almost as though [they] were in on a very special secret." After the campers ended the night of performances by singing Yiddish songs to the "audience of bewildered up-starters," Jo experienced "an inescapable feeling of authenticity." Drawing a clear line of distinction between the audience—vacationing, middle-class Jews from New York's city and suburbs for whom *Fiddler* reflected a nostalgic past—and the Hemshekh campers and counselors, who saw themselves as active defenders of and participants in the culture onstage, Jo distinguished camp life, and the kinds of Jews campers became through it, from mainstream American Jewish culture, detached from their cultural inheritance and from real Jewishness as she understood it.[1]

Placing Yiddishism, a nineteenth-century Jewish linguistic nationalism, and Bundism, a Jewish form of socialism rooted in Europe, at the center of its mission, the leaders of Camp Hemshekh, many of them Holocaust survivors, operated on a different political wavelength from the vast majority of American Jews at the time. By the late 1960s, not only had Yiddish ceased to be an everyday vernacular among most American Jews; most Jews had also worked to disentangle themselves from the kinds of socialist or communist ideas that Hemshekh promoted in response to the intense scrutiny Jews faced under McCarthyism.[2] In comparison to well-known summer camp networks like Ramah, Hemshekh had a small population, serving around a hundred campers each year at one campsite. But while Hemshekh represented a marginal ideology with a shrinking audience, Jo's description of the camp's *Fiddler* excursion mirrored the purposes of a much wider variety of postwar Jewish summer camps: to bring children and teenagers closer to their leaders' or movements' particular visions of authentic Jewishness, conceptions based on those of Jews from other times, like prewar Eastern Europe, or fantasies of an ideal, contemporary elsewhere, primarily in Israel.

Camp leaders' interests in simulating other times and places had much to do with how they felt about their current moment and locale: postwar America. While American Jews had steadily begun their climb into middle-classness prior to World War II, Jewish soldiers returning home from the war found themselves catapulted into middle-class comfort, benefiting from housing loans and educational scholarships offered to white veterans. As they moved from cities to suburbs, the synagogue center, with its sisterhoods, men's clubs, and other social offerings, provided new Jewish suburbanites official and tangible ways to affiliate with Judaism, replacing the informal, neighborhood-based affiliations of urban communities earlier in the century. Furthermore, mirroring middle-class America's mounting focus on the child during the baby boom, children and adolescents became the center of Jewish communal priorities.[3] Coinciding with what many have described as a "golden age" for American Judaism—a time marked by social

Hemshekh campers dressed as Jewish tailors from the
turn of the twentieth century, late 1960s.
Source: Kolodny Family Photos. Printed with permission.

mobility, affluence, and suburbanization, and the development of what Herbert Gans coined as "child-centered Judaism"—the period saw the dramatic growth of synagogue Hebrew schools, nursery schools, youth groups, and, indeed, summer camps.[4]

Growing affluence and rising social status clearly afforded American Jews great benefits. As they climbed the educational and professional ladder, most happily embraced their new standing and the material and psychological comforts that came with it. The sizable and attractive synagogue buildings and Jewish community centers that Jews built reflected their comfort in postwar suburbia and their plans to stay there for the long haul. At the same time, these dramatic socioeconomic transitions also provoked deep anxieties among communal leaders. As historians Rachel Kranson and Lila Corwin Berman have demonstrated, many Jews felt intensely ambivalent about their socioeconomic ascent, worrying that Jewish cultural authenticity would not survive the ease of affluence.[5] Rather than celebrating their new place in American society, educators, rabbis, lay leaders, journalists, and others projected these concerns onto youth and parents in particular, citing a growing need to develop Jewish identity in children.[6]

Ironically, the affluence at the heart of their concerns about authenticity proved essential in the Jewish camping sector's ability to flourish. In the early twentieth century, thousands of Jewish children attended philanthropic camps that served immigrants and the children of immigrants, or smaller, private camps for the middle- and upper-class Jewish elite. But postwar Jews had more resources to put toward their children's education and recreation and the enjoyment of their own child-free summers. The more that families could afford to send children to camp, the more the yearly migration of the young from Jewish urban neighborhoods and suburbs to the American countryside became a distinguishing element of Jewish middle-classness and, for thousands of young Jews, a rite of passage.[7] This sunny economic picture also meant that Jewish movements and institutions had the ability to purchase acres of land, where they built modern, comfortable, and permanent campsites and could provide scholarships for families who could not afford camp without assistance. The Jewish summer camp thus offers a unique lens for examining tensions between the postwar period's goldenness and ambivalence. Rather than sitting in contradiction, the affluence, comfort, social mobility, and anxiety over cultural decline that Jews experienced fed off of each other, pushing Jewish culture and communal life into new directions. The educational or ideological summer camp was one such direction, the dazzling homogeneity of camps' structures and methods over the course of the postwar period revealing their leaders' underlying shared hopes and dreams: that camping could counteract the downsides of the present, propelling "positive," "real," or "authentic" Jewishness forward into the future.

The full realizations of the Holocaust's devastation added a level of urgency to their distress about the state of postwar Jewishness. Without European Jewry to look to and with Israel's future uncertain, postwar American Jewish leaders saw themselves as responsible for carrying Judaism and Jewish culture forward into the future. At Camp Hemshekh, remembering the Holocaust played an exceptionally central role in everyday life. To Jo and other Hemshekh attendees at the performance, *Fiddler on the Roof* represented not only a nostalgic picture of shtetl life but an all-but-vanished Ashkenazi Yiddish-speaking civilization that the camp memorialized and tried to resurrect in a new form. Many Hemshekh campers also had parents who had survived the Holocaust and found at their small camp a community of fellow second-generation survivors who understood the specific pains and difficulties that came with having survivor parents. While Hemshekh's profile was specific, memorializing the Holocaust permeated camps across the ideological spectrum, the genocide's very recency employed by camp leaders to make counselors and campers take their camp's mission seriously. For many Jewish educators, producing educational, immersive, and affective Jewish camp experiences in the Holocaust's aftermath was a matter of cultural life or death, of continuity or discontinuity.

For all these reasons, a vast array of Jewish movements and organizations founded dozens of heavily educational camps in the 1940s and 1950s, while many of the Jewish camps that had been established in the 1920s transformed their missions to answer to the new concerns of the postwar moment. Camps affiliated with Zionist movements, Yiddish cultural institutions, and the Conservative and Reform movements of Judaism were by far the most emblematic of these trends. These were not the only Jewish camps of the period. Dozens of camps sponsored by the Young Men's Hebrew Association or Jewish Community Center movement included some cultural and religious practices throughout the postwar era, as did some private summer camps owned by Jewish families. But the amount of Jewish education such camps integrated into their programs varied immensely from site to site, director to director, and year to year. Communal camps eventually came to put a more intense focus on Jewish education as child-serving Jewish institutions of all kinds became more deeply influenced by rising concerns over assimilation. From the 1940s through the 1960s, however, Zionist, Yiddishist, Reform, and Conservative camps stood out in the degree to which religious, political, and linguistic ideologies shaped the details of everyday camp life and how much energy their leaders invested in inculcating youth with their Jewish beliefs, practices, cultural touchstones, and political attitudes. While other Jewish camps make cameos in this book, these four kinds sit at the center of its analysis.

Camping leaders of these four ideological types disagreed with one another on a variety of issues; even those of the same type held conflicting ideas when it came to the details of their Zionism, Yiddishism, Jewish-language ideologies, religiosity, or secularism. Their camps also differed in the kinds of Jewish families they served when it came to religious observance, economic background, and politics. Because of these differences, most of the previous scholarship on Jewish camping has looked at camps of one type or another, emphasizing the uniqueness of their programs, ideologies, and missions, describing what made such camps distinctive.[8] Much of the literature has also focused on the founders and ideologues behind Jewish summer camping, painting a picture of the emergence of camping within the history of Jewish education or the unique histories of different movements. The essential book on the history of American summer camping in the early twentieth century, Leslie Paris's *Children's Nature: The Rise of the American Summer Camp*, included some private and philanthropic Jewish camps within its broader range of subjects, contextualizing their place in the foundational years of American camping writ large. More recently, Sarah Bunin Benor, Jonathan Krasner, and Sharon Avni's *Hebrew Infusion: Language and Community at American Jewish Summer Camps* offered a unique historical and linguistic study of how camps' Hebrew "infusion practices" evolved over the course of the twentieth century and continue to play out in the present.[9] These works, alongside myriad other social-scientific, educational, and historical studies, have combined to make Jewish camping far and away what one Christian camping scholar called "the most well-researched branch of religious camping."[10]

Building off these works, *The Jews of Summer* takes the subject of Jewish camping in several new directions. First and foremost, this book focuses less on what makes these camps unique than on how diverse movements employed the camping idea in strikingly similar ways. Camping leaders had distinctive visions regarding which Jewish language should take precedence, whether to invest their energies in Israel or the diaspora, or how much religious ritual to include. Much of the focus of the following chapters is placed on how these differences shaped everyday life within various kinds of camps. While holding their differences in mind, however, this book focuses more on how camps' diverse leaders came to agree that nationalism, language, and various forms of Jewish practice should be harnessed to transform Jewish children. What this mutual agreement and mission articulated about the anxieties that pervaded postwar Jewish culture and how those anxieties shaped the everyday experiences of campers are the central topics driving this book.

Second, *The Jews of Summer* pays long-overdue attention to the history of Yiddish summer camps, and of Yiddishism more broadly, in postwar America. Scholars of American Jewish history have chronicled the rise of Reform and Conservative camping movements, highlighting how they transformed Jewish camping to match their visions of an intelligent and capable lay leadership; others have centered their work on Zionist camps, where camp leaders promoted Hebrew culture and aimed to build support for the Jewish state. While work on prewar secular Yiddish education lay the foundation for future studies, however, practically nothing has been written until now about these camps after World War II, as if they simply ceased to exist.[11] This lack of attention matches trends in scholarship regarding postwar Yiddish more generally. As Jeffrey Shandler has argued, "More often than not, discussions of Yiddish culture terminate in 1939, 1948, or some other date, with any later phenomena involving the language either characterized as vestigial or not mentioned at all."[12]

Yiddish culture undoubtedly declined during the postwar decades due to the loss of millions of Yiddish speakers during the Holocaust, American Jewish linguistic assimilation, Soviet repression, Zionist anti-Yiddish attitudes, and American anticommunism. And yet it did not disappear entirely from the American scene, remaining particularly integral to the educational missions of several summer camps. Instead, American Yiddishists and their institutions struggled with their purposes and ideologies in the decades following the Holocaust and ultimately transformed them into symbolic tools that better fit a monolingual American context. Studying their camps not only reveals something about American Yiddishism's evolution after the Holocaust, however; it also helps to explain how and why Yiddish cultural and linguistic activism have become meaningful engines of identity for thousands of Jewish young people in more recent decades. Rather than emerging suddenly, the perceived Yiddish revival that began around the mid-2000s actually relied on an unbroken generational chain of cultural keepers, creators, and teachers, many of whom were educated and inspired by camps like Hemshekh, Boiberik, and Kinderland.[13] For a broader range of readers who may have no interest in Yiddish, moreover, Yiddish camps may expose something even more significant: that Jewish educational camps once nurtured a larger range of Jewish ideas and identities, not only looking to Israel and religious practice as their primary transformational tools, but toward diaspora Jewish culture, cosmopolitanism, social justice, and notions of Jewish secularism. The diverse ideologies of Jewish camps past reveal the possibilities within a broadened American Jewish educational, political, and cultural paradigm.

As a history of Jewish youth and childhood, *The Jews of Summer* also represents a turn in the studies of both postwar Jewry and American Jewish education. The story of Jewish summer camping has thus far been told mainly through the eyes of the educators, ideologues, and rabbis—mostly male and many middle-aged—who constructed and directed camps with dreams of molding the next generation of young Jews. But while this book pays significant attention to this cohort, adults ultimately constituted the minority of camps' populations, their missions and plans representing only one side of a more nuanced story. Indeed, all American summer camps, as Leslie Paris writes, "flourished through intergenerational negotiation, a significant degree of permissiveness, and attention to children's peer culture."[14] Jewish children and teenagers were no different from their non-Jewish peers, arriving seeking fun, freedom, play, escape, and romance, and generally prioritizing these other elements over camps' ideological missions. While leaders formulated their missions in advance of the summer, life at camp proved much more complicated. To make a mark on campers, staff had to endeavor to get their buy-in, answering to their needs, desires, and interests. This dynamic made Jewish camps sites of ongoing intergenerational negotiation, debates, and dialogues that occurred both aloud and in the unspoken space between what adults wanted camps to accomplish and what actually happened on the ground.

Dynamics between adult and youth, child and teen, staff and camper not only shaped the texture of everyday life within camps, but reconstituted American Jewish culture in and outside them, with lasting implications. Using oral history, sources about children and teenagers from the point of view of adults, and sources written by children and teens themselves, I aim to bring out the myriad ways that young people shaped camp life. Because camps' abilities to succeed educationally and economically fundamentally required the buy-in of campers, children and teenagers wielded tremendous power within the camp environment in their everyday reactions, their decisions to engage or disengage, to nod in agreement or roll an eye in defiance. As the following chapters show, the desires and interests of campers guided

Campers at Cejwin having an impromptu water fight, late 1960s.
Source: Marlene Greenman Heller. Printed with permission.

how much camp leaders pushed campers to speak Yiddish and Hebrew, the kinds of educational programs staff created to support their approaches to Jewish practice and ritual, and how they would come to employ campers' interests in sex and romance toward the goal of encouraging Jewish marriages. Campers and young counselors also influenced the very ideologies camp leaders came to highlight. From the 1960s onward, for instance, modes of Zionist camping once unique to socialist Zionist youth movements like Habonim and Hashomer Hatzair became popular in a much wider array of Jewish camps, including those of the Reform and Conservative movements. A growing focus on Israel correlated with the broader American Jewish embrace of a prouder, louder, and more public Zionism matched the fervent Zionism of many camping leaders themselves. But focusing on Israeli heroism and pride proved more inspirational to young people than looking at the past in the wake of the Holocaust. The collective nature of the kibbutz also provided a natural bridge with the youthful Jewish counterculture of the period, and images of Israeli strength and beauty meshed well with an embrace of Jewish ethnicity also fueled by the countercultural young. Looking at camps from the top down and bottom up reveals that leaders of the postwar period came to harness Zionist symbols, ideas, and practices not only as a result of their own growing Zionist sentiments, but because doing so resonated with the American youth in their midst.

By highlighting and acknowledging the sway campers held in the camp environment, I do not mean to minimize the more overt power and authority of adults. As the leaders, builders, and funders of American Jewish summer camps, adults played main roles, generating the environment for camper culture to flourish. Parents held tremendous power as they chose which camps to send their children to, basing their decisions on not only programmatic offerings and ideologies but cost and location. Jewish groups chose what kinds of camps to promote to their members and which to support financially, while prominent organizations such as the American Camping Association created codes of conduct for staff, as well as systems of accreditation, exercising serious control over camping writ large.[15] State and local governments also played an important role in the daily running of camps as they updated and expanded laws regarding conduct with children and health and safety regulations throughout the 1960s and 1970s.

At the same time, even the seemingly simple categories such as "adult" and "youth" require reconsideration when studying summer camps. Only a few years older than the eldest campers, counselors occupied a crucial yet blurry in-between position within this generational divide. Serving as the on-the-ground enactors of their leaders' visions of a repaired American Jewish culture, counselors ultimately implemented most of camps' daily programs and worked most directly and intimately with the children in their bunks. In late high school or college, counselors brought their own youth culture to camp with them, arriving with similar interests in fun, freedom, dating, and sexuality as did adolescent campers.[16] With only a handful of middle-aged and older adults in attendance at a given time, summer camps were overwhelmingly shaped by the desires and interests of the young, and even sometimes the very young, with campers starting as early as age six or seven in the postwar decades. *The Jews of Summer* places special attention on these age-based categories, providing an opportunity to consider the crucial yet often unexamined roles of intergenerational negotiation, age, children, and youth in American Jewish life.

I highlight the voices of campers wherever possible, and much of my focus is on the experiences and reactions of teenagers. While younger children ages seven to twelve appear in various parts of the book and attended many of the same activities and programs as did older ones, teenage campers left more of a mark on camp archives. Although I offer their voices, I also seek to avoid the pitfalls of focusing on the question of agency, which has occupied historians of children and youth since the beginning of the field's coalescence, often to the detriment of other fruitful questions.[17] Due to the field's connection to children's rights and the fact that historians of childhood and youth are often pressed by other historians to defend their focus on the young as worthwhile, this examination of agency is understandable: it gives the subject of children and youth immediate importance and connects the field to the kinds of questions that once occupied scholars of the history of women. But as historian Mona Gleason has argued, historians of youth and children must begin to go beyond the "agency trap," the field's focus on proving the agency of the young often in ways that obscure other questions and subjects, if they want to bring youth's "contributions to change over time [to] emerge in sharper relief." Using empathic reference, or "the ability to imagine and to interpret historical events and sources from the point of view of young people," this book aims to do just that, offering an assessment of not only "the messier 'in between' of more nuanced and negotiated exchanges between and among children" but also their negotiations with leaders and educators of various ages and stages. Campers, moreover, shaped life at camp not only in moments of rebellion, but in moments of acquiescence to their elders; not only in times of agency and separation from adult authority but in times of coalescence and meeting in the middle.[18] In this way, *The Jews of Summer* points to the importance of considering age in the study of Jewish history and to the uses of going beyond agency in the history of childhood and youth.

Finally, this book sets the stage for further research on the history of postwar American camping more broadly. Jews were far from alone in recognizing the potential power of sleepaway camps after World War II. As a growth period for both religious denominations and the American economy, Christians similarly expanded their summer camping sector in the postwar years, with leaders in "the major Protestant traditions . . . convinced of the potential of the summer camp experience for Christian education," according to Sorensen, and evangelicals "identif[ying] the summer camp model as fertile ground for conversion and religious experience."[19] That Jews followed a similar time line as Christians provides a new and important layer of understanding to what made the early 1940s through the early 1950s what Jonathan Sarna called Jewish camping's "crucial decade."[20] At the same time, Jewish and Christian camps also diverged in significant ways. Christian camps operated for a standard session of only five to seven days, taking inspiration from the conference model and camp meetings of the Second Great Awakening, a period of Protestant religious revival that took place in the early nineteenth century. While some postwar Christian camps, particularly those in the Northeast serving a clientele of middle- and upper-middle-class Protestants, operated for longer sessions, these camps proved less common within the world of Christian camping both postwar and today.[21] Catholic organizational camps and the handful of contemporary camps for Muslim children in the United States and Canada have also adopted this shorter-term conference model.[22] While the Reform movement's summer camps emerged out of five- to ten-day youth conclaves that matched the conference model, Jewish camps generally came to embrace a four- to eight-week summer camping model rooted in the turn-of-the-century Northeast and Midwest. In the case of Zionist, Reform, and Conservative movements, camp sessions lasting two to four weeks became the norm, in many cases even as their camps expanded to the South and the West, where camp sessions longer than a week proved far less common in the broader American camping sector. Religiously affiliated sleepaway camps are by no means unique to Jews, but Jews are seemingly the only religious or ethnic group in the United States that has embraced these longer sessions as standard. That most Jewish campers spend more time at camp each year and often return to the same camp year after year undoubtedly adds to the weight that camping has taken on in American Jewish culture and childhood, helping to explain why camps serving a tiny minority of Americans constitute some of the most studied American camps. Further historical research regarding a more diverse set of postwar camps, including Christian, Muslim, nonsectarian, scouting, sport, and arts camps would allow for more fruitful and detailed comparisons. It is my hope that this book is the first stone laid in the foundation of a much broader history of postwar American camping.

## A Brief Historical Overview

The paradigm of the postwar Jewish camp cannot be understood without examining the foundational years of American and American Jewish camping that preceded it. In the Progressive Era, Jews, alongside fresh air reformers, the Boy Scouts of America, settlement house organizations, and Christian congregations, began to build residential summer camps for children. Providing a reprieve from what progressives saw as the deleterious effects of urban life on immigrant children, philanthropic Jewish camps offered recreation in nature with the comfort of socializing with one's coreligionists, while private camps for middle-class children offered an opportunity for families denied entry to, or left unaccommodated by, predominantly Christian camps. In the 1920s, a small number of new camps, built by Hebraist, Yiddish-oriented, Zionist, and Jewish educational organizations, were established, incorporating some elements of Jewish study, leadership training, and language learning.

In an industry focused on recreation, immersion in nature, socialization, and Americanization, camps with intensely Jewish missions were originally on the margins of the Jewish camping sector, although this began to change in the years between the two world wars.[23] With origins in the European Haskalah, nineteenth-century Zionism, Hebraism, and Yiddishism developed as distinct and often clashing cultural and nationalistic worldviews, while German advocates for Reform and Positive Historical Judaism, Conservative Judaism's forerunner, offered two different paths to religious liberalization and modernization.[24] When they arrived on American soil, however, all of these movements moved in new directions, aiming to reconcile Judaism with modernity while seeking to balance their new status in American society. As they sought this balance, all five of these movements turned their attention to the next generation, seeing residential summer camps as particularly valuable to their goals.

Zionist movements built some of the earliest summer camps, beginning in the late 1920s. They revved up in earnest in the 1940s, buoyed by increasing American enthusiasm for the project in the years leading up to and following Israel's establishment in 1948. Affiliated with the youth movements such as Young Judaea, Hashomer Hatzair, Habonim, and B'nei Akiva, or with Hebraist organizations and Hebrew teachers' colleges, these camps engaged with "Hebrew culture," focusing their educational agenda on promoting Zionism and, after 1948, teaching about the nascent State of Israel.[25] Zionism was not a singular enterprise, and neither was Zionist summer camping. Young Judaea's camps imbued campers with a pluralist approach to Zionism, while Habonim and Hashomer Hatzair's camps were explicitly socialist; B'nei Akiva, serving a more Orthodox clientele, centered itself on religious Zionism, while Camp Massad focused its Zionist energies chiefly on Hebraism. Nevertheless, these movements shared many of the same methods, ideals, and visions, with the imagined lifestyles of the "New Jews" of Palestine and, later, Israel permeating life throughout all their camps.[26] No matter the kind of Zionism a camp adhered to, Israel and Israeliness functioned as a counterpoint to American postwar comfort that educators used in their efforts to foster pride, identity, and purpose in campers.[27]

At their outsets, Yiddish-oriented summer camps of the 1920s primarily provided recreational escapes from the city for Yiddish supplementary school students or the children of labor movement members, mainly Yiddish-speaking children of recent immigrants to the United States. But by the beginning of the postwar period, the leaders of Camps Boiberik, Kinderring, Kinderland, and Hemshekh came to hold similar concerns about the decline of Jewish culture in America as their Zionist counterparts, citing the diminishing place of Yiddish in American life as concrete evidence. As campers arrived with less and less Yiddish knowledge, these once-mixed Yiddish- and English-speaking camps became increasingly educational and ideological, their responses to linguistic decline amplified by the Holocaust's role in the near decimation of European Jewish culture.[28] Like Zionist camps, Yiddish camps had a variety of political affinities: some promoted socialism, others communism, some socialist Zionism, and others Bundism. But as the Cold War and McCarthyism made these affiliations precarious, the specificities of their politics faded somewhat in exchange for a focus on Yiddish culture, cosmopolitanism, and social justice. Role-playing the Jews of Eastern Europe, Yiddish writers and intellectuals, and labor movement activists, these camps worked to bring campers' cultural inheritance to life, performing as stand-ins for a world destroyed by concentration camps. For generations of American children who would never know that world first-hand, Yiddish summer camps became "Yiddishlands."[29]

Reform and Conservative movement summer camps entered the sector in the late 1940s.[30] In their efforts to produce ideal future movement leaders, these camps modeled immersive Jewish lifestyles and focused on teaching Jewish texts, prayers, songs, and the Hebrew language, and interwove Jewish religious rituals into everyday life. These camps shared many qualities. Both movements gradually expanded their camps across the country, emphasized leadership development, wrestled at their outsets with the place of Zionism in camp, involved campers in leading prayer and ritual, and ultimately came to influence their streams of Judaism back at home. But the myriad differences between Reform and Conservative Judaism also exposed themselves in camp life. The Ramah camps proved more traditional in their approaches to religion than their Reform counterparts, had more rigorous formal education programs and selective admissions processes, and proved more Hebraist in orientation. Reform camps, in contrast, experimented with formal education and eventually came to uniformly embrace Hebrew learning but came to more enthusiastically embrace informal education, role-playing activities, and emphatic song sessions than did Ramah camps. And yet both sets of camps similarly functioned as incubators for their movements, inspiring campers through Jewish practice, text, and language, an immersive experience of "Jewish living."[31]

As Jews experienced new economic and social conditions, and along with them new anxieties about the Jewish future, the 1940s through the early 1950s irrefutably marked a moment of dramatic expansion in the field of educational Jewish camping, with the notion of using camps to transform Jewish youth taking on a new weight. Several new independent educational camps, like Camp Lown, Camp Sharon, and Camp Yavneh, opened in the mid-1940s as extensions of Jewish community organizations, schools, and teachers' colleges.[32] Zionist camping grew significantly as American Jewry's passion for the cause of Zionism grew in the years up to 1948, with passionate Hebraists founding Hebrew-speaking Camp Massad in 1941, and with Young Judaea's first flagship program for teenagers, Camp Tel Yehu-dah, starting in 1948.[33] By 1966, twenty-eight Zionist camps existed, with the number of campers at an average of six thousand each year.[34] Even the Yiddish camps changed in the postwar years, becoming more overtly educa-tional and ideological in the face of Yiddish decline.[35]

The most influential and robust products of the 1940s and 1950s, however, were the camps affiliated with the Reform and Conservative movements of Judaism. Stimulated by the growth of their movements in postwar suburbia, Reform and Conservative summer camps centered their programs on Jewish religion, culture, and ritual, with the aim of supplementing their movements' religious schools and youth groups by "giv[ing] each camper a direct personal experience in Jewish living."[36] The Ramah camps, run by the Jewish Theolog-ical Seminary of the Conservative movement, began with the goal of "cre-at[ing] an indigenous Conservative movement—both lay and rabbinic—that would perpetuate the movement into the next generation."[37] The first Ramah site opened in Wisconsin in 1947, with the establishment of other Ramah sites across the country following throughout the 1950s and 1960s: Ramah Poconos in Pennsylvania in 1950, Ramah New England in Massachusetts in 1953, Ramah California in 1956, Ramah Canada in 1960, and Ramah Berk-shires in New York in 1964.[38] Working to offer a more balanced approach to Jewish education, these camps included a great deal of Jewish ritual, text study, and philosophy alongside instruction in modern Hebrew.

Short-term retreats for the teenage leaders of the National Federation of Temple Youth (NFTY) group in the 1940s set the stage for the foun-dation of Reform Jewish summer camps across the United States.[39] Reform movement leaders of the Pacific Association of Reform Rabbis opened the movement's first permanent, full-summer camp, Camp Saratoga, in 1947, changing its name to Swig Camp Institute in 1964.[40] The Union of Amer-ican Hebrew Congregations established its first national movement camp, the Union Institute (also known as the Olin-Sang-Ruby Union Institute, or OSRUI), in Wisconsin in 1952, beginning first with most campers attending the camp "for two weeks or less," a "pattern of short 'institutes' rather than a full summer of 'immersion.'"[41] But this shorter-term model did not prevail for long. While continuing to run some shorter sessions, OSRUI began to hold longer sessions in the later 1950s. New Reform camps with lengthier sessions grew across the United States throughout the 1950s and 1960s as well, including Camp Harlam in Pennsylvania in 1958, Myron S. Goldman Union Camp Institute (also known as GUCI) in Indiana in 1958, and Camp Kutz in New York in 1965. All of these camps fell under the Reform movement's umbrella of youth programs, but they never became centralized to the same degree as the Ramah camps, allowing each camp director a significant degree of autonomy.[42]

Modern Orthodox, Hasidic, and Haredi Jews followed a distinctive time line in the development of their youth programs, their camps thus mirroring a different set of concerns and historical circumstances. Some recreational camps for Orthodox clientele were founded in the early twentieth century. Many Orthodox children of the 1940s and 1950s attended camps like Massad, Tel Yehudah, or Yavneh, where traditional or halachic Sabbath and kosher practices were upheld, a small minority of camps defined through the lens of Orthodox Judaism or the religious Zionism of the youth movement Bnei Akiva. A larger and more defined Orthodox camping sector emerged in earnest only in the late 1960s, as Modern Orthodoxy began to grow in size and self-assuredness as a community and began its delayed transition into affluence and Jewish suburbia.[43] Their divergent time lines situate most Orthodox camps outside the realm of this book's thematic chapters, but they do receive treatment in both the first and last chapters, which contextualize Jewish camping before and after the postwar period, respectively.

### Sources, Archives, and Methodologies

The subjects I address here represent a wide range of camp types and locations around the United States, using deep archival research to uncover several aspects of the lived experience. Nevertheless, the book does not address every kind of Jewish camp or every element of the camp experience with uniform attention. As American summer camping, and in particular Jewish camping, began predominantly in the northeastern United States, this study mainly considers camps in rural areas near New York City and Boston and, to a lesser extent, in the Midwest, where camps serving Chicago and Detroit made the region the second most populous area for the Jewish sector. However, the book does touch on the development of camps in the South and on the West Coast, which served both established southern Jewish communities and new arrivals in the sunbelt cities of Miami, Los Angeles, Phoenix, Houston, and Dallas.[44]

The book's detailing of camp life is derived chiefly from archival research, placing its focus on the experiences of campers and staff at the time. But as I observed and became an occasional participant in alumni Facebook groups over the course of several years, I also had the pleasure of connecting with dozens of former campers of the 1950s, 1960s, and 1970s who generously donated helpful sources, photographs, and memoir literature they wrote of their time at camp. I conducted over thirty in-depth oral history interviews with former campers, making a special effort to get as diverse a set of participants as possible in terms of which camp they attended and in what decade, as well as their gender and sexual identities. Their recollections appear in various parts of the book, but are most prevalent in chapters 6 and 7, which concentrate on camper culture most intensely.

Photographs have been important sources for me as a researcher, and a selection of the most evocative of them appear throughout this book. Some camps are visually represented more than others due to logistical and availability issues. However, the photos generally reflect the similarities among camps at the level of everyday life, making them usefully reminiscent not only of the specific camp from which they came but of the whole Jewish camp experience. Given my focus on the experiences of the young, I made an intentional effort to use photos taken by campers and young counselors whenever possible, although some photographs from camp archives, likely taken by older staff members, are included as well.

These photographs will no doubt entertain you, as they have me over the years; I invite you to enjoy their playfulness, humor, and the nostalgia they might generate. Beyond allowing them to amuse you, however, I encourage you to use them as paths toward understanding the lived experiences of campers more deeply. As you come across each photograph, consider which moments campers prioritized capturing with their limited rolls of film. What parts of camp life seemed to matter most to them? What do you see in the expressions on their faces? In the case of the photographs sourced from camp archives, what can you take away from the photos that camp leaders ensured were kept for posterity? These photographs helpfully portray what camps looked like as physical environments and what kinds of activities took place. What makes them invaluable, however, is their utility as windows into the emotional experience of camp life.

## Age and Gender as Categories of Analysis

Although the boundaries between campers and counselors proved culturally and generationally porous, most summer camps had clear and defined hierarchies. Camp directors and other members of the year-round head staff held the top position on camps' pyramids of official authority, setting their missions and managing all the staff members below them, including the education staff, group supervisors, and program specialists. The directors and the supervisors managed the counselors who lived in bunks with campers, interfacing with them day in and day out. Campers of different ages occupied the bottom of the authority pyramid, subject to the plans, rules, and restrictions of the staff members above them.

Camps' hierarchies matched the approximate age differences of staff members, with each ascending stratum occupied by people a few years older than those in the strata below. Some camps had a younger-leaning staff than others. At postwar Zionist camps, for instance, where staff members mostly came out of a camp's affiliated year-round youth movement, the director, typically the oldest person at camp, was often merely twenty-five years old. At Reform and Conservative camps, rabbis, teachers, and other professionals occupied higher positions of power, and thus the camp had larger age differentials between the strata of camp's hierarchies, as counselors remained in their late teens and early twenties.[45] These differences displayed their different institutional backgrounds but also their values. Leadership training for young movement leaders proved central to the purposes of Zionist movement camps, while professional, seasoned, and well-prepared educators made sense for the Ramah camps, where educators aimed to teach Jewish content at a higher level and directors could recruit rabbis and educators from the Jewish Theological Seminary with relative ease.

In this sense, both the age of an individual at camp and the role they played can prove difficult to parse out, let alone label. An eighteen-year-old counselor, a fifty-year-old rabbi, and a twenty-five-year-old teacher, for instance, all had very different credentials within and approaches to education. Nevertheless, all of them took on educational roles within the world of the summer camp, each of them indispensable in their own ways. Counselors had much more contact with campers, and in this sense they exercised considerable educational, social, and cultural influence on them. Older, out-of-bunk staff members had the time and ability to thoughtfully sketch out their programs and shape a camp's educational mission from the top down, deciding the themes for the summer and organizing the daily, weekly, and monthly schedules to match their goals. While acknowledging these variations, the uses of the terms *educator* and *leader* in this book necessarily refer to a large range of people. When sources allow, I use more specific terms— *counselor*, *rabbi*, *director*, or *specialist*—to reference staff members. But staff members often appear in archives as anonymous, genderless, and ageless. Precious few educational programs, play scripts, counselor training manuals, or other archival documents attributed their writing to a single person or group of persons, since planning and curriculum development at camp proved a collaborative process, often layering on or lightly modifying programs of earlier summers.

Such ambiguities make the study of the texture of camp life difficult and help to explain why many scholars have focused on the individual founders or directors of educational Jewish camping, whose influences on the enterprise are more easily traceable. But looking at camps' more diffuse and diverse leadership offers an important opportunity to see how Jews of different ages, genders, and life stages played roles in shaping camps as affective and effective educational opportunities. Camp founders or directors had an essential function in controlling a camp's missions from the top down and made their visions of ideal or authentic Jewishness the benchmark by which they judged the summer a success. And yet camp directors had less day-to-day interaction with campers than counselors did. Under such circumstances, who had the chance to influence campers' identities and lives more: older, semiprofessional educators, or teenage or college-aged counselors? That the case could be made either way indicates that age can serve as an important lens within the study of history and education history. Individuals of different ages and stages not only experienced camp differently but had their own roles to play in the making of the lived experience, the sum of which influenced the trajectories of American Zionism, Yiddishism, and Jewish practice for decades to come.[46]

Camps' hierarchies also followed certain common patterns when it came to gender. While women were ever-present in the camping enterprise and directed several communal or private Jewish camps, only one of the Jewish educational and ideological camps examined in this book employed a female camp director before the 1970s. The wives of camp directors and founders worked in crucial but often untitled roles, while younger women and college students worked as the counselors of female campers, area specialists, office workers, and education staff. In Hashomer Hatzair, reflected one former camper, the Israeli emissary that ran the camp's educational activities "was always the husband," while "the wife was always the nurse" or "the teacher for dancing and the singing."[47] Most camps also hired a female staff member for the extremely gendered position labeled "Camp Mom," typically tasked with emotionally supporting homesick campers, encouraging bunk cleanliness, and serving as camp therapists (with and without the professional degrees to support such work) and parent liaisons. Camps' staffing structures mirrored the traditional, patriarchal family, with, as Nancy Mykoff explains, "Jewish

Boys playing guitar, Camp Hemshekh, late 1960s.
Source: Kolodny Family Photos. Printed with permission.

women justif[ying] their camping activities in terms of extending their child-rearing duties to a more public sphere."[48] The roles of women in Jewish camping undoubtedly expanded during the postwar years alongside the status of women in American life, but the face of Jewish educational camp leadership remained overwhelmingly male until the 1980s. The fact of the maleness of camp leadership in those decades must not be treated as simply a given. As the following chapters show, many of their notions of Jewish authenticity, whether relating to the New Jew ideal of Zionism or the notion of Yiddishism as a legitimizing project of a derided, feminized jargon, related directly to ideas of Jewish masculinity and the perceived pitfalls of the Judaism campers experienced at home, primarily by the efforts of mothers.

When it comes to campers, the issue of gender proves much less clear-cut. Female campers at educational Jewish camps generally took part in the same daily programming as boys, while the experimental ambiance of the camps led to somewhat alternative renderings of femininity and masculinity.[49] At certain camps, for instance, leading Jewish rituals and playing guitar, as modeled by adult male staff members, became peak expressions of Jewish masculinity, alongside more traditional ones like athleticism. Female campers sometimes reflected on how camp relieved them of some of the pressures surrounding their looks, ditching the makeup and hair routines of the city and suburb for plain faces and ponytails. Cross-dressing, which both transgressed and reified gender boundaries, proved common at camps both Jewish and more broadly American. Still, expressions of Jewish girl-hood and boyhood at camp proved a far cry from revolutionary, and camp leaders stopped short of actively encouraging new ways of thinking about gender and Jewishness. Boys still competed and ridiculed one another over the boundaries of masculinity, and girls still fell victim to beauty standards, shame surrounding sexual conduct, and self-image issues; both sexes experienced the compulsory heterosexuality of camps' romantic atmospheres. In this way, gender, age, and the way both attributes influence power dynamics all provide a window into how camps operated both inside and outside mainstream culture, pushing cultural boundaries in some cases while echoing societal norms in others.

### "Does Camp Work?"

At nearly every public and scholarly lecture I have given, I have been asked something along the lines of whether Jewish summer camps "work." In 2019, Brandeis University's Mandel Center for Jewish Education sponsored a conference, "The Power of Jewish Camp." As the name of the conference implied, the consensus among stakeholders today is that Jewish camps largely succeed in their goals in transforming young Jews.[50] Studies of camps' impact, often subsidized by Jewish organizations such as the Foundation for Jewish Camp, have backed up this assertion since the 1970s with data that display lower rates of intermarriage, higher rates of membership in Jewish organizations and synagogues, and more support for or attachment to Israel among camp alumni many years later.[51] The coronavirus pandemic put the issue into even fuller, more intensive focus. When it was not yet clear whether Jewish camps would open for summer 2020 due to health concerns, parents, educators, and even teenagers took to the Jewish press to argue over the ethics of camps' eventual decisions given their important role in communal life and, later, when almost all decided not to open, to lament the loss of a precious Jewish summer.[52]

Postwar educators, journalists, and camp staff similarly lauded the perceived impacts of camp on youth, marveling at how "gloriously motivated" Jewish children became after the summer as they experienced Jewishness in "its fullest and its unadulterated form with no compromises."[53] They too would have no doubt mourned the loss of a summer at camp. But while I understand why Jews want to understand if Jewish camp "works," this book is centered on a different kind of question. Just as most studies have framed the impact of camping on children as something that happens from the top down, an experience fostered by adults with clear results in mind, most postwar leaders initially underestimated the power of youth in the camp environment. As the growing youth activist ethos of the 1960s spread to camps, it became clearer to adult leaders that their programs' transformative properties relied on nuanced dynamics between themselves and the children and adolescents in their care. The successful implementation of their educational missions and plans required campers to buy in. Camps' yardsticks of success moved not only according to historical and social trends, but because campers, in their everyday decisions to accept or not accept their leaders' values, shaped what adults at camp could and would accomplish. When the generations did not align, camp leaders had to alter their programs, forced to reconsider the idea of success as they went along.

Considering youth as active rather than passive, the question of whether camps of past "worked," or if camps today "work," becomes rather difficult to answer. Who decides what constitutes success? If a camp's yardstick of success habitually moved, what truly constituted a failure? The fact that many of the questions researchers have posed to gauge camps' impacts have political implications complicates these inquiries even further. Asking whether former campers support Israel, for instance, does not leave room for critics of Israel who see their politics as an expression of attachment to Israel rather than a rejection, even as the ultimate proof, perhaps, of their camp's success in making Israel important and relevant to their lives. It also does not leave room for those who took the kinds of critical analysis their educational camps encouraged into directions that push the boundaries of their former camps' ideologies. Probes into the marriage choices of former campers, moreover, start with an assumption that is less and less accepted by American Jews writ large: that intermarriage is a problem that communal organizations must fight against. As a 2020 debate over the question of how many Jews of Color there are in the United States put on display, the Jews who do the counting have the "inordinate power to include and exclude populations," Ari Kelman writes, "not only on the basis of sampling approaches, but on the basis of the questions they ask."[34] Research into the influences of Jewish education can certainly be worthwhile, and there are many open-ended questions one can ask former or current campers to better understand what kinds of educational impacts take place during and after camp. As a historical work, however, *The Jews of Summer* takes a decidedly different approach, focusing instead on how the very notion of camp's powers to transform children, repair the perceived inauthenticity of American Jewish culture, stem assimilation, curb intermarriage, and build up support for Israel came to shape the experience of going to Jewish camp in the first place. In so doing, I hope that this history of Jewish childhood, youth, and camping leads readers of all ages, stages, backgrounds, and professions to reflect on their own visions of "good," "authentic," or "real" Jewishness (or Muslimness, Christianness,

Americanness, as the cases may be), and how those conceptions could be productively expanded, especially in the case of the young.

———

This book's chapters are organized by theme, with each focused on one part of the overall camp experience. The first several chapters examine the foundational fantasies Jewish educators held about the powers within camp to redefine and reproduce American Jewishness according to their movement's molds. Presenting the historical conditions that allowed for the postwar rise in Jewish educational, nationalistic, and religious camping, chapter 1 shows how the sector emerged at a transitional moment for youth, education, and Jews in America. As Jews climbed the socioeconomic ladder, many came to worry that their new-found status threatened the future of Jewish life in America, arguing that affluence and acceptance had negative impacts on Jewish authenticity. At the same time, Americans increasingly problematized youth, first with a panic over juvenile delinquency in the 1950s and then over the politicization and rapidly changing youth culture of the 1960s. These trends, with the backbone of a longer legacy of American camping dating back to the turn of the century, coalesced to allow Jewish summer camps to rise in number and importance within American Jewish culture writ large.

Despite their ideological differences, the founders of Jewish summer camps shared a central hope about the power of Jewish camping: that immersing children in Jewish lifestyles for one or two months of the summer would yield a more authentically Jewish generation, curbing the decline of Jewish culture as educators understood it. Chapter 2 describes how this underlying impulse guided the construction of camp life in the 1940s, 1950s, and 1960s. At the most basic level, leaders organized time at camp to simulate the lifestyles of Jews from other times and places. Through the content and overall flow of camps' daily, weekly, and monthly schedules, camp leaders projected and enacted their fantasies on campers, inflecting every hour with their specific visions of ideal Jewishness. Chapter 2, which details the average weekday and Sabbath, brings the intensity of camp life into view.

From the beginning of American summer camping, progressive educational philosophies underpinned the enterprise, with camp leaders arguing that play and recreation proved vital to social development and education.

Jewish educators of the early twentieth century adopted these ideas too, aided by the heavily Jewish professions of social work and social science. However, the games they had campers play took on new forms and purposes in the postwar decades. Through role-playing games, sociodrama, and color war and special pageants, chapter 3 shows how play at camp worked to make the simulation of Jewish lifestyles apparent in daily schedules all the more direct. Orchestrated and curated by directors and educators influenced by Jewish social science, campers took on the roles of historical and contemporary Jews from other parts of the world through imaginative, performative, and competitive play. The performative practices traced in chapter 3 boldly highlight the intentions and fantasies of educators, as they hoped campers would come to take on the identities and behaviors of Jews untouched by middle-class American comfort.

In the years following the Holocaust, Jewish educators faced the question of how to broach the recent genocide. While camps emphasized stories of Jewish life and renewal more often than death and suffering, all Jewish educational camps integrated one day into the schedule in which they would memorialize the six million. As chapter 4 shows, camps used the Jewish holy day of Tisha B'Av, the only holiday to fall in the summer months, as the main moment for marking the recent tragedy alongside a host of other Jewish tragedies, while avowedly secular Yiddish camps created alternatives to it. Their differing political and religious standpoints infused the days with different messages and goals, but their camp-wide programs proved remarkably similar in tone and order. All camps used stories of Jewish heroism as counterbalances for the sadness of the day, drawing inspiration from Warsaw ghetto resistance fighters, Israeli soldiers, or both, depending on their ideological orientations. Addressing the Holocaust, educators came to believe, functioned as a particularly powerful tool in their efforts to change Jewish culture through the next generation, not only because it offered a chance to underscore the relevance of their camps' nationalist, religious, and linguistic ideologies, but because campers sourced deep commitments to their Jewishness through stories of Jewish suffering.

For most of their history, Jews were multilingual, able to speak both Jewish languages and the majority language of the wider society in which they lived. Postwar American Jews, however, were overwhelmingly monolingual, following in the footsteps of immigrant generations that quickly embraced English as their lingua franca. As they sought to turn the tides of what they saw as a decline in Jewish authenticity, chapter 5 shows how Jewish educators across the ideological spectrum came to see Jewish languages as paramount in their efforts, the abandonment of Yiddish or lack of interest in spoken and written Hebrew as indications of just how far their culture had fallen. Integrating Hebrew or Yiddish into camp life from the 1940s onward, they hoped to not only connect campers to their Ashkenazi roots or the Hebrew culture of the nascent State of Israel but also to transform them into Jews they envisioned as more ideal or authentic. The fantasy of the Hebrew- or Yiddish-speaking camp quickly clashed with the broader linguistic realities of the Jewish community: campers' lack of enthusiasm challenged their educators' plans, and the issue of language was a source of substantial hand wringing and intergenerational tension. And yet that very tension would ultimately lead to new uses for Yiddish and Hebrew in the 1960s and beyond, reconstituting symbolic engagements with language into vehicles toward expressing different political affinities and staking claim to a more authentic vision of Jewish culture.

As camp leaders laid out the missions and ideal trajectories of their programs, they understood that their success required getting campers onboard. But adolescents inevitably arrived with their own desires and aspirations for their summers, increasingly expecting substantial degrees of freedom within the camp environment. Guided by John Dewey's theories of democratic education, chapter 6 reveals how Jewish educators created camper governments, newspapers, and camp-wide voting assemblies, hoping to make the youth in their midst feel as though they had the power and agency to have an impact on their own experiences. With campers having the reins over certain aspects of camp life, educators believed that the sense of freedom and laxity they fostered in the environment would bring campers to happily accept their leaders' ideals as their own. However, age-based categories of camper, counselor, and head staff member clashed both in and out of these structures. Negotiating power and place in the camp milieu, the interactions between generations often proved tenuous. But the groups also found ways to converge on paths forward, fostering camp life and shaping their political, linguistic, and religious ideologies in tandem with one another.

While campers struggled with staff over the limits of their freedoms, such limits did not stop them from fostering lively and complex youth cultures. Dating, romance, and sexuality all came to play central roles in camper culture, with adolescents expressing their interests in the opposite sex in newspapers, inside jokes, songs, and in their clashes with staff for more freedom. Their desires to engage in sexual and romantic relationships inevitably challenged adult leaders to consider what freedoms and privileges campers should have, a loaded question in a time between growing sexual openness, on the one hand, and a loud condemnation of youth's liberal sexual mores, on the other. But as camp leaders came to invest greater energy in curbing intermarriage, their evolving missions and the youth culture came to converge once again, with educators finding their own reasons to allow a romantic and relatively sexually free environment.[55] Chapter 7 charts the beginning of this complicated dynamic, which continued to shape debates and conversations about Jewish youth sexuality and interfaith marriage well beyond the early 1970s.

Finally, chapter 8 addresses the trajectories of Jewish camps from the 1970s through the present. Beginning in the late 1960s, leaders of Jewish Welfare Board, "communal" or Jewish Community Center camps joined in a broad discussion centered on what educators called "Jewish survival," expressing increasing interest in bringing Jewish content into camp than in earlier decades. These efforts continued throughout the 1980s and 1990s, increasing once again in the wake of the 1990 Jewish Population Survey, which heightened communal concerns over intermarriage. In the same years, Israel grew to be the central focus of many Jewish camps beyond the Zionist sector, while the economic impacts of the 1970s recession and growing competition (teen travel programs, organized trips to Israel) prompted major changes in the offerings of camps. So too did the decline of Yiddish institutional life, which contributed to the closures of Boiberik and Hemshekh. The anti-occupation group IfNotNow's #YouNeverToldMe campaign, the impacts of #MeToo at camp, the recent revival of a Hemshekh-style diasporism, and the fiery discourse surrounding whether camps should open during the coronavirus pandemic highlight just how intensely Jews continue to uphold the power and importance of the Jewish summer. Using educational research and the Jewish press, the final chapter brings readers up to the present while placing the postwar camping paradigm in bold relief.

# "Under Optimum Conditions"

### American Jews and
### the Rise of the Summer Camp

IN JANUARY 1969, Rabbi David Mogilner, director of the Conservative movement's network of Ramah summer camps, attended the three-day National Conference on Jewish Camping sponsored by the National Jewish Welfare Board (NJWB). Addressing camp directors, social workers, and educators from across geographic, political, and denominational lines, Mogilner used his moment at the lectern to focus on Israel's function as "spiritual, cultural, secular and national center of Jewish life" through which campers "can draw strength, encouragement, pride and self-fulfillment as American Jews." Within this Israel-centered address, however, Mogilner also took a moment to speak to what he saw as the broader function of residential summer camps in American Jewish culture. Since he saw "little indication that the second and third generations have the intellectual and spiritual wherewithal to evolve an indigenous Jewish religious and cultural life," Mogilner argued that camps played a critical role as a strengthening agent of Jewish life, ensuring the "continuity" of Judaism "under optimum conditions." Through these conditions—24/7, contained, and protected from the pressures and pull of mainstream culture—Jewishness would find its way into the souls of American children and teens and remain with them for the long haul.[1]

The first conference of its kind, the 1969 meeting introduced a new and more formalized approach to cross-movement collaboration. Although camps had shared programs and ideas through ad hoc and localized means, the NJWB's conferences, program guides, and overall oversight helped camp leaders share knowledge nationwide, leading Jewish camps to become steadily more similar in their educational goals and methods from the 1970s on. This small moment in American Jewish history marked an important turning point in the trajectory of Jewish camping, its effects still felt today through the highly organized and coordinated Jewish camping sector. Jews in the immediate postwar decades harnessed summer camps with a distinctive kind of urgency, hoping to cure the perceived communal ills specific to their time. Jews of the latter part of the postwar period, in the 1960s and 1970s, would find even more urgency and motivation for camping as rates of intermarriage rose to new heights, seeing marriages between Jews and non-Jews as emblematic of a broader and more extreme kind of assimilation.

And yet Mogilner and his colleagues were hardly the first to see the mission and potentiality of the sleepaway camp as one of serious import, their rise to the status of a rite of American Jewish childhood owed to camps that Jews and Christians founded at the turn of the century. By the time the conference took place, summer camps for Jewish children had already enjoyed a decades-long history in the United States. While the conditions of the postwar period stimulated growth and evolution, the Jewish camps detailed in this book owed their existence to the hundreds of camps, Jewish and Christian, that predated them. This chapter addresses this longer history of American summer camping to bring what made the postwar moment detailed in later chapters in full relief, tracing the sector's nineteenth-century beginnings, its nineteenth-century rise during the Progressive Era, the period from the 1890s to the 1920s, and its modernizing years between the two world wars.

The educational and ideological Jewish sleepaway camp, moreover, came about during the twentieth century's twists and turns, its trajectory inextricable from the history of education in the United States, youth history, and the course of modern Jewish history. That Mogilner and his colleagues came to see camps as ensuring the continuity of Jewishness itself proved specific to their moment in history, an idea that had specific resonance in the wake of the Holocaust's destruction. But broader anxieties about the state of American youth, gender, modernity, and urban life set the stage for the rise of their specifically Jewish project in the centuries prior. Who were the Jewish leaders, kids, and parents, this chapter asks, who attended, led, and paid tuition for Jewish camps in of the postwar period? What historical conditions, Jewish and American, contributed to their choices and actions in the camp environment? Treating this range of circumstances in quick succession, the following sections offer the historical background required to best appreciate the deep dives offered in later chapters.

### US Jewish Immigration History and Postwar Social Mobility

The first Jewish migrants arrived in the American colonies from Brazil in 1654. The vast majority of postwar American Jews, however, descended from the 2.5 million European immigrants who arrived in America between 1820 and 1920.[2] Settling mainly in large urban centers like New York and Chicago, immigrant Jews formed tightly knit communities in ethnic enclaves, organizing through mutual aid organizations, labor unions, and cultural production and consumption. Yiddish, the ancestral language of most European Jews, initially served as the language of social, familial, and cultural life. As families embraced public education, however, Jewish children learned English, their new language quickly becoming the everyday vernacular of most American Jews.[3]

In the initial years following immigration, Jews experienced economic strife, abusive working conditions, and cramped, unhealthy dwellings. With backgrounds in socialist movements in Europe, Jews took major roles in the development of the American labor movement at the turn of the century, developing networks of solidarity with other new immigrants who faced the same poverty and harsh labor conditions upon arrival.[4] As they sought paths out of their poverty, moreover, they came to face discrimination in the form of university quotas and businesses that made not hiring Jews a policy. The nativism of the 1920s and the assaults on Jews in the 1940s and 1950s as communist sympathizers placed them in even more vulnerable positions.[5] At the same time, Jewish immigrants and their first-generation children encountered opportunities unimaginable for the vast majority of Jews in Eastern Europe. Climbing the social and economic ladder generation by generation, Jews of the early twentieth century laid the groundwork for the community's economic ascendance in the postwar years.[6] The changing perception of Jews' racial status in midcentury America also greatly affected their capacities to ascend. Like their Italian and Irish immigrant predecessors, Jews became white within American conceptions of race, and their nascent whiteness bestowed on them new forms of economic, educational, professional, and social privilege. The GI Bill's scholarships and housing loans for white veterans of World War II further catapulted Jews into the growing middle class. Jews departed the cramped tenements of America's cities for the comfortable glory of the new postwar suburbs, participating in broader trends of white flight.[7] As their living standards, educational backgrounds, and professional status rose, many first- and second-generation Jews came to see themselves as experiencing the actualization of the American dream that had drawn their families to the United States in the first place.

Suburbanization also transformed Jewish life. While for earlier generations, being Jewish meant existing within an informal, decentralized, and neighborhood-based set of associations, postwar Judaism required formal affiliation, with membership in synagogues, the new centers of Jewish communities, emerging as central.[8] The growing role of the synagogue, which housed not only worship but a variety of social clubs and youth programs, also mirrored the rising place of religious affiliation in postwar life writ large.[9] As Cold War anxieties triggered more Americans to embrace conservative "family values," moralism, and religion, denominational Judaism, with the synagogue center as its engine, thrived.

Affluence and whiteness undoubtedly offered Jews myriad benefits, amenities, and opportunities for further advancement. Nevertheless, not all Jews welcomed the period's golden hue with unfettered excitement, as many postwar Jews continued to "identify with the Jewish history of poverty . . . [understanding] economic and social marginality" as "integral to the Jewish experience." Seeing authentic Jewish life as incompatible with conditions of comfort, communal leaders, Rachel Kranson has argued, pronounced "middle-class Jewish life in postwar America as tragically complacent, superficial, and incapable of nurturing future generations of committed Jews."[10] Many Jews, particularly those in positions of leadership, responded to their success with a great deal of ambivalence, enjoying what their nascent affluence afforded them while troubled by how it distorted what they understood as authentic Jewish culture. Jews were not alone in pointing out the potential downsides of what appeared, on the face of it, to be a period of unquestionably beneficial progress and economic mobility. Other middle-class white Americans raised similar concerns about their new lifestyles, claiming that suburbia led to loneliness, isolation, and a detrimental sense of materialism, but the aftermath of the Holocaust added a particular layer of urgency to Jews' concerns.[11] While Jews had perhaps never experienced quite the degree of safety and comfort as they did in postwar America, Hitler's Europe cast its shadow over their communal agendas and activities.[12]

In an effort toward bridging their new status with their historical visions of Jews as disenfranchised outsiders, many Jews found an outlet in activist movements of the 1960s. Jews had participated in the struggle for civil rights from the beginning of the twentieth century, finding common cause with African Americans as they sought out their own equal treatment in American society. But the 1960s brought about a new kind of Jewish activism for the cause, their rising status and sense of security allowing them to scale up their engagement and to do so consciously, organizationally, and openly as Jews. Connecting the lessons of the Holocaust and the legacy of anti-Semitic violence in Europe to their fights for racial equality, Jews founded their own civil rights initiatives and worked with African American movements and organizations to institute civil rights into law.[13] Their roles in civil rights proved far from simple. Some activists pointed to their fellow Jews' participation in white flight as an acceptance of racial privilege that stood in contradiction with their supposed commitment to equal rights. The Ocean Hill–Brownsville strike of 1968, a teacher's strike that pitted white and mostly Jewish teachers union members against the local Black community, and disputes over Black Power's embrace of the Palestinian cause soured Black-Jewish relations on a national basis. Nevertheless, the civil rights ethos presented Jews with a way to square their contemporaneous privilege with their histories of marginality. Civil rights also led Jews to see their own personal quests for roots as progressive political acts. Under trends of multi-culturalism and white ethnic revival, Jews in the 1960s, and in particular the younger generation, emerged more publicly proud of their own cultural heritage.[14]

The vast popularity of *Fiddler on the Roof*, onstage and on screen, re-flected this return-to-roots trend. In the Holocaust's wake, pre-Holocaust Eastern European Jewish life received creative attention in fiction, film, theater, and art through which Jews "crafted a sentimentalized vision of the impoverished shtetl as both a primary source of Jewish authenticity and the antithesis of their spiritual weakness."[15] Although Yiddish continued to de-cline in everyday use, a new sense of nostalgia for the language and its culture arose in its place.[16] At the same time, American Jews gravitated to visions of the Israeli state. Serving as a symbol of hope after the Holocaust, admiration of and philanthropic and political support for Israel flourished dramatically over the postwar decades. Israeli culture also became embedded in Ameri-can Jewish culture, with Israeli pronunciation replacing Ashkenazi Hebrew in synagogues' soundscapes, *bimahs* (synagogue stages) becoming flanked with both the American and Israeli flags, and with Israeli dance styles and songs entering American Jews' repertoires.[17]

All of these transformations influenced the experiences of Jewish chil-dren and teenagers in the postwar period. As synagogues developed into centers of Jewish life, flourishing programs for youth, including religious schools, youth groups, and summer camps, were established, providing new avenues for education and recreation. This "child-centered Judaism" in many ways mirrored the period's goldenness. As Jewish families, now predomi-nantly middle class, had more means to invest in their children's psycholog-ical and social growth, the world of Jewish youth programming expanded in kind.[18] But it also reflected communal anxieties over the post-Holocaust future as Jewish leaders came to see educating and socializing their youth as a path toward curbing cultural decline. The affluence of the period both enabled and provoked this focus on the child, blurring the lines between the period's economic goldenness and the ambivalence its comforts engendered.

### Childhood, Youth, and Cultural Anxiety

This tension between the golden and the anxious ultimately spurred the vast expansion of educational and ideological Jewish summer camping in the postwar period. But a whole host of earlier American trends concerning youth, the family, and education that began in the Progressive Era served as essential building blocks for Jewish camping. During this period, characterized by pervasive, wide-ranging social reform, Americans increasingly came to see childhood as a "time apart, protected from 'adult' culture" in which "play, education" and "freedom from productive labor" encompassed new rights of childhood.[19] Industrialization and urbanization transformed schooling from decentralized and community-run into an elaborate system with consolidated governance, administrative structures, and professional expertise. Child labor and mandatory schooling laws enshrined certain basic rights of childhood into law, while progressive educational philosophies like those of John Dewey transformed American education. The fresh air movement, which saw industrialization and urbanization as anathema to healthy childhoods, established parks, youth programs, and summer camps, taking urban youth into nature for recreational reformation. In 1904, moreover, G. Stanley Hall coined the term *adolescence* to describe the time between childhood and adulthood as a distinct period of life that, like childhood, required certain protections, rights, and systems of support.[20]

While progressivism spurred these innovations, the two world wars changed Americans' priorities and outlook, entering the postwar era with increasingly conservative notions surrounding youth, family life, and education. As politicians came to characterize the domestic ideal as a triumph of capitalism, journalists, politicians, and child-rearing experts portrayed failing mothers and families as the source of many of society's ills, with special attention to a growing societal concern: a perceived rise in juvenile delinquency. Amid geopolitical uncertainty, prompted by Cold War–era anxieties over mass society, fascism, and communism, the home came to represent both a bulwark against the dangers of the outside world and the most vulnerable site to those very same dangers, in need of scrupulous attention and protection for the sake of children and, by extension, the entire nation.[21]

The family-focused postwar decades also transformed American demography. During the baby boom period of 1946 through 1964, roughly 77 million children were born in the United States. As these children reached school age, American adults turned their attention further toward education, their growing conservatism leading many parents and politicians to blame progressive educators for cultivating permissiveness, lowering scholastic standards, and instigating the problem of delinquency.[22] Schools shifted toward older, more stringent forms of pedagogy and came to focus more on the sciences as the country engaged in a nationalistic competition with the Soviet Union over nuclear bombs and the space race. Parents demanded higher standards of education for their children, struggled over the content of schools' curriculum, and fought over racial integration in the years surrounding the 1954 ruling of *Brown v. Board of Education*, which deemed segregated schools unconstitutional.[23]

As American children and teenagers faced these changes within their families and schools, they fostered new youth cultures on local and national scales. Progressive Era child protection laws had not only led to safer and more educated children; they also offered youth the time and space to socialize with one another more consistently. In the schools and streets of the 1920s, 1930s, and 1940s, youth culture, expressed in fashion, dance, and dating trends, began to blossom. The rise of television, the baby boom, and the growing middle class of the 1950s and 1960s brought about an even more cohesive and visible youth culture, and with more money and free time than ever before, youth became a highly sought-after consumer market. Teen society expressed itself once again through new fashions, behaviors, and dating, with "going steady" becoming a rite of passage.[24]

While businesses happily capitalized on youth's penchant for trends and entertainment, however, many American parents, educators, and politicians came to see this developing youth culture as problematic and dangerous. Terms such as *high school dropout, juvenile delinquent,* and *teenage rebel* grew ever more common in the press, alongside condemnations of what many perceived as a more permissive dating and sexual culture.[25] City and state agencies, often led by the public schools, imposed a variety of controls on youth and worked to create teen centers and supervised activities like the prom and homecoming, all in an effort to take teen leisure off the streets.[26] Although concerns over delinquency were often fueled by a sense of hysteria, students in high schools and colleges across the country did begin to challenge adult authorities more loudly and consciously beginning in the 1950s, with rowdy panty raids flouting campus rules and with students demonstrating against dress codes, courtship, sex, and censorship rules.[27] Jews expressed concern over issues of juvenile delinquency too, writing about the issue frequently in local Jewish newspapers around the country throughout the 1950s and 1960s.[28]

These developments set the stage for the larger and more political challenges posed by the youth of the sixties, who pushed universities and public schools further regarding their rights of freedom of speech and expression. After the 1969 Supreme Court case of *Tinker v. Des Moines Independent School District*, which ruled that the suspension of students who protested the Vietnam War by wearing black armbands violated the First Amendment, a whole slew of litigation came to broaden the rights of students to express themselves through dress, hairstyles, and public displays of affection on school grounds, instigating a broader "realignment of children's relation to authority."[29] Amid the student-led movements and the growth of the counterculture, more permissive and progressive forms of education returned to the forefront of American education.[30] Youth not only continued to protest on their own behalf in the 1960s, but also engaged in political unrest on the front lines of the civil rights, women's, gay rights, and antiwar movements, making them overall more "radical than students of the 1940s and 1950s" and "more activist in temper."[31]

Jewish children attended America's public schools, embraced the flourishing youth culture, and became teens and young adults involved in the sixties counterculture and protest movements.[32] As they participated in these wider American struggles, they also came to challenge the complacency of their own elders and communities, establishing a distinctly Jewish arm of the counterculture. *Havurot*, lay-led independent prayer groups, rejected the dull, institutional postwar synagogue, reinstating traditional rituals and forms of prayer as their new norms.[33] Young Jews also formed collectives, residential communes, and political action groups that supported both the broader causes of the countercultural Left and a set of specifically Jewish causes, including the plight of Soviet Jewry and the rights of women, gays, and lesbians in Jewish ritual.[34] While the Jewish counterculture mostly harmonized with the broader countercultural New Left's politics and styles, the issue of Israel caused significant discord, as many American leftists, particularly in the years following the Six-Day War of 1967, came to see Israel as a Western imperialist nation. And yet the growing alienation many Jews felt in the broader Left further fueled the specifically Jewish counterculture, in which supporting or even visiting Israel as a volunteer on a kibbutz could function as an expression of hippie, communitarian values, not as a contradiction of them.[35]

Reckoning with the younger generation, Jewish communal leaders largely lamented the style and tenor of their children's critiques, trends, and behaviors, distressed that the products of their synagogues and Hebrew schools turned their backs on these very institutions.[36] And yet Jews of both generations shared rather similar critiques of middle-class American life, describing postwar Jewishness as disappointing, complacent, and lifeless. Their differences, then, lay less in the critiques themselves than in the actions that followed them. To many postwar parents, the problems of American Jewishness could be answered by institutions themselves, in part by the growing, substantial Jewish youth sector of programs tasked with inculcating Jewishness in the next generation. But to the younger generation who grew up in these child-centered Jewish communities, the answers lay in the creation of their own "meaningful alternatives": collectives and communities that addressed what they saw "as the problems of middle-class Jewish life."[37]

As sites of intergenerational negotiation, creativity, and cultural production, educational Jewish summer camps emerged as vibrant microcosms for all of these trends and turning points. The Jewish campers and counselors infused the camps with their own generational values, ideas, and goals, entering the camp setting influenced and shaped by the trends and gradual politicization of the youth culture. In contrast, working to turn back cultural decline in the shadow of the Holocaust, Jewish educators came to see camps as unparalleled sites for an educational immersion in Jewishness, child-centered Judaism of the fullest expression.

## Summer Camps: American and American Jewish

While the conditions of the postwar period brought educational camping into the spotlight, using camps as sites for mitigating cultural anxieties was not, in and of itself, an American Jewish innovation, and sleepaway camping did not first appear in the postwar period. As pioneer-style experiences, turn-of-the-century summer camps illustrated anxieties that held currency on both sides of the Atlantic. European and North American reformers similarly believed that urban life posed problems for the nurturing of healthy, well-behaved, moral children. But while youth movements in Europe such as Germany's Wandervogel and the British scouting movement revealed how "fresh air" ideas influenced children on both continents, organized, longer-term summer camping experiences flourished in North America much more so than in Europe.

Jewish summer camping's long history in America shifted alongside both Jewish history, American life, and the parallel growth of the broader American camping sector, beginning at the onset of the Progressive Era.[38] In light of changing understandings of childhood, progressive activists came to believe "that children's physical and social environments" had tremendous import.[39] The fresh air reformers saw camps as ideal settings for providing children with recreation, character development, and physical health, "translat[ing] anti-modern anxieties into youth-specific terms."[40] Progressive camping also responded to a particular set of gender-based anxieties, provoked by the idea that industrialization and urbanization threatened traditional forms of masculinity. Women, male camping leaders argued, had too strong an influence in cultural life and in the home; boys and young men, cut off from traditional forms of gendered labor, needed to acquire their sense of masculinity through retreats into the wilderness.[41]

Jewish families embraced sleepaway camp from the movement's fresh air rise, their earliest options mainly including philanthropic summer camps like those of the settlement house movement, which served immigrant and first-generation youth at low cost or completely free. But with their emphases on acclimating children to American life, these camps made very few concessions for religious and cultural difference, prompting the concurrent development of camps sponsored by Jewish philanthropic agencies.[42] In 1893,

Camp Lehman, for working-class Jewish boys run by the 92nd Street Y in New York, and the Jewish Working Girls' Vacation Society's Camp Isabella Freedman both opened their doors, with the Educational Alliance's Surprise Lake Camp following shortly afterward in 1901. Private Jewish camps also began to appear, primarily serving middle-class Jewish youth whose families had arrived in the United States a few decades earlier than the peak of mass immigration in the 1880s. One of the first private Jewish camps, Schroon Lake in New York, was founded in 1906 by Rabbi Isaac Moses of Manhattan's Central Synagogue. Beginning with just the rabbi, his son, and eleven other boys from his congregation, the camp demonstrated a theme in early twentieth-century camping writ large, as most camps started out with one or two enthusiastic leaders, a small group of campers, and a relatively undeveloped piece of land.[43] Jewish leaders like Rabbi Moses adopted this camping style from Christian clergy, whose earliest experiments in camping predated camps like Lehman and Schroon Lake by two decades.[44]

While only a few thousand American children went to camp in the late 1800s, 15 percent of children nationwide attended a summer camp in the interwar years, signifying camping's rising popularity among middle- and upper-class whites. Camp attendance reached 1 million campers each summer in the 1920s and doubled to 2 million each summer in the 1930s, its staggering growth attributing to the growing middle class, the expansion of high school attendance, and evolving perceptions of childhood and adolescence. Interwar camps also experienced myriad stylistic and philosophical changes; whereas early camps housed children in tents, lacked indoor plumbing, and had few or no permanent structures, camps of the interwar period began to build up and modernize their facilities, attracting increasingly middle-class families that had come to expect better conditions.

Established as bulwarks of antimodernism, camp leaders both Christian and Jewish wondered if "the new cabins" were "truly an illustration of the camp's rising quality of life," as Leslie Paris explained, or if they "were a sign that the boys were no longer truly and authentically camping."[45] Nevertheless, modernized facilities and permanent campsites prevailed by the beginning of the postwar period, as did an evolving system of camp oversight and cooperation in regard to health and safety. While the first association to organize camping leaders was the Camp Directors' Association (CDA), founded in

1910, camping slowly became more organized and controlled in the 1920s through the 1940s.[46] After several smaller organizations merged, the American Camping Association (ACA) was established in 1935, immediately suggesting recommended standards for camps regarding health, sanitation, and program goals. The ACA's role in camping expanded dramatically in the postwar years as it saw itself tasked with protecting "children by examining the operation of the camps in the light of proven, acceptable, high-level performance." But it was the modernization of camping in the interwar period that set these changes into motion.[47] As their focus on antimodernism dissipated, American camps came to address an array of new social concerns, including the increasingly visible and problematized youth culture, Cold War anxieties over education and democratic values, and a sense that moral and religious values were in a state of decline.

In these foundational decades of American camping, "the search for camps attuned to one's cultural and religious heritage was not uniquely Jewish."[48] In the Progressive Era, Christian camping found inspiration in both the fresh air and Social Gospel movements and from the "outdoor revivals of the Second Great Awakening."[49] Some early Christian camps functioned as conversionary experiences, with goals of instilling "religious fervor" in youth, while most came to embrace Horace Bushnell's critique of crisis conversion encapsulated in his philosophy of "Christian Nurture," which held that the purpose of Christian education is to lead children to "grow up in Christ."[50] At the same time, private Christian camps and those sponsored by the Young Men's Christian Association embedded their programs with the philosophy of muscular Christianity, taking "white males out of the squalor of city living and domestic feminization to pursue the more manly pursuits of wilderness, self-reliance, and Christian values" as their main goals.[51] Most Christian camps gathered groups of children for long-weekend and week-long programs, although many in the Northeast, particularly for the Protestant elite, developed as four- to eight-week programs.

While these different kinds of Christian camps certainly demonstrate the American camping sector's long-standing diversity, American Jews have embraced a particular kind of residential sleepaway camps with unique gusto, owing in large part to their significant population size in the northeastern United States, where sleepaway camping began and predominated.

While religious Christian camps typically took place over short periods of time and while Muslims would adopt a similar conference style as they began to create camps in the 1970s and 1980s, Jews overwhelmingly followed the northeastern style of long camp sessions lasting somewhere between three weeks to two months, even as their camps expanded to other parts of the country where lengthy camping programs proved rare.[52] As an expression of their zeal, Jewish camping emerged over time as diverse as American Jewry itself, with camps serving local Jewish communities, ideological movements, and, eventually, every movement of Judaism, from Reform to various sects of Hasidism.

Considering American Jewry's overwhelming enthusiasm for public schooling and the diversity of their urban neighborhoods in the early twentieth century, the development of a separate Jewish camping sector was hardly a given.[53] But while public schools, as agents of the state, had a mandate to serve all children, American recreation during the early- to mid-twentieth century proved quite segregated. Like the Jewish hotels and bungalows of the Catskills made famous in the movie *Dirty Dancing* or the more recent TV show *The Marvelous Mrs. Maisel*, Jewish summer camps came about because Jews were often blocked out of other vacation options, either rejected due to anti-Semitism and nativism or finding the camps unaccommodating to their religious and cultural needs like kosher or kosher-style food.[54] Between private camps serving middle-class Protestant youth, congregational Christian camps, and philanthropic camps with assimilationist missions, Jews had few options other than to create a camping world of their own. The proliferation of Jewish camps, however, offered families more than a set of options for their children. As the nativism of the 1920s and the general pressures of Americanization led many Jews to abandon their languages, mute their cultural distinctiveness, and modify their religious practices, the social safety of Jewish summer camps, even those without significant degrees of educational or religious content in their daily schedules, provided children an opening to express their Jewishness in a welcoming and secure environment. Exclusion played an important role in initiating the founding of Jewish camps in the Progressive Era, but the enthusiasm these camps inspired came to fuel the sector's growth and transition into Jewish education-focused camping, a process that began in the interwar period and intensified in the immediate postwar years.

### Jewish Summer Camps Embrace Jewish Education

A Jewish camping sector of one sort or another has remained a constant since the earliest years of American camping. But the reasons that families chose Jewish camps, the types of camps that proved most common, and the degree of institutional investment and professionalization in the enterprise evolved alongside twentieth-century Jewish developments at home and abroad. Communal and philanthropic camps like Surprise Lake and Lehman and private camps like Schroon Lake continued to dot the northeastern United States in the 1910s and 1920s, and even expanded to Jewish communities in other parts of the country, particularly the Midwest. In 1934, the Jewish Welfare Board (JWB) began to financially support and promote camps, and by 1936, its "Directory of Summer Camps under the Auspices of Jewish Communal Organizations" listed "eighty-eight camps in the United States and Canada," not including "the many privately run summer camps" that American Jews had also established.[55]

A new set of camps, decidedly educational in their missions, also came about in the 1920s, for the most part as extensions of year-round Zionist movements and Yiddish organizations. Yiddish-oriented camping began with the Sholem Aleichem Folk Institute's (SAFI) camping experiment of 1919, when the institute's *folkshul* (Yiddish school) leader, Leibush Lehrer, brought a group of just ten students out into nature. Eventually naming their barebones, rugged program "Boiberik," an ironic reference to the vacation colonies of wealthy Jews of Yehupetz in Sholem Aleichem's stories, the camp swiftly became more organized, purchasing a permanent site in Rhinebeck, New York, where a structured program permeated with Yiddish culture and language began.[56] Boiberik also developed a separate side of its site for adult guests.

Other Yiddish-oriented summer camps emerged out of labor movements and fraternal organizations. The New York Labor Zionist Farband established Camp Kindervelt in 1925. In the same year, the International

Workers Order organized Camp Kinderland, while the Workmen's Circle's first camp, Camp Kinder Ring, was founded in 1927. These camps deviated from one another according to the ideologies of the organizations that ran them: the Farband camps promoted Zionism, the International Workers Order camps promoted communism, and Workmen's Circle camps promoted socialism. But they shared a core interest in educating children about and infusing their camps with Yiddish culture. They also all expanded over the course of the early twentieth century to sponsor several camps each in the United States and Canada. Around twenty-five Yiddish camps existed at some time before 1945, mostly on rented campsites and lasting only a few years each.[57] However, camps established on purchased campsites, particularly in the Northeast, where these movements all had their strongholds, lasted much longer. While the last Kindervelt closed in 1971 and Boiberik followed in 1980, the New York camps Kinder Ring and Kinderland both continue as Yiddish and socialist-imbued programs through the current day.

Zionist camping began in the 1920s as small, experimental programs on farms or underdeveloped tracts of land, primarily in the northeastern United States. The first Zionist camp, founded by the Labor Zionist movement Hashomer Hatzair in 1928, functioned as a training farm where young adults trained for life on the kibbutzim of the Jewish settlements in Palestine. This concept of preparing for immigration by simulating life in Palestine emerged in Europe, taking on the Hebrew name *hachshara*, meaning preparation. The Habonim youth movement quickly followed with a similar venture in 1932, gathering fourteen members to live together in one tent in Highland Mills, New York. One year later, the Young Poale Zion Alliance, Habonim's affiliated forerunner, established Camp Kvutzah in the Catskills, a more modernized camp in terms of its site and its program, in which campers learned the movement's fundamentals of "collective-democratic living, a full Jewish life, and self-labor." The Young Poale Zion Alliance established two more camps in 1935, one near Montreal and another, named Tel Hai, in Michigan, for Jewish youth of the Midwest. The religious Zionist youth movement Bnei Akiva developed on a similar course, running its first summer camp in 1936 on a tract of land rented for just twenty-five dollars, establishing a farm in Livingston Manor, New York, for the purpose of *hachshara* in 1941, and finally developing its first modernized camping facility in Pennsylvania in 1949. Like those of the Yiddish organizations, many of the camps eventually established themselves on permanent sites and lasted for decades, while others were on-again, off-again ventures that moved from place to place.[58]

Some early educational camps also grew out of independent Jewish educational initiatives. The Central Jewish Institute's Camp Cejwin, led by Albert P. and Bertha Schoolman, as well as Camp Modin, a private Jewish educational camp developed in part by the Schoolmans, began in 1919 and 1922, respectively. These camps emphasized a centrist style of Zionism, Hebrew learning, and pluralistic approaches to Jewish practice. Samson Benderly, a pioneering progressive Jewish educator, founded Camp Achvah in 1927 to expand and enrich the educational experiences of the Kvutzah, a group of students from Hebrew High School in New York.[59] Although the camp lasted only five years, Achvah proved influential to a wide array of educational camps, including the Brandeis Camp Institute, founded in 1941 by Shlomo Bardin. Beginning first in New Hampshire, BCI ran short-term, high-level Jewish educational programs for youth from the ages of eighteen to twenty-six.[60] Primarily Zionist in orientation at the start, BCI received sponsorship from the Zionist Organization of America for its first several years. But unlike the camps of the various Zionist youth movements, Bardin quickly moved away from a strict focus on Zionism and toward a more pluralistic vision of Judaism, inviting secular, Reform, Conservative, and Orthodox youth for BCI sessions. After three moves around the East Coast, BCI settled in its permanent home in 1947 in Simi Valley, California, where it also established a children's program, Camp Alonim, in 1953.[61]

The years between BCI's establishment in 1941 and the foundation of the Reform movement's Union Institute summer camp in 1952 constitute what historian Jonathan Sarna has termed the "crucial decade" in Jewish camping. Whereas before 1940, around "two-thirds of all new Jewish camps were either philanthropic . . . or community-based camps founded by Jewish federations and community centers," the number of educational camps grew precipitously in the decades after 1940, with "almost 40 percent of them trumpet[ing] educational and religious aims." While Sarna drew these rough data from the "admittedly imprecise figures" from an early camping scholar named Daniel Isaacman, this designation of a crucial decade correctly describes the enormous expansion of educational camping in the 1940s and into the 1950s.

The histories of Yiddish and Zionist camping, however, place the idea that "the core of camping's educational potential" reached its full realization only in the 1940s into question.[62] Taking these camps into serious consideration, the decade from 1942 to 1952 represents less the crucial decade of Jewish camping than a link in a longer chain of events: Cejwin and Massad served as models for camps like Ramah, but Boiberik, Moshava, and Kinder Ring, their predecessors, were models in their own right for camps like Massad. Still, the establishment of Reform and Conservative movement camps, which quickly became become larger and more influential than these earlier camps and camping movements, marked an important moment of growth for the sector. The development of Reform and Conservative camping also mirrored the expansion of their movements more broadly, as both gained substantial energy, popularity, and resources under the new suburban conditions of postwar American Jewry.

Camps for Orthodox Jews similarly reflected the state of Orthodoxy itself. However, their camps followed a rather dissimilar historical trajectory from those of the more liberal movements of Judaism. A handful of camps for the children of traditional or Orthodox families, loosely affiliated with Yeshiva University, began in the 1920s as fresh air experiences for urban youth. One such camp, Machanaim, advertising itself as "The American Camp with Jewish Spirit," served as an escape "from the hot expanses of city streets . . . [and] the dangers of play on unprotected avenues." Recruiting campers mainly from the *yeshivot* and Talmud Torahs of New York City, Camps Machanaim and Shari focused not on Jewish education but on providing children with a "happy vacation," returning home as "better Americans, more appreciative Jews and healthier children."[63] But Shari and Machanaim were different from other Jewish camps of the progressive and interwar periods in their strict abidance to kosher laws, regularly scheduled times for prayer, and observance of the Sabbath according to *halacha* (Jewish law). Indeed, Camp Shari placed its kosher adherence so much at the core of its character that it promoted itself with the simple tagline, "The Recognized Camp of *Kashrut*."[64] Although they lacked organized educational programs, these camps did have Jewish goals, aiming to introduce in children "the flames of Judaism in so subtle a fashion that it is inculcated and molded into their consciousness without any effort on their part."[65] By the forties, there were also several private Orthodox camps for middle- and upper-middle-class families that focused on recreation rather than education.

Religious Zionist summer camps emerged too, such as the Bnei Akiva youth movement's Camp Moshava, the first location of which was founded in 1936. While it placed its educational focus mainly on Zionism and Israel, it similarly provided an opportunity for youth to live as traditional Jews. Orthodox Jews also sent their children to a handful of pluralistic Jewish summer camps including Massad, where, as Sarna writes, children "from Orthodox Zionist homes . . . and the socio-cultural elite of Conservative and Reform Judaism lived together with children from secular Zionist homes." Camps for children from more strictly observant Orthodox Jewish families also slowly developed beginning in the 1940s. At Camp Agudah, founded by Agudath Israel of America in 1941, religious boys would have "the chance to spend their vacation in a truly Torah-loyal atmosphere, where their faith in the Almighty will be strengthened, not demoralized."[66]

Agudah, its eventual sister camp, Camp Bnos, and Camp Monk formally established in 1955 by Rav Yechiel Aryeh Monk, exhibit that the use of Jewish camping as a form of education was not only the domain of liberal Jews of the postwar period. These camps actively sought to inspire children to embrace Jewish ideas and practices through education and immersion, in some cases leading campers to become more Orthodox in worldview than their own tuition-paying parents. But while camps like Agudah and Monk provided a vital starting point for a later boom in Orthodox camping, the crucial period of Orthodox camping truly began only in the late 1960s, a full two decades after more liberal Jewish movements, reflecting not only Orthodoxy's divergent time line and diversity but its postwar metamorphosis. As what was becoming known as Modern Orthodoxy grew in population size, self-assuredness, and affluence in the 1960s, its communities emerged more organized than and more distinct from other kinds of more traditional, *frum*, or Hasidic Jewish communities. While many liberal Orthodox families had once embraced pluralistic camps like Massad, a burgeoning and more structurally clear Modern Orthodox society meant that camps serving the specific tastes of these families could truly prosper, leading to the estab-

lishment of a new set of camps serving an increasingly affluent and subur-
banized religious community.[67]

Jewish camps' trajectories mirrored the status of their religious denominations or ideologies as they waxed and waned in popularity and relevance,
the sector evolving to present families with options that most appealed to
their sensibilities at the time. At the same time, a camp's longevity proved inextricable from other economic and logistical realities, including the strength
of their sponsoring institutions and the class status of their clientele. As the
American Association for Jewish Education found in 1963, fees for the average Jewish camp "were high—the average minimum weekly charge was
$66.67, and the maximum $71.28"—but they also differed by denomination,
with Orthodox camps having the lowest weekly rates, "usually between $39
and $43," and Conservative having the highest, with an average minimum
weekly cost of $72, reflecting their clienteles' differing class status.[68] While
92 percent of Jewish camps offered some scholarship assistance for campers
from lower-income families, the children of synagogue and temple members
"attending their own denominational camps" had the extra help of fundraising from their home communities, a fact that fortified their successes.
Of the 7 percent that did not offer scholarships, 50 percent were sponsored
by Yiddish cultural institutions, an outsized number that demonstrates the
troubling financial realities of their sponsoring organizations that contributed to the closing of most Yiddish camps by the end of the 1970s.[69]

Reform and Conservative camps not only enjoyed by far the most consistent and durable systems of fundraising and recruiting, receiving campers
from local synagogue and temple leadership who supported and promoted
these camps to congregants; they also had better resources for finding qualified staff members from their rabbinical and education schools.[70] All of
these advantages led Ramah and the UAHC camps to eclipse many of their
educational predecessors, most notably Cejwin and Massad, which suffered
their final blows during and after the recession of the 1970s. Zionist camps'
affiliations with larger movements, like the Zionist Organization of America and Hadassah in Young Judaea's case, also provided a ready pool of potential campers in the children of these organizations' members, as well as
built-in models of financial support. Zionist camps also originally had steady
supplies of young leaders who worked at camp as part of their commitment

to the year-round movement. But as their youth movements shrank in size and activity, their pool of qualified counselors shrank too. Beginning in the 1970s, many of these camps became increasingly reliant on Israeli *shlichim*, or emissaries, from the Jewish Agency to fill essential roles at camp, working alongside American movement members.[71] Up through the 1950s, Yiddish camps had a similar automatic system of recruitment for campers and staff members: camps affiliated with schools typically populated their camps with their school-year students, while the camps of unions and fraternal organizations appealed to members to send their kids to their camps. But as the number of students in Yiddish schools and number of members in unions and fraternal organizations declined along with Yiddish itself, recruiting campers and staff became a more difficult task.[72] Their lack of direct staff and camper recruitment, and their resulting financial instabilities, made camps Hemshekh, Boiberik, and Kindervelt all close by 1980, citing shrinking enrollments and struggling finances.[73]

―――――――

The historical turning points and trends of the twentieth century crafted a unique moment for the expansion of American summer camping, as anxieties surrounding child development, education, and modernity had served as catalysts for the foundation and evolution of all sorts of American camps, continuing to play roles even as camps changed their missions and purposes. Postwar American camps came to reflect trends in Christianity, American education, and youth culture too. But for postwar Jews, who experienced the changes of the period as they processed the devastations of the recent Holocaust, summer camps were evolving into sites of tremendous importance and investment. To Jewish leaders like Mogilner, who crafted these camps' programs with an eye toward transformation, the stakes were high and the mission was clear. Citing camps' potential to curb the decline of Jewish culture via children and teenagers, postwar camp leaders saw the successful implementation of their programs as a matter of cultural life and death. As the next chapter shows, these historical circumstances shaped the content and the purpose of life at camp from dawn until dusk, inflecting the everyday with the heavy weight of the American Jewish future.

# A Matter of Time

## Constructing Time for "Creative Survival"

IN 1955, MORRIS FREEDMAN, a writer, visited Camp Ramah in Connecticut to report on the new summer camp for the Jewish magazine *Commentary*. Growing up in a secular, Yiddish-speaking home, Freedman approached the Conservative camp a skeptic, noting with surprise that the campers proved rather "normal" despite their passion for Hebrew and Judaism, and asking camp educators whether Ramah "ought to be using the group pressures . . . to put over its religious program." But his interrogations did not ruffle the feathers of the Ramah camp leaders, who saw the power of camp in a different light. " 'What better place than a summer camp to teach Judaism to youngsters," replied one rabbi, "since you can control their daily lives in every way?' "[1]

The term *control* may evoke the brainwashing of religious cults more so than the fun-in-the-sun promise of the summer camp. And yet the notion that camp's transformative powers laid in its control over "the child's environment for 24 hours a day, 8 weeks a year" proved nearly universal among postwar Jewish camping's diverse stakeholders. As Jewish education scholar Daniel Isaacman wrote in 1966, camp allowed "the experience of Jewish living" to be more effectively conveyed in a couple of months in the summer than in "an entire school year of class instruction."[2] A decade earlier, Camp Boiberik's Leibush Lehrer similarly described that once his staff "had the children under our control for 24 hours a day," they would have "a free hand" to shape campers as they wished, making every hour of the day "where humanly possible related to Jewish life."[3] Jewish educator Asher Melzer echoed that sentiment in the 1970s, describing camp as a "total life experience," with all parts of the "daily routine of camp life" infused with Jewish "meaning and significance."[4] Scholars of Jewish summer camping have also portrayed camps in similar terms, describing them as "islands of Judaism," "total environments," and unparalleled sites for "foster[ing] in children a Jewish identity" in a "venue independent of their home environment."[5]

Sequestered in the countryside, sleepaway camps of all kinds are defined by their spatial remove from the everyday and by the act of entering a separated, devoted site with its own culture, norms, and routines.[6] The constructed environments of Jewish camps, with dedicated spaces for play, prayer, swimming, assembly, sleeping, eating, and strolling, designated typically with a name in Hebrew or Yiddish, mirrored a given camp's values,

Campers arriving at Camp Hemshekh, late 1960s.
Source: Kolodny Family Photos. Printed with permission.

ideologies, and priorities. Campsites also came to matter deeply to campers and staff, who often described their camp's scenic locale as a home away from home. But while some camps founded permanent sites immediately, making lasting marks on camp space with buildings, signage, flagpoles, statues, bunks, and other structures, many others moved from site to site one or several times before finding what became their final location; indeed, many camps both past and present operate on leased sites, their locations semipermanent.

Their precise locales and physical environments certainly mattered to the overall experience of being at camp, with campers and staff finding themselves attached to certain buildings, areas, views, and natural areas. So too did the architectural designs and quality of their facilities, which increasingly struck a balance between embracing the natural setting and meeting the material expectations of middle-class families. Nevertheless, the sites' sleepaway camps operate on proved less stable and influential than their fundamental insularity, which furnished educators with a "unique opportunity for coordinating the entire living experience of a child."[7] Much like the prisons, asylums, and monasteries evoked by Erving Goffman's concept of total institutions, residential camps have their own "hidden rhythms," or, as Eviatar Zerubavel put it, "unusual or innovative social order[s]" that "incubate and develop quite independently of the surrounding social environment."[8] The recreational quality of summer camp distinguishes them from these other sites, and unlike prisoners, campers ordinarily arrive of their own volition (although parents can certainly apply pressure). And yet camps are isolated environments in which one population controls the daily lives of another by supervising and structuring their every activity, nurturing routines, social orders, and rhythms that prove exceptional to life on the outside. While some postwar camps "retained the relatively unstructured approach of Fresh Air" camps in which "sports and games arose spontaneously," the schedules of American sleepaway camps became more planned and rigid from the interwar period onward, with limited hours of designated free time per day.[9] The power of camp space is the opportunity it offers to control inhabitants' time.

The special, palpable, and well-known effect of time within camp life earned its own designation within the world: "camp time." When camp leaders and participants invoked the term, they often used it to refer to one particularly common practice. At many camps, both Jewish and not, staff members moved the clocks back an hour in order to best use their days and make it easier for counselors to get younger children to go to sleep at earlier hours. At Jewish camps, moving the clocks back also provided the opportunity to shorten the lengthy summer Sabbath. Resetting watches on the first day, many camps quite literally operated on their own "private daylight-savings plan." But while operating on a clock different from the townspeople down the road served largely logistical purposes, existing in time zones of their own also strengthened the totalizing feeling of being at camp, fostering, as Jonathan Krasner put it, a "sense that camp existed as its own world divorced from the realities of everyday life."[10] A 2017 listicle published by the Foundation for Jewish Camp, "15 Ways You Know You Went to Jewish Summer Camp," captured this idea succinctly: a former camper "think[s] of time in two ways: camp time and real time. Camp has a very specific and distinct timeline that defies the time-space continuum: One camp day = one real world week, one camp week = one real world month, one camp month = six real world months. But somehow, an entire summer goes so fast that it feels like one real world day."[11] This variation on the common maxim, "a camp day feels like a week, a week feels like a month, and a month feels like a year," reveals that camp time is not only a logistical time zone some camps adopted but an emotional experience. As one former Ramah camper reflected in the pages of the *Forward*, "During the rest of the year, a few weeks can pass by in a blink, with little to 'write home' about. But in camp, a person can grow up in a month, or two. A person can fall in love. A person can change, forever."[12] At camp, a three-day-old friendship can feel closer and deeper than a three-year-long one at home; a week-long fling can feel like the romance of a lifetime; the initial surprises new campers experienced lost their peculiarity within a matter of a couple of days, if not hours. With so few moments left unoccupied, campers often expressed how long, intense, and significant their times at camp felt, the accumulation of jam-packed days for one or two months making the total experience epic in its proportions.[13]

The daily and weekly course of camp time proved remarkably similar from camp to camp, proceeding in comparable orders and including many of the same activities. Camps' schedules also appeared strikingly consistent over the decades, the structuring of time becoming a ritual of camp life that offered a sense of stability and tradition. While slight variations in the schedule meant that some campers worked in the early morning and learned in midafternoon, and others vice versa, Jewish leaders across the spectrum largely harnessed and organized time at camp to their ideological ends, using morning rituals, active afternoons, performative evenings, and the Sabbath to mark the end of the week. They also similarly embraced the sorts of activities present in American camps of all kinds, including flag raising, sports, swimming, hiking, and competitive games like capture the flag. In this sense, the story of camp time is one of similarity. Jewish leaders, whether Zionist, Yiddishist, Reform, or Conservative in background, all employed the totalizing qualities of camp time to their various ideological, religious, and nationalist ends, imbuing every hour of the day with their values and visions for the Jewish future.

At the same time, what occurred inside the printed boxes of camps' timetables played out in extraordinarily diverse ways in practice, with a camp's specific beliefs and values presented prominently in the details. The flags a camp raised in the morning, the songs campers sang, the plays they performed at night, and the ways they marked the Sabbath all mirrored a camp's precise purpose and ideology. Even as their names and orders rarely changed, the different scheduled parts of camp life reflected the historical conditions on the outside: the content of camp time evolved over the course of the postwar period alongside broader transitions in American and American Jewish life, including the broadening embrace of Zionism, the 1960s Jewish counterculture, and fluctuating popularity of progressive education.

No single chapter can account for all of the activities involved in everyday camp life or the manifold ways those activities each changed over time. Later chapters provide deeper analyses of camps' engagements with Jewish languages, mourning rituals, play, simulation, youth culture, and democracy, particular significant elements of camp cultures and norms. I offer this overview of camps' schedules, and a visual representation of an average daily schedule in Table 1, to demonstrate how camps' full and thoughtfully ordered timetables served as frameworks of the total experience. From activity to activity, hour to hour, and day to day, camp leaders wasted few opportunities to imbue life at camp with their visions of ideal Jewishness.[14] Moving through time from wake-up until lights out, from Sunday to the Sabbath, allows us to feel the shape and flow of camp life in our own imaginations. In so doing, we might come to understand on a visceral level how camp leaders used time and how campers experienced.

### Boker Tov, Chanichim! Prayer, Flags, and Calisthenics

The average morning in a Jewish summer camp normally began with one or two practices that intended to ground campers spiritually, physically, and mentally for the jam-packed day. The most common morning activities, prayer services and flag raising, had ample precedent in the broader world of American camping and were easily infused with religious or nationalist messages.[15] A 1963 survey of sixty-one Jewish summer camps found that 32 percent of camps that summer had included prayer in their morning routines, reciting either part or all of the traditional *shaharit* (morning) service. Holding services outdoors, having campers lead, and creating camp *siddurim* (prayer books) geared toward making prayer more evocative and accessible made the experience of *tfillot* (prayer) different at camp than in synagogues at home.[16] In 1948, for example, Zionist Camp Tel Yehudah's "musical and meaningful" prayer services took place under the leadership of teen campers, preparing the movement's youth for Jewish communal leadership and "render[ing] prayer meaningful and alive for the young people."[17] But while only some Zionist camps prayed each day, services represented a particularly important part of the experience at both the Ramah and Reform movement summer camps. Reform camp OSRUI advertised itself to parents as a place that combined "recreation, study, prayer, outdoor living and fellowship" in order to lead campers to an "appreciation of our religious and cultural heritage."[18] As one former *Ramahnik* explained, prayer at Ramah "was anything but passive," "the daily obligation of prayer with a unique blend of the modern and the traditional," and Ramah also held activities that allowed campers to better learn, understand, and reflect on their morning prayers.[19] In one such program, a group of counselors divided campers into groups and gave each one a prayer to discuss together, asking them what in the prayer could have "meaning for you today" and what they would "be called on to do" if they were to take the prayer seriously. Encouraging the children to ex-

Table 1. Amalgamation of Various Camps' Schedules

| Time | Zionist | Yiddishist | Reform and Conservative |
|---|---|---|---|
| 7:30 a.m. | *Hitamlut* (calisthenics) or *Tfillot* (morning prayers) | *Farzamlung* (a line-up assembly that often included a flag raising) | *Shacharit/Tfillot* (morning prayers) |
| 7:45 a.m. | *Ha-Ramat HaDegel* or *Mifkad Boker* (flag raising) | *Gimnastik* (calisthenics) | Flag raising or *HaRamat HaDegel* |
| 8:15 a.m. | *Aruchat Boker* (breakfast) | *Frishtik* (breakfast) | *Aruchat Boker* (breakfast) |
| 9:15 a.m. | Cleaning | Cleaning | *Nikayon* (cleanup) |
| 10:00 a.m. | Hebrew Learning | Yiddish Hour | *Chinuch* (education) |
| 11:00 a.m. | Sichot/Study Groups | *Yidish-sho* (Education or Jewish Hour) | Chinuch |
| 12:00 p.m. | Rotation: *Shira* (singing), *Rikud* (dancing), Drama, *Tsofiut* (scouting), Sports | Rotation: *Muzik* (singing), *Tantsn* (dancing), *Teater* (drama), Sports | Rotation: *Shira* (singing), *Rikud* (dancing), or Drama, Sports |
| 1:00 p.m. | *Aruchat Tsohorayim* (lunch) | *Mitog* (lunch) | *Aruch Tsohorayim* (lunch) |
| 2:00 p.m. | *Menucha* or *Chofesh* | Rest Hour or *Fraye-tsayt* (free time) | *Menucha* or *Chofesh* |
| 3:00 p.m. | Work Hour | Work Hour | *Chinuch* II or Work Hour |
| 4:00 p.m. | Rotation II | Rotation II | Rotation II |
| 5:00 p.m. | *Chugim* (choice period) | Choice Period | *Chugim* (choice period) |
| 6:00 p.m. | *Asepha* (assembly) | *Farzamlung/Zitsung/* (assembly) | *Asepha* or Assembly |
| 6:15 p.m. | Dinner | Dinner | Dinner |
| 8:00 p.m. | *Peulat Erev* (evening activity) | *Nakht-Aktivitet* (evening activity) | Evening Activity |
| 9:00 p.m. | Free time or lights out | | |
| 10:00 p.m. | Lights out | | |

Note: This table shows side-by-side examples of different kinds of Jewish camps' schedules throughout the postwar decades. The term *rotational activities* refers to moments in the schedule when the various age groups or bunk groups attended different activities around camp.

press what they felt "in their hearts," campers described their feelings to the rest of the camp during prayer services, their inward reflections becoming outward performances of spirituality and belief.[20]

Prayer at both the Ramah and Reform camps also developed in similarly experimental spirits, the stances and styles of campers and counselors eventually influencing the practices of their movements at home.[21] As many of Ramah's teenage and twenty-something counselors became influenced by the independent prayer groups of the Havurah movement, the do-it-yourself culture of the rejection of "the way Jews observe the Sabbath and their Jewishness in general in America," they pushed Ramah's religious practices into a simultaneously more traditional and more radical direction. Conceiving of themselves as different from the Jews of a "well-to-do synagogue," with their "minks, Cadillacs, diamonds, a Bar Mitzvah show, constant chatter," Ramahniks prayed exclusively in Hebrew, "recaptur[ed] the participatory quality of the pre-emancipation synagogue," revived spiritual tunes, or *niggunim*, and donned prayer shawls and tefillin, practices more ascribed to traditional Jews than the members of most Conservative synagogues in postwar suburbia. The younger generation's approach to gender also made Ramah's morning prayer services more egalitarian than the Conservative movement from which it emerged.[22] While Ramah "steadily increased the amount of participation allowed to women in the religious life of the community" throughout the 1950s and 1960s, the Conservative movement's synagogues, assemblies, and seminaries "responded sluggishly to the needs of youngsters who had tasted the probing and passion of the Ramah *nusah* (style)."[23] This tension, between camps influenced by the counterculture and a postwar Judaism molded by middle-class suburbia, eventually fertilized Conservative synagogues with new styles, traditions, and approaches to prayer and gender, but it took time for the movement to catch up with Ramah's progressivism, with the Jewish Theological Seminary beginning to grant women rabbinic ordination only in 1984.[24]

Prayer at Reform camps similarly "impressed the campers as very special and different from those they knew at their home congregations," particularly as "the normal service" at camp included "a lot of singing."[25] Camps' participatory prayer style, directed by a guitar-strumming song leader, filtered into the movement's temples via their youth movement, NFTY, start-

Prayer services at Camp Ramah California.
Source: Courtesy of the National Ramah Commission. Printed with permission.

ing in the mid-1960s, slowly but surely replacing the kinds of quiet "liturgical music played on the organ and performed by the cantor and a professional four-part choir." Indeed, UAHC camps have played significant roles as incubators for Jewish musicians—for example, Michael Isaacson, Daniel Freelander, Debbie Friedman, and Jeff Klepper—who used the camp environment to experiment, refine, and try their music out on youth. In both cases, prayer at the Ramah and UAHC camps demonstrates that the camps were not merely shaped by their movements from the top down, but also came to shape their movements back home from the bottom up.[26]

For the roughly 70 percent of camps that did not hold religious services, other practices came to take the first slot in the schedule after wake-up. The custom of flag raisings and morning assemblies provided all sorts of American camps with daily moments for gathering as an entire camp body, setting intentions, making announcements, and expressing patriotism. But for Jewish camps, reveille practices, often called *haramat hadegel* (flag raising), *mifkad* (roll call or morning assembly), or *khavershaft farzamlung* (literally "camaraderie gathering," but also a kind of morning roll assembly) also became infused with their ideologies, beginning with the question of which flags should be raised in the first place.

While Zionist camps actively embraced raising the Israeli flag and singing "Hativkah," the Israeli anthem, alongside the American flag and the "Star-Spangled Banner," the question proved less clear-cut in both the Reform and Conservative camps.[27] As Ramah first identified as an "American camp and not an Israel-oriented one," many of its original leaders from the seminary "ambivalent about Zionism," the camps debated the question of flag raising in their first foundational five years. As Shuly Rubin Schwartz explained, when "older campers raise the question of dual loyalty," feeling that "the raising of the Israeli flag was un-American and perhaps illegal," Camp Ramah in the Poconos struck a compromise, creating a "Jewish people's flag," with the Ten Commandments between two blue stripes to fly instead of the Israeli one. The controversy and the criticism it brought Ramah from outside the camp (when Camp Massad caught wind of the decision, the nearby camp notoriously raided Ramah by foot and by plane to drop Israeli flags all over the campgrounds) eventually led some of the Ramah camps to eliminate flag raising for a few years.[28] This ambivalence, however, did not last long. As a 1958 photograph from Ramah in the Poconos shows, raising the Israeli flag had begun by that year. In 1967, the campers and counselors of the Reform Swig Camp Institute similarly deliberated whether raising the Israeli flag proved disloyal to America or disrespected Israelis, since, as American Jews, they had not fought in Israel's wars.[29] But by the end of the 1960s, Jewish camps, including both Swig and Ramah, largely settled on raising the Israeli flag alongside the American flag, mirroring the wider embrace of Zionism in the years coming up to and following the Six-Day War.

Yiddishist camps like Hemshekh prove fascinating exceptions to this general rule. As an expression of their Bundist politics, Hemshekh raised the American flag at its daily khavershaft farzamlung but never an Israeli one, raising instead a special red and white Hemshekh flag adorned with a falcon, the symbol of several socialist movements including the Jewish Labor

Bund's youth movement in Europe and Australia, SKIF.[30] As counselors instructed campers to line up in the shape of the letter *khes* [ח], so began a ritual call and response between campers and staff, repeating the word *khavershaft* (friendship). The camp's director, Mikhl Baran, then made announcements about the camp schedule and read sports scores and "headlines from the *NY Times* and from the Yiddish *Forverts*." The assembly ended with a chosen bunk leading the whole camp in the camp's anthem, "Mir Kumen On."

Following flag raising, many Jewish socialist and communist camps, including Hemshekh, Kinderring, Kinderland, and Shomria, included a short period of group exercises, scheduled as *gimanstik* (Yiddish) or *hitamlut* (Hebrew). Calisthenics hearkened back to some of the activities in socialist Eastern European youth movements as well as to various Zionist "preparation" or *hachshara* programs in Europe, which sought to train young Jews for the climate and labor awaiting them after immigration to Palestine. While hitamlut fit the overall Labor Zionist vision of the New Jew, however, the idea of strengthening the body to build up the land, Yiddish camps' *gimnas-*

*Khavershaft Farzamlung*, or morning meeting and flag raising, at Camp Hemshekh, 1972.
Source: Henry Nusbaum. Printed with permission.

*tik* or *genitung* (exercise) programs reflected the idea that physical culture was part of a being a socialist.[31] Although it is unclear how long or how consistently these camps included calisthenics on their schedules, evidence of the activity on camps' schedules shows how even the earliest rituals of the morning mirrored camps' diverse ideological visions of Jewish culture.

### Cleanup

After one or two of these morning customs, campers entered their camp's *chadar ochel* or *ess-tsimer* (cafeteria) for breakfast. During mealtime, campers chatted, sang, and cheered while they ate and listened to announcements from staff about the day's schedule. At denominational as well as more religiously oriented Zionist camps, a short prayer for bread preceded the meal and the longer *Birkat HaMazon* (grace after meals) followed it. At every meal, older campers worked as servers or designated cleaners, usually one camper from each bunk playing the role of waiter each day, cycling through all of campers by the end of the summer. Many camps named this role after the Hebrew term *toranut*, referencing the cyclical duties taken on by members of kibbutzim or as soldiers in the Israeli army, while other camps used the word *waiter* or the Yiddish word, *kelner*.

When it came to standards of cleanliness inside their bunks, campers were given similar responsibilities. Indeed, camps often followed breakfast with a period of in-bunk cleaning (*nikayon* in Hebrew). At Labor Zionist camps like Shomria, the camp's lack of amenities served as a socialist badge of honor, with campers cleaning together, posing an integral part of living as a collective.[32] But periods for communal cleaning appeared in most camp schedules, regardless of their stance on socialism. One Ramah educator, for instance, held that *nikayon* contributed to the education and character building of children, teaching them a skill toward their own independence.[33] Taken together, toranut and nikayon both fostered an expectation that campers would take part in the maintenance of camp, contributing to the experience as participants or members of a camp society rather than as consumers.

## Education Hour

Zionist, Yiddishist, Reform, and Conservative camps typically held their educational programming midmorning, when campers' minds and attention spans proved freshest. As counselors, rabbis, and Jewish educators led campers through discussions, lesson plans, and experiential programs related to cultural, religious, linguistic, and political themes, education hour, called by many names, including Jewish hour, *lern-sho* (education hour), *yidish-sho* (Yiddish/Jewish hour), or *peulat chinuch* (educational activity), revealed the ideological orientations of camps most blatantly. Using both formal and informal pedagogical styles and even vacillating between the two over the course of the postwar decades, a camp's given methods also reflected its particular values and goals. "How one learned [was] as important" an indicator, wrote Riv-Ellen Prell, "as what one learned."[34]

Guided discussions, role-playing games, and debates over political or religious issues and group projects all fell into the broad category of informal education, the most common set of pedagogical techniques used by Jewish camps. Zionist camps, for instance, used discussion circles (from the Hebrew word *sicha,* meaning discussion) as their main vehicle for education. During a sicha, counselors and campers spoke about politics, Zionist thought, Judaism, and history. Using a discussion format, educators hoped campers would come to understand topics through the lens of their and their peers' own responses, showing the topic's relevance to campers' lives. One camper described Tel Yehudah's discussion sessions in a poem: "The act of learning can be so beautiful / It's all encompassing, here, there every minute / *Sichot*, discussion, sitting Indian fashion / Under shady trees, raised hands, quizzical eyes."[35] But even as some campers clearly gained something from the sicha method, others pushed back against it through humor: one Shomria camper wrote in the camp's newspaper, "You try to have a sicha about something deep / half of them are talkin', the other half's asleep."[36]

Yiddishist camps like Kinderland, Kinder Ring, and Hemshekh focused their education hours primarily on Yiddish culture, Jewish history, and the ideologies of socialism, communism, or Bundism, using discussion groups, storytelling, interactive projects, and skits. As fewer and fewer campers arrived speaking Yiddish from the home, however, with the number declining throughout the postwar decades, all of these camps increased their focus on teaching the Yiddish language itself. Boiberik, unique among Yiddish camps in its embrace of religious traditions and ideas, also taught campers about Jewish holidays, rituals, and the Bible. The camp differed from others in its embrace of classroom-style teaching methods. In part as a means of mitigating the decline of vernacular Yiddish, the camp's "Jewish Hour" experimented with more formal educational methods in the late 1940s and 1950s. But by the 1960s, the camp had turned to a fully informal and experiential approach to Jewish education, finding that campers did not respond well to programs that seemed in any way akin to school.

Frontal or more classroom-style instruction had a longer-lasting presence in the Ramah camps due to its affiliation with the Jewish Theological Seminary, and camps like Yavneh, an outgrowth of the Hebrew Teachers College of Boston. Their relative formality not only reflected their educational goals and their professionalized pools of staff but developments in American education during their foundational years, a moment of pedagogical conservatism prompted by a backlash to progressive education against the backdrop of the Cold War. In the 1950s, children of these camps took part in educational programs that closely resembled classes in schools, with teachers or rabbis teaching in a frontal manner. Course topics at both camps varied but centered mostly on religious texts, Hebrew, and Jewish history, slowly integrating more and more content regarding Israel beginning in the 1960s. Ramah's educators found formal methods compelling as "a vehicle for teaching the 'basics' and essentials of Jewish religious life and literature," communicating "the information, facts, and conceptions which are judged to be most essential for a camper to acquire during his years at camp." The formality of Ramah's courses included not only frontal teaching but essays, group work, textbooks, and worksheets. But by the early 1970s, Ramah's informal programs proved themselves to be, according to one educator, "the central medium of inculcating Jewish life in the campers."[37] While some formality remained, the Ramah camps of the 1960s had moved more toward project-based learning, role-playing activities, debates, discussions, and other informal methods that had become the norm in Jewish camps, as educators more widely reembraced progressive educational ideas and formats in response to the youth culture and the realignment of children to authority.

## An Active Afternoon

Following lunch, campers typically went to rest for an hour in their bunks or had a period of free time around the camp's grounds to relax, play, and socialize. It was in these hours and during other moments between programs that the camper culture described in more detail in later chapters flourished. After the break, many camps held a work hour, as either a separate activity or part of a rotating set of activities that included arts and crafts, music, dance, sports, drama, and scouting. Infusing a mélange of Zionist, socialist, and essential American messaging influenced by the Protestant work ethic, work hour created opportunities for campers to beautify, build, and take responsibility for and within the camp environment. At Zionist camps, *avodah* was purposed with connecting campers with the Jews of Palestine, and later Israel, simulating kibbutz life. Thus, the work projects that camp leaders crafted often matched those that would theoretically occupy kibbutz members, including farming, tending to animals, cooking, and building structures. An article by a Tel Yehudah attendee in the *Senior*, Young Judaea's newspaper, glorified the experience of kibbutz-inflected notion of avodah at camp, poetically bemoaning the difficulties of work while acknowledging the joy found in labor and a recognition of its necessity:

> Lift the shovel, wield the hoe, one, two, squeeze (look, there's milk). Feed the chickens, peel some carrots, scrub the floor, turn about, do some more. . . . Sun beats down, sweat trickles, so hot—do I have to? I will not answer. Come to the *gan* [garden] first. Look you planted here— and now the seed lives and grows. Can you understand now? Taut, rigid muscles, sweet surging exhaustion. If I did not work, these worlds would perish.[38]

A Tel Yehudah advertising pamphlet similarly stressed how campers participated "actively and physically in the camp maintenance and general welfare. The garden . . . the grounds, the dining hall, the clean-up of the bunks and special projects such as painting, carpentry, form a regular part of the camp program." Work gave the campers not only "the feeling that that they are an integral part of Tel Yehudah, helping and improving," but also allowed them to "learn the value of working with the hands in a congenial atmosphere."[39] While Tel Yehudah was technically centrist and pluralistic in its Zionism, idealistic visions of labor Zionist kibbutzim pervaded its Zionism, guiding its inclusion of work on the camp's schedule.

Typically holding daily labor hours for campers of all ages and stages, work represented a crucial part of Zionist camp culture from the 1940s through the 1970s as leaders aimed for camp life to simulate the lifestyles of new Israelis and produce better movement leaders. But at the explicitly Labor Zionist camps like Shomria and Tavor, work encompassed an especially important and defining aspect of camp life. "The basic concept" of the camp "is that of work and human interrelations" explained one Shomria advertisement geared to parents. Camp was not an "idle pastime," but a place "that calls for direct involvement which ultimately gives the campers a sense of achievement and inner fulfillment."[40] Through a mixture of "fun, work, and study in a group framework," the camp hoped "to help Jewish youth identify more closely with their Jewish heritage, Israel, and humanitarian ideals."[41] At Habonim camps, campers took an active role in camp for a similar purpose. "Unless the individual is part of the day's activity," one camp leader explained, "we will fail in our attempt to develop him into the person we want," a leader of the movement or a future immigrant to Israel.[42] As an embodiment of their commitments to socialism, Bundism, or communism, furthermore, Yiddish camps emphasized labor in camp life in similar ways to Labor Zionist camps. Both Kinderring and Kinderland placed a period of work on their daily schedules, and when Hemshekh came along in 1959, it followed this established practice. Calling the period *arbet-sho* (work hour), Hemshekh's leaders espoused that "every child should perform some useful job for the camp, in order to make it better and more beautiful."[43]

Socialists and Zionists did not hold a monopoly on labor as a value, and neither did their camps. Indeed, American camps of all kinds shared a general rhetoric about the benefits of work for the development of children, emphasizing the importance of gaining of skills, responsibility, and independence. The Ramah camps mirrored this general outlook in the world of camping, viewing daily work as crucial to the development of the ideal Jewish child, one who "exhibits the common personal qualities and work habits needed for success . . . [and] respects all kinds of socially useful work."[44] Joining a work project each summer, the Ramah camper of the 1950s and 1960s encountered "an opportunity . . . to lose himself in hard physical labor and see some tangible results," developing a strong work ethic, "intellectual and emotional non-dependence on his family" and "a greater sense of responsibility for the physical maintenance of his life conditions," an "alternative lifestyle" in comparison to the comfortable home lives in postwar suburbia from which most campers came. Ramah's educators also saw "a side benefit" to working throughout the week: the Sabbath took on "a special complexion when the body is truly weary and in need of rest."[45]

As the afternoon went on, most camps held an hour or two of rotational activities in which campers visited various specialty areas around camp, while others included rotational activities plus an hour of elective activities, which allowed campers to choose an area of camp programs they wanted to delve more deeply into, including something in the arts (for example, guitar lessons, needlecraft, knitting, ceramics) or sports. Electives also sometimes included running a camp radio station, a book club, a garden, camper government meetings, or writing and editing a camper newspaper. Not all electives propelled forward a camp's ideals. While some camps provided a Hebrew literature *chug*, bar and bat mitzvah lessons, or additional Hebrew or Yiddish lessons, most campers chose an activity that would provide a chance to learn a practical skill or simply provide fun and recreation.[46] But most other activities campers rotated through did mirror a camp's given purpose, offering informal and active ways to engage in Zionism, Judaism, and Yiddishism.

Scouting proved one of such active choices, holding particular resonance in Zionist camps. Providing a simulated opportunity to live like youth in Israel who participated in youth movements like the Israeli scouts (*tsofim* in Hebrew) or the "pioneers" (*halutzim*) of the Yishuv, *tsofiut* (scouting) typically included learning skills like tying knots, building fires, and constructing simple structures.[47] Hashomer's Shomria used scouting to campers in order to "build bodies and train minds," as the campers "tramp(ed) through forests and fields" simulating Zionist "pioneers."[48] Young Judaea's partnership with the Hebrew Scouts, which dates back to 1924, proved particularly central to their camps' programs. Bringing a group of scouts to camp beginning in the 1960s allowed them to imbue the camps with skills and traditions from the movement in Israel. Ramah also included scouting activities in its

Machaneh Avodah program of the 1960s, concentrating on teaching teenagers the skills of basic knots, how to handle and use tools, "how to build a fire including a trench and altar-fire," and "simple first-aid techniques."⁴⁹

Sports and swimming also proved common parts of camps' active afternoons, providing campers opportunities to engage with thoroughly American pastimes like basketball, baseball, and volleyball, inflected with a few Hebrew or Yiddish words on the court or in the field. But at Zionist camps, even the most American sports like baseball could take on messages about building the body for the sake of the nation. At Habonim camps, for instance, sports were made "explicitly related physical activity to *halutziut*, building the land of Israel." Beginning in the 1960s, furthermore, Gaga, a purportedly Israeli form of dodgeball in which players use their hands to hit their opponent's ankles with the ball, began to spread in Jewish camps across the country. While Gaga's Israeli origins are likely mythological (some sources credit the game to Australia, while others credit it to Jewish summer camps themselves), the notion of Gaga as an Israeli sport successfully infused the least explicitly educational hours of day with a healthy dose of Zionism.⁵⁰

Campers playing Gaga at Camp Cejwin, 1976.
Source: Jeffrey Young. Printed with permission.

## Music, Art, and Evening Activities

Whether through work or play, Jewish camps' dynamic afternoons provided educators opportunities to infuse recreation with their educational and ideological goals. The remaining afternoon activities tended to focus on art, music, and various forms of performance.

During arts and crafts (*omanut* in Hebrew; *hantarbet un kunst* in Yiddish), campers made Judaica and maps of Israel and beautified their camp environments with mosaics and murals. At one Zionist camp in the 1940s, a group named after the first kibbutz, Deganiah, "built a model of the cooperative colony for which they were named," the Tel Aviv group "made a model of the all-Jewish city," and the "Jerusalem group depicted the Holy City with its ancient historic sites and modern buildings," allowing the arts and crafts specialist to teach "the geography and history of Palestine."[51] But much like sports, arts and crafts did not always directly touch on Jewish or nationalist themes, providing a more free-form creative outlet for campers.

Group singing played a sweeping and integral role in camp life, taking place at weekday meals, around the campfire, at Friday night meals, after Shabbat lunch, at prayer services, and more. During scheduled music hours (*shira*, song, in Hebrew or *muzik*, music, in Yiddish), campers sang familiar camp favorites and learned new songs with a song leader. While enthusiasm for Jewish music proved rather consistent across the board, camps had different song repertoires and explained their enthusiasm for song in different ways.[52] Yiddish-speaking camps, for instance, integrated group singing in order to connect campers to prewar Yiddish culture, believing that the "singing of Yiddish songs . . . should play an important part in the life of the camp" and that the camp "should be a singing one."[53] While Yiddish camps of the 1920s through the early 1940s usually included some English songs in their repertoires, American songs disappeared from their songbooks in the 1940s, underlining their prioritization of Yiddish songs as a tool for Yiddish engagement and learning.[54] Zionist movement leaders also praised communal singing, believing that songs with Zionist themes would inculcate the spirit of halutziut in campers. Reform and Conservative camps similarly prioritized singing but drew on much more diverse repertoires, including religious songs, an occasional Yiddish tune, and some American folk songs.[55]

As Zionism grew in popularity, both Reform and Conservative camps embraced more Israeli songs too.

Educators approached their camps' dance and theater programs with similar enthusiasm. During dance hour, campers learned the steps to the dozens of dances that featured prominently in camp festivals and cultural activities. Zionist camps enthusiastically emphasized dance as one aspect of a broader simulation of the pioneer ideal early in their histories.[56] Watching Camp Massad's dance festivals, for instance, Israeli visitors noted that as they saw the children dance, "they felt as though they were in a youth village or kibbutz in Israel, and that they would have never expected to find such a magnificent Hebrew spectacle in the far corner of the Pocono Mountains."[57] Mirroring the growing popularity of Zionist culture in American Jewish life, Israeli dance also became a part of Reform and Conservative camping of the 1960s. At GUCI and OSRUI, campers learned the steps to Israeli dances, with a group of campers who were part of the Israeli dance *chug* at OSRUI in 1962 finding that the dances both helped them develop physical coordination, as well as a familiarity and connection with Israeli culture.[58] Learning the popular folk dances of a camp also became a part of what it meant to belong in that camp's internal culture. "I had something new to learn, something very hard, before I could become a part of this camp," wrote one camper in a reflection of her first summer at a Habonim summer camp. Not only did she need to learn Hebrew, "but there were still those Hebrew songs that sounded as if somebody was chewing too much bubble gum. Then, don't ask me how I did it. I'll never know, but, I, too, learned to sing all the songs. . . . There was still the Israeli dance to learn. Those fast and whirly dances, but this, too, I conquered!" "Conquering" both song and dance helped the girl feel not "like a stranger or an outsider but someone who belonged to the wonderful group at Camp Habonim."[59]

As with dance, drama programs played a role in the daily schedules as periods for preparing evening performances and special camp festivals. But unlike sports or arts and crafts, "dramatics takes a primary place as an activity sated with the tensions of life experiences," wrote a staff member at Camp Massad, teaching campers about Jewish life both "directly and indirectly."[60] Indeed, theater at camp functioned both as a practice of embodiment, with campers performing visions of Jews from other times and places on stage,

Boys, cross-dressed, and Israeli dancing, Camp Cejwin, 1976.
Source: Jeffrey Young. Printed with permission.

and as a performance, with the audience of campers and staff seeing Jewish stories and historical events brought to life. The plays that camps produced, some of which they wrote themselves and others they sourced from other camps and cultural institutions, mirrored their ideological underpinnings and provided an opportunity to take on roles and perform visions of Jewishness for camper and counselor audiences. At Zionist camps, for instance, theater programs placed the theme of Israel front and center. At Camp Cejwin, the play *Alizah in Wonderland* glorified the experience of arriving in Israel as a young newcomer; at Tel Yehudah, *My Fair Sabra* glorified the story of immigration to Palestine, while *Portrait of the Shtetl* painted Jewish life in Eastern Europe as sad and backward, with migration to Palestine depicted in comparison as the realization of Jewish redemption.[61] At Ramah, the Hebrew language took center stage more so than any other particular theme or ideology. In the summer of 1967 alone, the Ramah camps put on sixty-two Hebrew-language plays collectively, "the presentation of a Broadway musical translated into Hebrew," wrote Walter Ackerman, "so institutionalized as to be beyond question."[62] At Orthodox Zionist Camp Morasha, where the "dramatic program was [a] . . . source of pride," the camp also put on Hebraized Broadway shows, culminating in one mid-1960s season with a "Hebrew presentation of 'My Fair Lady,' beautifully done."[63]

Yiddishist camps proved especially enthusiastic about dramatics, using plays to instill pride and interest in Yiddish culture while finding inspiration and sources in the rich history of Yiddish theater. As a rotational afternoon activity, dramatics prepared campers at Hemshekh for their weekly *Kulturnakht* (culture night), which featured onstage performances of Yiddish plays that often had Bundist and socialist undertones. The camp also held two "bigger dramatic functions" on visiting days, with parents and guests as the audience.[64] In 1968, one such "dramatic function" depicted the suffering of a group of factory workers in Russia, proclaiming in Yiddish, "This is how the Yiddish worker lived, worked, and suffered. . . . They only had one hope: The Bund." Other plays had similar themes, including the play *Amkho Sher un Ayzn*, which the camp newspaper described as "a smash" that all "Yiddish-loving people" just had to witness for themselves.[65] Some Yiddish camps also used the stage to perform Yiddish fluency, creating dual-language play scripts to make the shows comprehensible to campers, who increasingly arrived without much prior Yiddish knowledge.

Reform camps put on a notably diverse selection of plays. In 1968, one year after the monumental Six-Day War, GUCI performed several plays with Zionist messages. In *To the American People*, a Holocaust survivor meets American soldiers and tells them to go home and get the US government to support the building of a Jewish state in Palestine. *Proclamation of the State of Israel* recreated "the events that led to the rebirth of a land, a language and a people so beautifully stated by Mr. Abba Eban," while plays about Bar Kohkba or the death of Akiba connected a distant past to the Jewish future with a focus on resistance and martyrdom.[66] But Reform camps also performed plays based on traditional Chassidic tales, stories by Y. L. Peretz, and a whole host of more American themes. In GUCI's 1972 season, the history of slavery and the civil rights movement took center stage with the play *Debt of a People*. That same year, the camp put on a "short playlet," *The Jewish American Princess*, a satire centered on "a young Jewish girl growing up and becoming a woman."[67] The camp even put on plays about "Jewish conflicts in school and how to deal with them." One such play, *Is It Worth It?*, centered itself on Jewish life on America's college campuses, bemoaning how the majority of students did not attend or express interest in Jewish experiences.[68]

Ideological and educational camps used their theater programs not only as a form of entertainment and expression, but as a path toward presenting and representing their given values and missions. As campers rehearsed by day and sat in the audience at night, plays transported both actors and spectators to other Jewish times and places and presented Jewish languages in fuller, memorized fluency. But theatrical presentations were just one of many kinds of nighttime activities, such as capture the flag, scavenger hunts, "socials" or camp dances, campfire singalongs, pool parties, and talent shows. While infused with Jewish themes at times, many of these activities existed as opportunities to socialize and let loose after a long day. For older campers, evening programs typically ended with time to meander slowly back to their bunks, an opportunity for camp romances to find time for canoodling. But by a certain hour, all campers, regardless of age, returned to their bunks to get ready for bed. Another long day awaited them at sunrise.

### The Day of Rest: *Shabbat* and *Shabbes*

Packed with learning, singing, dancing, playing, scouting, performing, and working, the daily schedules of camps illustrated how educators' diverse visions of cultural renewal and continuity entered the lived experience of Jewish summer camps. But camps' schedules took on more than just a daily form, with Jewish camps of all kinds ending their weeks in some form with the marking of the Sabbath (*shabbat* in the Hebrew-inflected camps and *shabbes* in the Yiddish ones). The Sabbath's significance to the camp milieu, and the sweeping choice to mark it in ways both traditional and novel, married camp time to Jewish time, concluding the week with emotional reflection, ritual, joy, and pleasure.

The particulars of Sabbath observance at camps differed mainly depending on their overall missions and approaches to religious practices. Ramah's staff members, for instance, taught campers how to observe the day in accordance with Jewish law; more traditionally observant Orthodox camps, like Morasha, Massad, and Moshava, also kept the Sabbath according to the fullest expression of halacha, refraining from all use of technology and from labor. Conservative, Reform, and more traditional pluralistic camps all prayed on Friday night and Shabbat morning, while Ramah and other camps that served some Orthodox youth also held services on Saturday afternoon and evening.[69] Reform camps observed some of the laws of the Sabbath more liberally, but still generally marked the entirety of it with activities that highlighted its religious and spiritual significance, including Bible study, prayers, singing, and a communal *Havdalah* (a religious ritual that concludes the Sabbath). Indeed, certain core elements of the Sabbath schedule, including Torah learning, prayer, singing, Havdalah, free time, and ample time to rest prevailed at all denominational camps, as well some Hebraist and Zionist camps. At Camp Yavneh, one camper described how Shabbat was "different from the regular days at camp and that's how it has to be. Already during the evening everyone looks beautiful and happy, and I love very much the spirit of Shabbat at camp."[70] A Tel Yehudah camper similarly reflected on how camp time made Shabbat observance so "natural," "something to look towards with reverence and thankfulness."[71] Most camps also held an *oneg shabbat* (literally "joy of Sabbath") event after Friday night dinner, incorporating different kinds of fun activities and performances to mark the evening as special.[72]

While Tel Yehudah, pluralistic in its approach to religion, observed Shabbat much as Conservative Jews did (including prayers Friday evening and Saturday morning, refraining from work and technology), the socialist Zionist camps of the postwar period deemphasized traditional Sabbath observances, holding other sorts of activities to come together as a full camp community. Hashomer Hatzair's camps held special flag-raising ceremonies and gathering activities on Friday night, encouraging campers to wear white as they moved from mifkad to a festive meal.[73] Most Yiddish camps observed shabbes with a similarly untraditional approach. As an expression of its avowed secularism, for instance, Camp Hemshekh did not observe the Sabbath in a religiously traditional way. And yet the kitchen cooked a tastier meal on Friday nights, campers and staff dressed in white, and they marked the evening as special with the camp's weekly "culture night." On Saturdays, Hemshekh campers ceased work, awoke to a breakfast of fresh babka, and all wore blue work shirts with a red bandanna around their necks, a uniform reminiscent of those in socialist youth movements in prewar Europe.[74] As one former camper explained in an interview, "Shabbes [at Boiberik] wasn't religious at all, but to me, it felt different, more peaceful."[75]

Boiberik differed from other Yiddish camps, administering a much more traditional Shabbes program to bring campers "closer to the sphere of our history and heritage."As the camp's Sabbath services developed over the years, they became "gradually more elaborate," wrote Leibush Lehrer in 1959, with melodies based on "traditional Jewish liturgy."[76] The camp also lit and blessed shabbes candles communally, recited the traditional blessing over wine, and held a morning service that included a reading of the weekly Torah portion in both Yiddish and English. Since most campers came from secular Jewish homes, the rituals performed at camp often represented their first experiences of traditional Sabbath observance. As former camper Mara Sokolsky reflected on her Friday nights at Boiberik, "Dressed all in white, we sang haunting, lilting melodies about the sun setting and the Sabbath peace descending. There was no mention of God that I remember. But it was quite an ushering in of the Sabbath for secular socialists."[77] This very uniqueness made Boiberik's embrace of Sabbath rituals quite controversial, leading fellow staff members, parents, and leaders of the Sholem Aleichem Folk Institute in New York City of the 1940s and 1950s to take issue with the camp's departure from Yiddishist secularism.[78] But Leibush Lehrer stood by his long-standing belief that secular Yiddish culture on its own would not be enough to instill postwar American youth with a profound sense of Jewishness, and that to use camp time to transform campers, time itself had to illustrate and model Jewish sensibilities.

For leaders like Lehrer, the fusing of camp time with Jewish time showed campers that Jewishness could be as natural and organic as other routines, practices, and rhythms of the week. In both its daily and weekly constructions, then, camp time provided educators a "rare opportunity for creating an atmosphere of Jewish living" within a "self-contained community," a one- to two-month period dedicated to strengthening youth's "Jewish consciousness . . . culturally, spiritually, and emotionally."[79]

———

Daily and weekly schedules provided the scaffolding for all that occurred in camp life, serving as the essential, organizing backbone for what adult leaders saw as camps' transformative properties. Even as camp leaders across the spectrum sought to balance education with recreation and creativity, the camp day placed ideology front and center. Camps' schedules shared similar orders and labels on paper. The intensity of camp life, which left campers only a few unprogrammed hours for rest and free time, contributed to a sweeping "strange time-bending phenomenon that makes a few weeks feel like years."[80] Every activity on camps' schedules contributed to this inherent, affective experience. For Jewish camping leaders, their sense of control of campers' time was what made camps impeccable sites for cultural transformation. But their specific political and religious tilts determined the contents and shape of daily life, leaving campers with different lessons about how to best live as Jews.

The total experience of being at camp constituted more than just its scheduled parts. Within, between, and beyond the boxes of camps' timetables, camp leaders aimed to teach campers to play, mourn, speak, govern, and find love in Jewish ways as they employed camp's totalizing qualities toward their diverse visions of an ideal Jewishness. The next chapters focus on each of these elements of camp life in kind, offering a chance to see how camp leaders used camps toward their various ends and how campers responded to them, shaping the culture of the Jewish summer camp on their own accords.

# Jews Playing Games

## Role-Play, Sociodrama, and Color War

IN SUMMER 1964, CAMP HABONIM Midwest, a socialist-Zionist camp in Michigan, held "four days and nites [sic] of special days," each full of "enough excitement and drama" for an entire summer. After recounting a few challenging hikes, a counselor named Jackie described one special day, "Yom Hityashvut," an elaborate, twenty-four-hour activity that turned a moment in Zionism's history into an action-packed role-play. "The usual ruse," wrote Jackie in her camp's newspaper, began with a mock illegal im-migration game, in which campers played "poor defenseless Jews trying to get to Israel" during the British Mandate. Counselors had roles too, playing the "British soldiers and dense Arab rabble-rousers" blocking the campers from their goal. Despite their originally "poor" position, the "Jews" made it "home, proceeding to build their kibbutz," and after listening to "a won-derfully told tale of Israeli heroism," the campers went to bed, waking up in the morning for more "building and carousing." The game ultimately ended when the Jewish group won, "as they always do out here," wrote Jackie. "A good time was had by all."[1]

Starting in the 1960s, games centered on the history of Jewish migration to and settlement in Palestine emerged as common in Zionist camps. Thanks to educational guides for camping leaders, renditions of Hityashvut and similar games surrounding Jewish migration to Palestine also became widely circulated, with versions appearing in the programs of Reform, Conservative, and some communal camps growing in the decades after. Passed down from generation to generation, such games evolved into long-lasting traditions. Like Habonim, the camp of my childhood was a place where Zionism permeated nearly every element of daily life, even the precious time we got to spend cooling off at the pool. One day in summer 2002, counselors and lifeguards led my peers and me through a similar game, tasking us with "migrating to Palestine" by swimming to the other side of the pool. Only when we managed to swim past the counselors, representing "Arabs" and "British soldiers," did we successfully reach our "homeland." The pool was a different setting, and the focus was only on the act of immigration to Palestine rather than the settling of land that came afterward. And yet the nuts and bolts of the activity and its messaging were largely the same.

Performance of a Hityashvut-style activity or play, Camp Massad, 1949.
Source: Photo Courtesy of the American Jewish Historical Society. Printed with permission.

What explains the wide appeal and durability of games like Hityash-vut and Aliyah Bet? The answer, on the one hand, stems from the trajectory of Israeli politics in aftermath of the Six Day-War. By having campers play as "poor defenseless Jews" of the Yishuv and identifying Palestinians as "rabble-rousers," educators hoped to encourage identification with Zionism, especially as Israel's new occupation of the West Bank brought about more scrutiny to the new state and its supporters. Elevating the story of Jewish settlement while overlooking Palestinian dispossession perpetuated an over-simplified notion of pre-1948 Zionism as a story of "good guys" and "bad guys," with Jews always inhabiting the "good" side of the conflict. Games like Hityashvut became popular and widespread over the course of the late 1960s and 1970s because educators believed in their power to strengthen campers' identification with Israel, particularly before they reached college campuses where the countercultural and youth-powered New Left might challenge their stances. By the time I played Aliyah Bet, the occupation's continuation and the Second Intifada had only fueled more conflict on campuses over Israel, placing many Jewish students in the early 2000s in the position of needing to reevaluate, defend, or justify their relationships to Israel and Zionism. Part of what has helped these games endure, then, has been their utility as promoters of Zionist narratives. In a geopolitical conflict in which every term or designation is a potential land mine, role-playing communicates political messages almost wordlessly.

In this sense, these games' lasting appeal has had less to do with the specific message they propagated than the broader power their creators and implementers believed they contained. Renditions of Hityashvut and Aliyah Bet were some of the earliest gamified historical scenarios that camps generated, but they were just two of the dozens of role-playing activities that Jewish camp counselors and educators created in the postwar period. Centering games on their visions of Jews from other times and places—primarily settlers of British Mandate Palestine, citizens and soldiers of Israel, or the Jews of pre-Holocaust Eastern Europe—camp leaders embraced play as a transformational source of Jewish authenticity, pride, and identity. Educators even infused color war competitions and all-camp festivals, the recreational highlights of the season, in comparable ways, inserting and imbuing their activities with their values, goals, and similar forms of creative dramatics. In all of these cases, play served goals far beyond educating campers with political or historical information. In fact, games like Hityashvut did not pass on data or detail very well at all, the physicality and dynamism of these activities often eclipsing the educational discussions or lectures that set them up beforehand. The former campers I spoke with often could not remember the historical particulars of the games they played: Were they role-playing migration to Palestine or the War of Independence? Were they simulating pogroms, the Holocaust, or an ahistorical conflation of the two? And yet perhaps in their very eschewing of nuance, these games produced emotions, mood, and feeling in spades, from excitement and joy to fear and distress. Through play, educators crucially hoped campers would come to feel more like the Jews they embodied and, in some crucial way, become more like them, assuming their values, passions, dreams, struggles, and even their pain.

In his 1961 book *Man, Play, and Games*, philosopher Roger Caillois wrote that "it is not absurd to try diagnosing a civilization in terms of the games that are especially popular there," that "to a certain degree, a civilization and its content may be characterized by its games."[2] The concerns that motivated camp educators were in many ways unique to the Jewish postwar moment. Anxieties Jewish leaders held over growing affluence, suburbanization, and assimilation made themselves apparent in their camps' language programs, Holocaust memorialization, and even their romantic and sexual cultures. The rise of educational Jewish camping occurred in a moment of pronounced concern over the future of Jewishness, over a perceived cultural decline in the face of postwar comfort. But considering how camps approached play helps reveals the hopes camp educators held about their work with youth and the kinds of Jews they held up as models of authenticity, with profound specificity. Following Caillois, this chapter analyzes the games camps played as a mode of "diagnosing" the anxieties that postwar American Jewish adults held about their present and toward identifying the fantasies they held about the Jewish future they could build within their summer camps.

Although the anxieties that shaped the content of camps' games were Jewish specific, this chapter begins by situating Jewish camps within these entwined histories of social work and progressive education, tracing the rise of "purposed play" in the Jewish summer camp within its broader American context. Role-playing took campers time-traveling into the Jewish past or to a present-day elsewhere. Their American roots rarely factored into the games that campers played, the purpose of role-play being the ability to bring campers to sites and times of imagined Jewish authenticity through the power of imagination itself. And yet Jewish camps' approaches to play mirrored distinctly American developments in the fields of education and social science. The elaborate setups and ambitious missions of games like Habonim's Hityashvut reveal not only specific Jewish anxieties and motivations, but the long-lasting and profound influence of American educators and social workers such as John Dewey, Elbert Fretwell, William H. Kilpatrick, Joshua Lieberman, and Louis Blumenthal on camps both Jewish and not, where their theories on play, recreation, and education readily translated into action. With this two-pronged approach, this chapter places the role-plays intended to take kids out of their American context within the American story of camping itself.

### Social Science and Purposed Play

The games children play on their own are often expressions of their own autonomy, creativity, and inner world.[3] Make-believe, for instance, allows children to directly enact their desires, fantasies, and interests through acting out a scenario they imagined on their own or as a group. At camp, independent play flourished in bunk or during free time, and older campers certainly initiated games such as spin-the-bottle and truth or dare without adult involvement. So too did younger children find time to play on their own. This kind of play is what Caillois defines as "free, separate, uncertain, and unproductive" yet "regulated."[4] Within camps' jam-packed schedules, however, play in the educational Jewish camp mainly took place under the guidance of staff members, who rarely wasted the chance to infuse it with an educational or social function. In the Progressive Era, adults came to interpret childhood as "a stage apart, freed from productive labor." Early American camps "substituted" labor with "productive leisure," with reformers conceptualizing residential summer camps as locales for transforming what was viewed as the "aimless play" of urban children into something constructive.[5] Taking on the educational philosophies of thinkers like John Dewey, who argued that educators should use "native tendencies to explore" as a pedagogical tool, American camping leaders more broadly began using play toward educational ends.[6] In the interwar period, moreover, social workers began to see camps as ideal settings for the implementation of a method called "group work," which centered on cooperative learning, living, and playing as paths for improving the "social functioning" of youth.[7]

As camping leaders of the early to mid-twentieth century came to share a progressive vision of what camps could achieve, they shared and disseminated creative, fun, playful, and organized activities they viewed as consonant with their goals. Classic American camping games, such as capture the flag and color war, developed and spread through new, organized camping associations from the interwar years through the middle of the century, alongside other mainstays of camping like talent shows and end-of-season banquets.[8] These recreational activities provided outlets for campers' desires and rowdiness, helping camp leaders strike a balance between rules and recreation and fostering what Louis Blumenthal, a Jewish social worker and leader in American camping, called a "sense of unity."[9] With their "impressive settings, costumes, singing, acting, and music employed in rituals," all-camp festivals proved particularly helpful to camp leaders both Jewish and not in their tendency "to melt individual differences into a great oneness," producing "social control through an ideal." That ideal, as Blumenthal saw it, could be summarized in the expression "camp spirit," which he described as an "emotion evoked in the campers' reaction to their contacts and experiences in camp."[10] Recreation at camp did not need to be blatantly didactic to serve camps' educational and social purposes; fun and games helped American camping leaders from diverse backgrounds harness the summer camp's powers to educate and shape campers by simply cultivating a balance between what campers wanted out of their camp experience and what staff hoped camp life would achieve.

Progressive education and the field of social work were products of the Progressive Era. Play within early Jewish camps therefore was influenced by notions of group work, camp spirit, and cooperation. Camp festivals such as color war, which appeared prior to the postwar period, were often infused with Jewish themes and ideas. But Jewish educators began to take purposed play in increasingly educational directions starting in the postwar decades, mirroring both the mounting cultural anxieties of the period and the interconnected influence of social scientific thinking on American Jewish education and youth work. Jewish involvement in the social sciences began in late nineteenth-century Europe, but social science became particularly important for American Jews of the early to mid-twentieth century, who came to see sociology as a path for figuring out "where they belonged and which categories of personhood—bodily, communal, or religious ones— best described them." By the 1930s, "prominent Jewish leaders pledged fealty to social science as a means for Jewish redemption," with the field of Jewish social research "achiev[ing] unprecedented prominence" in the postwar era, writes historian Lila Corwin Berman, "irrevocably imprint[ing] itself on the way Jews talked about their Jewishness."[11]

These prominent leaders inevitably included, or at the least heavily influenced, the rabbis, educators, and social workers involved in the field of Jewish camping, for whom talk of Jewish "behaviors," "social values," "cultural survival," "identity," and "ethnicity" emerged as normal parts of the sector's parlance, ubiquitous in internal memos, at camping conferences, and even in educational activities and discussions aimed at prompting campers to consider their own Jewishness.[12] Although few young counselors would have arrived at camp with training in sociology, social science's influence on camping proved pervasive on the higher levels of leadership and on the level of camps' umbrella organizations. When sociological studies showed that the Six-Day War "had an impact on the feeling of Jewish identity, particularly with Israel," for example, those attending the National Conference on Jewish Camping asked themselves how they could "translate this concern and relevancy into program at our camps."[13] As sociological vocabulary came to filter "into rabbis' normative pronouncements" against rising rates of intermarriage in the 1960s, the relationship between Jewish education and social science became even more blatant as camp educators and social scientists teamed up in a mutual fight to influence the future dating habits of young Jews.[14] By the late 1960s, social scientists not only influenced the language of camping but emerged as trusted researchers on and consultants to Jewish camps, their authority within the sector continuing to the current day.

In certain ways, role-playing activities like Hityashvut, which proliferated in the postwar decades, reveal how social science's influence on camping translated into action. Through simulating a moment in Zionist history, educators believed that Habonim's campers would come to identify with Israeliness, internalize Zionism's role in Jewish "cultural survival," and reap Jewish pride from stories of Israeli heroism. The notion of pride proved particularly important in the wake of the Holocaust, when framing Jews as courageous, muscular, and victorious soldiers, pioneers, and builders of the land served as a counterpoint to stories of diasporic tragedy and victimhood. Simulations of Jewish wedding ceremonies, furthermore, in which counselors usually role-played as bride and groom in front of the entire camp community, taught campers the traditions associated with Jewish weddings in a fun manner and communicated the value of marrying Jewish just as a growing number of American Jewish young people were choosing not to do so. As camps became increasingly permeated with social scientific language and data, role-play gained popularity for its transformational potential.

The concept of using dramatics in Jewish education in fact emerged before the postwar period, with progressive Jewish educators of the early twentieth century embracing the form with notable enthusiasm. Samson Benderly, one of the leading Jewish educators of the period, was a known "bold experimenter" in "drama and pageantry," placing dramatics in the center of Camp Achvah's programs in the 1920s.[15] While a child watching a play onstage may "vicariously feel the emotions of the characters and lives through the situations portrayed," Benderly believed that the "ideal situation," educationally speaking, was "one in which we can activate every child in the play's development" by "eliminat[ing] the audience entirely," with "every child . . . taking an active part in the play."[16] Through his students, Benderly's enthusiasm for what became known as creative dramatics influenced the field of Jewish education for decades. As educator Samuel Citron, a self-described disciple of Benderly, who became the Jewish Education Committee's dramatics director, explained in 1949, "The skilled educator, aware of the tremendous potential of make-believe-play, of dramatization . . . utilizes this natural childhood activity for the furtherance of the educational process. . . . If in general education, Creative Dramatics has been found to be a useful tool, in Jewish education it is a real boon. The Jewish teachers who have become acquainted with its techniques have taken to it most avidly," as "a most potent ally in the attainment of their educational goals . . . irrespective of [their] ideologies."[17]

Fully immersive and without an audience, activities like Hityashvut are direct ancestors of what Benderly and Citron described, even as Citron's work typically involved scripted plays more so than unscripted simulations.

Just as the themes and goals of postwar camps' role-plays proved highly influenced by social scientific language and research, Jewish educational dramatics' evolution toward including unscripted role-playing demonstrates yet another way that social science shaped Jewish camping. Sociodrama, a role-playing practice invented by Jewish sociologist Jacob Levy Moreno, emerged on the American scene around the same time as progressive education reached its apex in the 1930s.[18] Born in Bucharest in 1889, Moreno began his career in Vienna as an artist in the expressionist movement. At the age of twenty, he founded a safe house for Jewish refugees arriving in Vienna from all over Eastern Europe called the "House of Encounter," where he not only provided food and shelter but developed and implemented what he first called "encounter practices," in which he used dramatics as a tool to help residents process their traumas, mainly those instigated by anti-Semitic violence.[19] By 1921, Moreno made a name for himself in Vienna for his mix of improvisation, role-play, and therapy, which he performed at the Stegreiftheater (Theater of Spontaneity). Moreno eventually coined these encounter practices with the term *psychodrama*.[20]

Following his immigration to the United States in 1925, Moreno invented a new practice, sociodrama, that similarly involved role-play, improvisation, and the notion of the "encounter." But instead of centering the practice on personal traumas, sociodramas brought groups together to experience, feel, and face their pasts "in a collective way." In New York, Moreno came to apply this practice to conflict resolution efforts between ethnic groups, as well as in the treatment of collective traumas, "the genesis of the drama and of its original aim" one "of collective catharsis."[21] To disseminate his techniques, Moreno lectured at educational institutions around the world. In the late 1930s, he held a guest lecturer position at Teachers College at Columbia University, a long-time destination for educators involved with American Jewish camping. He also taught briefly at the New School for Social Research, where he likely interacted with Horace Kallen, whose notion of cultural pluralism and noted relationship with John Dewey influenced Jewish educators like Alexander M. Dushkin and Isaac B. Berkson.[22]

Although Moreno is better known as the inventor of psychodrama, sociodrama reached American psychologists, sociologists, and educators, who transformed it over time to better match their differing goals. In the case of educational researchers Fannie and George Shaftel, who dedicated much of their research in the 1960s to the topic of role-play, sociodrama operated as the starting point for a wider world of "dramatic play," or "spontaneity experience[s] focused on exploring roles and acquiring content," while sociodrama in particular functioned as a "group learning procedure focused on providing practice in solving problems of human relations."[23] On a colloquial basis, many Jewish camps used the term *sociodrama* more loosely. At Camp Hemshekh, for instance, a Warsaw ghetto uprising sociodrama did not provide intended "practice in solving problems" but did deliver a moment of collective catharsis by proxy in the Moreno mode for its participants, many of whom had parents who had survived the Holocaust. At other Jewish camps, the term *sociodrama* specifically described "surprise" activities like those that the Shaftels referenced, with a unit head at one camp telling campers that "he had just received a phone-mail telling him that a group of neo-Nazis was an hour away driving towards the camp," prompting an "hour-long discussion of how to respond."[24]

While Benderly's fingerprints are all over Jewish camping, the direct influence of Moreno and the Shaftels on the field proves less simple to draw out. Although Jewish educators used the term *sociodrama* interchangeably with *role-play*, *simulation*, and *dramatic activity*, demonstrating familiarity with Moreno's practice at some point down the chain of influence, Moreno's name never appeared in camps' archives. Benderly, Dewey, Blumenthal, and Lieberman, who passed through many of the same academic institutions as Moreno, likely had contact with Moreno himself or with his practices. Fannie and George Shaftel republished a version of their book *Role-Playing for Social Values* with the National Conference of Christians and Jews in 1967 titled *Building Intelligent Concern for Others through Role-Playing*, which presented role-play to Jewish and Christian educators and clergy and referenced Moreno's pioneering influence on the process. The long-lasting popularity of educational dramatics, role-plays, and sociodramas in Jewish camping, then, is less likely owed to just one of these influences, but rather to the wide-ranging ways that progressive education, social work, popular psychology, and social science mixed and mingled in the American and American Jewish summer camping sector throughout the twentieth century.

### Role-Playing and Sociodrama in Practice

Sociodrama and role-play proved popular across Zionist, Yiddishist, Reform, and Conservative summer camps alike. Zionist educators seemed to be both the most prolific inventors of activities and the most organized disseminators of them, sharing their ideas through detailed program guides published by the Jewish National Fund and the American Zionist Youth Commission.[25] Zionist role-playing activities all reflected different historical events, but educators crafted them with the same purpose in mind, hoping to bring campers closer to Zionism and Israel by vicariously living through experiences of early Zionists and Israelis or by highlighting the struggles of diaspora Jews prior to the establishment of the State of Israel through Holocaust, pogrom, or "neo-Nazi" raid simulations.

Although Zionist role-plays differed in their precise details and were periodically updated with new events, one particularly detailed guide by educator Eli Weber described a few of the most common games with comprehensive instructions. Through interviews with ten camp leaders representing six different Zionist youth movements and a total of nearly "forty camp seasons" of experience, Weber intended his guide to take the most creative programs of the summer, demystifying and sharing them across camping movements, creating a written record of games that had existed for over a decade but had only been "passed on from the staff of one summer to the staff of the next as part of the ongoing culture of the camp." Alongside the internal program materials of camps, Weber's pamphlet gives a sense of the kinds of role-plays Zionist educators guided campers through, as they simulated the early Zionist movement, Zionist "pioneers," and Israeli soldiers.[26]

In Weber's version of Aliyah Bet, for instance, campers role-played the risky and illegal efforts of Jewish immigration to British Mandate Palestine over four days. Over the first few days, Weber suggested counselors "prepare the chanichim" for the activity "by having sichot [discussions] on the period of Aliyah Bet and showing the film *The Illegals*," noting the importance of

Massad camper or counselor dressed as David Ben-Gurion, 1950.
Source: Photo courtesy of the American Jewish Historical Society. Printed with permission.

campers' "develop[ing] sufficient feeling for the period, to enable them to understand the roles which they will be playing the evening of the game." Weber then recommended that counselors divide the campers into three teams: the British, the "Israelis" (a historically inaccurate term for the Jews living in Mandate Palestine), and the *Maapilim* (the illegal migrants coming from Europe). "The object of the game is for the Israelis to get the *Maapilim* through the British blockade and absorb them into the Israeli settlements before they are caught," wrote Weber, urging counselors to make the "educational preparations . . . intensive enough for the *chanichim* to actually be able to feel their roles."[27]

In Weber's version of Hityashvut, the activity should begin with a week of conversations "explaining Turkish law and its relation to the Choma-Migdal episode," referring to the years between 1936 and 1939 when Zionist settlers established new Jewish settlements under a legally restricted mandate authority by putting up walls or watchtowers, with the implicit cooperation of the British. After the historical background had been thoroughly established, counselors would awake campers "without warning at 3 AM" to divide them into five groups: three groups received the task of establishing kibbutzim, one group took on the role of British soldiers at a British Army base, and the last group played the part of Arabs in an Arab settlement. After each group received a set of building supplies, Weber instructed participants to walk to a designated area in the woodsy areas of camp in order to begin "construction" at dawn. Building continued for the greater part of the day, but at around 10:00 a.m., the British group identified itself and began "the inspection for guns and tools." Counselors, serving as the game's judges, gave points to "the Israelis" if "they manage to keep [their guns and tools] hidden during the day" and proved able to "transport them at night." After dinner, the last stage of the game took place, with counselors ordering the kibbutz groups to transport "their weapons" to various locations around camp, while "the Arabs and British . . . try to intercept them." The game continued until 3:00 a.m. the next day, a full twenty-four-hour experience of immersive role-play that ended with the whole camp singing Israeli songs around a campfire.[28]

Hityashvut and Aliyah Bet both centered on historical events of the late nineteenth or early twentieth century, intending to provide campers a chance to embody Jewish immigrants to Palestine during a desperate moment in European Jewish history. Such games proved particularly common, giving campers the feeling of an experience far away from their comfortable reality in order to bring campers closer to the *chalutz* (identity) their camps idealized. The guide also included games that simulated much more recent events, such as a role-play of the Six-Day War in which counselors split the camp-grounds into sections "corresponding to Israel and the border sections of her neighbors" and divided the campers into two groups: Israelis and "attackers" from neighboring Arab countries. Counselors scored the game based on campers' success "planting mines (made of paper plates), expanding borders, and capturing prisoners." Bringing the recent war to life, the game provided an updated version of the chalutz, focused on portraying the idealized heroism and strength of contemporary Israeli soldiers.[29]

In each of these militarized games, some players embodied the role of "Arabs" or the "British." But even when campers took on the role of so-called enemies, the games did not play out like true competitions. The Jewish side always emerged victorious, with the emphasis consistently placed on Jewish or Israeli heroism.[30] Not all Zionist role-plays proved quite so militaristic; some camps role-played political bodies like the Zionist Congress, bringing Zionist ideas to life through a form of sociodrama based more on discussion or debate. But most role-plays did involve a militaristic scenario, and many began in the middle of the night in order to heighten their emotional impact, adding an element of excitement as campers wandered in the dark. As Weber explained, campers' sleeplessness sometimes led to impromptu naps on the ground or in some cases to "problems of control." To prevent campers inhabiting their roles a little too realistically by way of violence, Weber suggested drafting "clearly defined rules governing the capturing and freeing of prisoners" to keep campers under control.[31]

Oral histories with campers supported the idea that Aliyah Bet and Hityashvut could be considered fun by one camper's measure and scary by another's. One former Habonim Camp Tavor camper of the 1960s recalled leading his campers in this same game as a counselor, playing the role of the British, searching the campgrounds "with flashlights, trying to send [the campers] back to Cyprus or something."[32] Judith, a former camper from Hashomer Hatzair, recalled a more detailed setup, beginning with a screening of the movie *Let My People Go*, a Holocaust film that framed Israel as the redemption of the Jewish people. As she recalled, the movie was graphic, with images of Jews in pits burned into her mind decades later. The camp's educators intended for the movie to provide a context for why Jews had been desperate enough to illegally immigrate to Palestine despite the risks. Although her camp called their version of the Aliyah Bet activity the Night Games, the basic idea was similar. "Whatever [role] you were," Judith explained, "you were either trying to sneak your way from one place to another or you were trying to help the people who were sneaking from one place to another." The movie and the activity terrified her—at the time, she was only ten years old—so she found "a bush to hide under and hung out there until they blew the whistle, and it was done."[33]

As a broader range of Jewish camps came to embrace Israel education in the late 1960s, games like Aliyah Bet started to become a part of the experience at some Reform and Conservative camps, as well as at some Jewish Community Center camps, like Surprise Lake.[34] During Swig's immersive Hebrew program *Solel*, for instance, campers took part in a diverse array of simulation activities focused on the historical evolution of Zionism. In a 1967 role-play, counselors led campers through an activity mimicking a meeting of Jewish leaders in Russia to discuss the violent Kishinev pogrom of 1903 and decide "what to do about it." One group, representing the Jews of Kishinev (now Chişinău, Moldova), began the program by reviewing what had happened in their town. A different group, whose campers were told to "side with the Bundists," offered the socialist solution to the problems of anti-Semitic pogroms, while another group represented Zionists and accordingly proposed the building of a Jewish home in Palestine. After all sides had a chance to express their opinions, "a vote was taken to determine what to do about our problem," and "the solution held by the Zionists . . . won the argument overwhelmingly."[35] In a different activity that same summer, groups of campers simulated the 1897 Zionist Congress in Basel, Switzerland, much as in Weber's game.[36]

At the same time, Ramah and the UAHC camps also fashioned a wider variety of sociodramas that hearkened back to a broader range of Jewish historical moments and experiences. In Reform camps such as Swig, OSRUI, and GUCI, a variety of role-playing games intended to provide campers opportunities to reenact historical events, their approaches to informal education "trigger[ing] the use of sociodrama and simulation," which became "legendary" in Reform camping.[37] In 1969, for instance, a group of GUCI campers took part in a month-long program, Shtetl, that began with counselors teaching campers the history of the Jews in Europe, Yiddish songs and stories, a bit about Hasidism, and finally Jewish humor. Five years after the premiere of *Fiddler on the Roof* on Broadway, the Shtetl program reflected growing American Jewish nostalgia for visions of shtetl life.[38] While notions of Eastern European Jewish life permeated the month's daily activities, the program reached its emotional climax with a dramatic simulation in which counselors, playing the role of Cossacks, "invaded camp." As the campers "gathered around the flagpole shortly before dinner . . . waves [of] ferocious raiders" poured "out of their hiding place." The activity, which aimed "to signify the period in Jewish history when huge numbers of Jews were cruelly slaughtered in terrible pogroms," was described in the camp newspaper as a "complete success."[39] Other camps also simulated events in the Holocaust or the pogroms of Eastern Europe or had campers imagine what it might be like to be attacked by Nazis now. The former camper Judith noted that "the older leadership" of her camp, Moshava in California, once "decided to leak that there were neo-Nazis coming to raid the camp" in the 1960s, leading campers to "escape" silently in the middle of the night. Without giving a hint that the leak was false, the camper recalled the experience "scar[ing] the shit out of people," but the staff eventually sat campers down in a local park to inform them that the rumor "wasn't real."[40]

Camp Swig put pronounced emphasis on role-playing activities in their educational sessions, setting the camp environment up with serious attention to detail. In a 1964, a month-long "hero-oriented" program, Our Jewish World, children arrived on the first day of camp to a role-play immigrant processing on Ellis Island, with staff playing the roles of immigration officials. Counselors also decorated cabins to look like barracks, covering the walls with "American slogans." Each camper received a tag with the "country of origin of [their] parents or grandparents"; counselors posted "incidental paraphernalia," such as Yiddish and German newspapers, around camp; and head staff made announcements over the loudspeaker "geared toward [an] immigrant processing atmosphere." Intended to teach campers their history in America, the activity set the stage for programs throughout the summer centered on American Jewish heroes such as Emma Lazarus, Lillian Wald, Louis Brandeis, and Stephen Wise. Later in the session, campers also had opportunities to "meet" Anne Frank and Theodore Herzl (counselors dressed in costume), integrating both the Holocaust and Zionism into this wider concept of the "Jewish world."[41] While Reform leaders would also come to embrace games like Hityashvut and Aliyah Bet, both the "Cossacks raid" and the simulation of Ellis Island reveal the diverse ways that Reform educators brought diaspora history to life, prompting campers to reflect on the trials and tribulations of their own ancestors through sociodrama.

Reform and Conservative role-playing games not only aimed to connect their campers to climactic moments in Jewish history but to bring them

closer to the history and ideology of their given movements. In a game entitled The Sabbath, for instance, Camp Ramah's counselors assigned campers
one of four roles, each representing an approach to Sabbath observance. The
first group played as Jews who observe the Sabbath according to Jewish law,
the second group representing Jews who mark the Sabbath "in a way that
fits the times . . . but not necessarily [observing] every custom," the third
representing Jews who do not observe at all, and the fourth group playing as
Jews who do not have the ability to observe because they need to go to work.
The campers discussed "the Sabbath from the role outlined," and the groups
debated with one another in their roles, the activity purportedly feeling
"very realistic."[42] While the game did not make the historical origins of these
positions explicit, it mimicked the sorts of debates about Sabbath practice
that marked the Conservative movement's history in both Germany and in
America and the ongoing conversations about what traditions to conserve
and which could be made more flexible to modern life.

In 1973, GUCI's campers were led through a similar sociodrama in
which they played rabbis in the Union of American Hebrew Congregations
writing various platforms regarding Jewish life and practice, simulating the
Reform movement's 1885 Pittsburgh Platform and 1937 Columbus Platform,
each of which clarified evolving positions on issues as diverse as Zionism,
God, social justice, and the Bible. GUCI's "Zionsville Platforms" role-play
(named after the camp's location in Zionsville, Indiana) included assigning
campers the roles of the "pioneers," who gathered "in an organized manner
in a tract of land near the municipality of Zionsville in Indiana, the holy
land. Despite hard rains, limited resources, and cruel overseers," counselors
informed campers that they had to form "a temporary society, based on the
values they shared," just like the "pioneers . . . our predecessors at this camp."
As the game begun, GUCI's educators instructed campers to come up with
their own values and statements on various issues, much like the 1885 and
1937 platforms critical to the history of the Reform movement. The campers and staff members focused on questions regarding how to interpret the
Torah, what women's roles in Judaism should be, and whether Jews could
marry Christians. On the issue of biblical interpretation, for instance, one
camper group explained, "While our Orthodox brothers base their entire
lives on the Bible, we as Reform Jews feel differently. Times have changed

since the Bible was written making it impossible to follow all the rules and regulations presented in this scripture." In some cases, the platforms that GUCI campers crafted mirrored the official stances of the Reform movement, but campers could also contradict them. For instance, the campers voted that the bar/bat mitzvah "need not occur at the age of 13, but [should] be decided upon ... at the time that he/she feels it most meaningful," and that confirmation "should not be practiced as is currently done in Reform Judaism, as it does not truly establish a commitment to Judaism. The confirmed should arrange the time according to his/her beliefs and his/her readiness to confirm them in the faith of Judaism and the minimum age ... should be 14 years."[43] These examples show the experimental quality of Reform camps, which taught campers the movement's official stances on Jewish issues while allowing space for questions and critique.

Jewish camp leaders had divergent conceptualizations of what Jewish identity and behavior could and should entail, and the issues that individual camps took on through play did change over time, mirroring changing historical circumstances. The growth of Zionist games outside Zionist camps in the 1960s, for instance, mirrored the growth of American Zionism, with "Israeliness" becoming an increasingly common communal shorthand for Jewish authenticity. Role-playing games also took on new issues, incorporating not only the Six-Day War in camp sessions following 1967, but the struggle for Soviet Jewry as well. In 1972, Asher Meltzer of the American Association of Jewish Education encouraged educators to create role-playing games that would bring campers closer to their Soviet Jewish brethren, inventing a sociodrama in which campers, playing "Soviet Jewish youth," had to try to "contact a person, obviously an American Jew carrying the Jewish Daily Forward quite demonstratively and ostentatiously," to help them get out of the Soviet Union.[44]

Not all Jewish camps embraced sociodrama to the same degree, the ideologies of camp leaders influencing what kinds of Jewishness they wanted campers to emulate and how they went about instilling them with Jewishness in the first place. Implementing sociodrama less frequently, Yiddish camps more heavily emphasized camp-wide festivals instead, allowing camp leaders to impart their values and ideologies through play, performance, and camp spirit.

## Special Days, Pageants, and Color War

In summer 1967, the campers of Camp Hemshekh took part in the *Hemshek-hyada*, or the "Yada," a special day "designed to bring every aspect of camp life into full play." With activities that struck "a balance between the physical and the cultural," wrote one counselor, the Yada involved two competing teams, assigned with a Yiddish cultural icon to symbolize, represent, and honor. Through the Yada's recreational, "entertaining and enlightening" activities, Hemshekh's educators hoped to pass on "the vast treasure of our Jewish cultural heritage." In that particular summer, the teams, representing the Yiddish authors Yehoash and Mendele Mocher Sforim, competed in sports, quizzes, and dramatic skits, all the while learning about, embodying, and drawing inspiration from their assigned author's life and work.[45]

In *Children's Nature*, Leslie Paris describes the prevalence of special days at American camps in the first half of the twentieth century, explaining how "at full-season camps, each week brought a new special event, whether a canoe trip, a national holiday like Independence Day, or a camp circus or pageant." A series of "exciting" events, including "large-scale competitions, theatrical performances, award ceremonies and final banquet," not only "raised the emotional pitch to its highest level" but marked "the passage of time," "heighten[ing] the sense that camp space and time stood outside the ordinary mundane world."[46] As Blumenthal explained, special days proved particularly effective when placed toward the end of the summer session, when campers began exhibiting "waning, tired, lagging spirits." Since "the intensity of group feeling, known as 'camp spirit,' fluctuates in the course of a camp season" and reaches its highest "peaks under the impetus of activities that give great joy and satisfaction," "special or occasional activities in which the whole camp participates" tended to lift campers' "lagging spirits," serving "as a means of social control."[47]

For Jewish camp leaders, the use of special days had all of these universal advantages but also served some specifically Jewish purposes. As with role-plays, days like the Yada helped camp leaders strike a balance between the recreational and the educational while offering them additional ways to highlight their camps' ideologies. Color war, which began appearing in American camps in the 1920s as an expansion of capture the flag, proved far and away the most widespread special day program at camps both Jewish and not.[48] Breaking the entire camper body into teams identified by colors, the competition, which involved an array of physical and intellectual challenges, occurred either over one full day or two to three consecutive days. Nearly every postwar Jewish camp put on some kind of color war (and continue to do so today), with most naming the competition *Maccabiah* (referencing both the Maccabees, the Jewish army central to the holiday of Chanukah, and the worldwide Jewish Olympic games called the Maccabiah or Maccabi Games, held first in Palestine in 1932).[49]

Massad's three sites proved central not only to campers' enjoyment but to the camps' educational mission, with staff using the three-day game "to impart to the campers broad knowledge of heroes, their personalities, and their language," "illustrat[ing] the theme of Eretz Yisrael" through the "formation and implementation of projects in the spirit of heroism and of the period in history."[50] From the 1950s through the 1970s, staff members divided campers into two teams, each representing a hero, idea, or movement in Jewish history, with campers receiving pamphlets describing their team's

Maccabiah at Camp Cejwin, 1976.
Source: Jeffrey Young. Printed with permission.

symbol and its relevance to Zionism. In 1956, for instance, counselors broke the campers into teams representing the geographical groups in Israel *kartanim* (cities), representing the "capital and major cities in Israel," and *kfarim* (villages), symbolizing "the agricultural settlements in Israel."[51] In 1973, teams *Tslilim* (notes or rings, but referring to bells), referencing a Chaim Nachman Bialik story, and *Galim* (waves), referencing Henrietta Szold, who "dedicated her life to waves of *aliyot* of children from Europe, through the waves of the sea of Eretz Yisrael," competed against one another in sports, song, and skits.[52] Providing campers with quotes from both Szold and Bialik, Massad encouraged both teams not only to fuse their team's symbols into their cheers and songs, but to embody the figures and ideas their teams represented throughout the day. In 1976, the teams *Migdal* (tower) and *Homah* (wall), which refer to a settlement method Zionist settlers used in Mandatory Palestine during the 1936–1939 Arab Revolt, helped educators bring "the idea of Zionism in the far past and in our days" to life, illuminating "the problems of *olim* (immigrants) then and now . . . the relationship of the inhabitants of Israel to the Jewish immigrants and today's *Aravim* (Arabs) . . . [and] the institutions of the settlement then . . . and today."[53]

Massad's rotating themes for Maccabiah mirrored the camp leadership's desire to encourage campers to identify with Zionism through learning Israel's history, culture, and geography. Through the three-day programmatic high, educators saw an opportunity to impart knowledge and ideology through a memorable experience, celebrating Hebrew culture through both education and athleticism. Maccabiah engaged both the body, through such sports activities as Newcomb (a variation of volleyball), kickball, boxing, swimming, running, and field game competitions, and the mind, through trivia quizzes, artistic performances, and anthem writing.

Other Jewish camps included similar activities but focused their color war themes to align with their ideological purposes. At Reform camp OSRUI, for instance, color war educated campers about the Reform movement and Judaism more broadly. In 1964, the camp's counselors put campers in teams that came to role-play different rabbis, the results of their competitions determining "which rabbis would enter the Hall of Fame." Relays "were held on land and water," and a "*Shiur* [lesson] competition," in which teams competitively learned and taught pieces of Torah, allowed teams to acquire points in hopes of "electing" their team's rabbi to the Hall of Fame.[54] While OSRUI's focus on Jewish tradition and the leadership of rabbis contrasts with the Zionist color wars of camps like Massad, it displays how camp leaders molded color war to match their ideological and educational missions.

Yiddish-focused Camp Hemshekh held several types of color war, infusing the days with its own particular ideologies. The Yada encompassed a similar format of competitive events to Massad's Maccabiah, similarly taking place over two or three days. But like all other versions of color war, the Yada was "designed to bring every aspect of camp life into full play," reflecting, in Hemshekh's case, the camp's Bundist and Yiddishist orientation.[55] "The Yada is not a competition for its own sake," wrote a staff member in 1971. "Through *Hemshekhyada*, we seek to strengthen our emotional ties to the Yiddish culture of our forefathers, while preparing ourselves to take an active role in its future development."[56] Much like Massad, Hemshekh's staff made the Yada educational and ideology laden by assigning teams Yiddish-related themes, typically naming them after Yiddish authors. In 1965, for instance, teams Sholem Aleichem and Y. L. Peretz competed against one an-

A flag for the Y. L. Peretz team, the Camp Hemshekh Hemshekhayda, 1960s.
Source: Photographed by Gabriel Ross. Printed with permission.

other and created team cheers and songs representing the lives and works of
their authors.[57]

Moreover, the camp's weekly culture night, which highlighted the lives
and works of authors and artists through performance, became part of the
competition, serving as the climax to the Yada's three days. The teams performed as their assigned personalities, and judges awarded teams points on
the quality of their scripts, songs, and costumes. Beginning with the "Parti-
san Hymn" and the "Bund Hymn," the Yada's culture night included each
team's forty-minute presentations of original skits and dances symbolizing
their Yiddish cultural icon in Yiddish and English, as well as a Yiddish folk
song that related to the work of their assigned author, playwright, or other
Yiddish cultural icon.[58]

Hemshekh's second color war of the summer similarly mixed competition with education. During *Di Yontefdike Teg* (the Festive Days, or simply
the Holidays), campers were "divided into the four holiday seasons: Pesach,
Sukkes, Shevuos, and Chanukah," in accordance with their birthday seasons. Like the Yada, Di Yontefdike Teg involved track and field events and
swim meets and concluded with presentations by each group depicting their
holiday with song and skits.[59] The special day also aimed to introduce the
Jewish holidays of the school year to campers "as an integral part of [Jewish]
tradition and culture." In accordance with the camp's Bundism, Hemshekh's
staff emphasized the secular, "social values" attributed to the holidays, such
as "the quest for freedom" epitomized by Passover, the "acceptance and
practice of a high standard of personal and national morality" presented
by Shavuoth, the preservation of "one's ideals and culture while enduring
hardships as evidenced in Succoth," and the "fight for a cultural identity and
against assimilation as seen in the story of Chanukah."[60] Campers cooked
special holiday foods, learned the songs that pertained to their holiday, and
performed the song about the name of the day, "Di Yontefdike Teg" by the
Yiddish-language composer and poet Mark Warshavsky.[61]

Like the Yada, Di Yontefdike Teg also culminated with the regularly
scheduled culture night, in which campers presented the essence of their
assigned holidays in front of the whole camp through song, dramatization,
dance, and decoration. In their dramatizations, campers emphasized the
ideals their holidays taught them and linked those ideals to their perception

of Camp Hemshekh. In one such play, the 1968 Chanukah group considered the "fight against assimilation" an ideal of their holiday, making a case for their particular view of secular Jewishness. "We secular Jews agree with the Jewish sages of old that Yiddishkayt—Jewishness—may be linked to *'mayim chayim'*—living, flowing water," the script explains. "We desire movement rather than rigidity; we seek friendship and understanding rather than laws and commandments. Instead of supernatural faith and dogma, our primary concern is with and for man and his fellows. Those are the ideas embodied in our celebration of *Yontefdike Teg*—festive days—here at Camp Hemshekh. Through song and dance, play and story, we cherish anew the treasures of our cultural heritage."[62] The *Shevuos* team's 1967 play, which bounced from ancient Israel to contemporary America and between English and Yiddish, similarly portrayed the immediate lessons to be gained from understanding the holiday as applied to the camp and its Yiddish-related convictions. "The children of Israel today are abandoning their culture as those who danced around the golden calf," explained the narrator. "The commandments become the building symbol for our growing and beautiful culture, which Hemshekh is preserving in the present world."[63] As with the Yada, Di Yontefdike Teg emphasized Hemshekh's vision of Jewishness, reframing the holidays to fit their Yiddishist and Bundist values.

Hemshekh's final competitive special day, the "Olympics," represented another common variety of color war. Hemshekh's Olympics shared some traits with the Yada, with similar activities and teams competing against one another in a variety of games. However, instead of embodying different Yiddish authors, the teams represented different countries in the world, imbuing the day with a cosmopolitan ethic. Through the Olympics, counselors hoped campers would learn the cultures of their assigned countries as they role-played its people, drawing inspiration from their flag, songs, and customs. In socialist spirit, staff wanted campers to "understand social and economic problems of the countries represented in light of their own history."[64] Other kinds of Jewish camps also conducted Olympic-style special days but placed more focus on specifically Jewish communities around the world. In 1964, Swig broke campers up into teams, each representing a different country, including Israel, Brazil, Denmark, Ireland, Turkey, and the United States, and instructed them to "learn about the Jewish community of its particular country, and to center its efforts during the pageant to presenting aspects of this Jewish community to the rest of the camp through song, dance, cheer, banner and costume."[65]

Through the Yada, Di Yontefdike Teg, and the Olympics, Hemshekh used the color war format to create an opportunity for campers to embody both Jews and non-Jews, drawing on the Yiddishist and Bundist education they received throughout the camp session. The cosmopolitan themes of the camp's Olympics had found inspiration in its predecessor, Camp Boiberik, where, from the 1920s onward, the camp marked a special day, *Di Felker Yontef* (the Festival of the Nations). As color war spread throughout American camps of all kinds, Boiberik's founder, Leibush Lehrer, expressed concern that competition would ruin the cooperative spirit his camp aimed to foster. Thus, in place of color war, Lehrer created a different kind of large-scale festival he felt served as a more fitting finale to the summer season. Felker, as it became called for short, expressed Lehrer's fantasy of "all of the countries liv[ing] in peace, where the lion lies down with the lamb, where they never make war anymore," with dance, song, and elaborate costumes.[66]

Role-playing games and special days differed in many ways. While Jewish educators often infused camps' color war games with educational concepts, embodying a team's Jewish theme or personality through learning, acting, singing, and cheering proved far less direct for campers than in acts of a sociodrama. And yet role-plays and color war shared certain core characteristics, breaking up the daily schedule with climaxes to the camp experience and serving as enjoyable camp rituals that gave staff, as Blumenthal put it, "social control." As Habonim's Hityashvut activity showed, some sociodramas occupied an entire day of the summer schedule, emerging as special days in and of themselves.

And yet what made special days and role-play most similar was their mutual, essential ingredient: play. Through a variety of play and games, educators used sociodrama and special days as climactic moments in which their camp's values and ideologies could not only be put on display, but embodied by campers otherwise engaged in exciting, recreational, and entertaining activities. At camps across the ideological spectrum, play instilled camp life with emotional highs and brought the broader idea that camps could pass on Jewishness through "Jewish living" to the next level. Intentionally placing

Children dressed in costume for Felker Yomtov,
Camp Boiberik, late 1960s/early 1970s.
Source: Susan Arnsten-Russell. Printed with permission.

special days toward the end of the summer or session schedules, camp leaders
trusted that these holidays and games would infuse campers with enough
passion for living like Jews of other times and other places, all in the service of carrying them through until their next summer of "maximum Jewish
life."⁶⁷ Jewish camp leaders had divergent conceptualizations of what Jewish
identity could and should entail but used a similar set of practices toward
their goals, transporting campers to imaginary worlds where they could play
ideal Jews on their paths toward becoming them.

———

Taken together, the simulations, special days, and festivals that Jewish camps
invented or tailored to their goals illuminate how diverse postwar Jews imagined and interpreted the ideal Jewish future. To Zionists, sociodrama and

Maccabiah provided two different paths to bring campers toward the chalutz ideal; to Reform and Conservative educators, they offered educational
impact and an infusion of ideal Jewishness through play; to Yiddishists,
Felker and the Yada aimed to mark campers with a sense of secular yiddishkayt. As the next chapter demonstrates, another set of special days also came
to heighten the senses, but in a very different direction, as educators crafted
programs centered on mourning and memorializing the six million Jews
murdered in the Holocaust.

# "A Little Suffering Goes a Long Way"

## Tisha B'Av, Ghetto Day, and the Shadow of the Holocaust

IN THE EARLY 1960S, Reuben, a camper at Camp Yavneh, wrote a reflection in his camp's yearbook describing Tisha B'Av, the Jewish holy day of mourning. "The *chadar ochel* [cafeteria] was set up in a way that was moving," wrote the camper. "All the benches were put on the floor, and on top of them candles." In the evening that Tisha B'Av began, he and his fellow campers listened to a reading of Lamentations, the traditional text that tells of the destruction of the Temple in Jerusalem, and to "explanations from our teachers and counselors about the background" of the day and its traditions. Campers and counselors past bar/bat mitzvah age followed the tradition of fasting from food and drink for the full twenty-five-hour, somber period. Toward the end of the next day, however, the mood changed dramatically: after a happy meal of breaking the fast, the whole camp came together for festive singing and dancing and eventually witnessed their Israeli counselors set a giant sign constructed out of wire and a flammable tarp on fire, the word *YISRAEL* [Israel] radiating against the dark night sky. After a day of grief, sorrow, and remembrance, the melancholic mood of Tisha B'Av transitioned into a joyful celebration of Zionist redemption, a stark contrast from the tearful rituals of the night before.[1]

Tisha B'Av is one of the most significant fast days in the Jewish calendar. According to the Mishnah, several historical tragedies occurred on Tisha B'Av (the Ninth of Av): the destruction of the First and Second Temples, the capturing of the city of Betar, and the plowing up of the Temple Mount by Roman commander Tarnus Rufus. Since the codification of the Mishnah, moreover, several other events, including the beginning of the First Crusade, the expulsion of the Jews from Spain in 1492, and the dissolution of the Warsaw ghetto in 1942, also took place on or near the date. To remember these tragedies, Jews observe Tisha B'Av by fasting; sitting on the floor rather than on chairs; refraining from greetings, swimming, and bathing; and communally reading the liturgical Book of Lamentations, or Eicha, a text that is part "traditional 'city lament' mourning the desertion of the city by God," part "funeral dirge."[2]

Its religious importance notwithstanding, Tisha B'Av has played an extremely minor role in American Jewish life.[3] Orthodox Jews observe it according to its traditional customs, but many American Jews outside the Orthodox community have never even heard of the day. Its American obscurity has a lot to do with its timing: overlapping with summer vacations, a time of emptied-out pews and paused Hebrew school programs, Reform temples and Conservative synagogues have had little reason to emphasize the one and only holy day that falls in July or August. In Tisha B'Av's place, liberal congregations have historically tended to emphasize other days, like the Tenth of Tevet, which typically falls in December, turning the minor fast day into a religious moment for Holocaust commemoration. Holocaust Remembrance Days have also offered opportunities for remembering the six million Jews murdered in the Holocaust within the synagogue since their various dates were chosen by the US government, the United Nations, and Israel.[4]

For the exact opposite reasons, the sparse summer holiday calendar left Jewish summer camp leaders with only Tisha B'Av—the least celebratory, most mournful day of the entire Jewish year, a day that diverges dramatically from the recreational moods and norms of life in a summer camp. Its traditions, rituals, and *halakhot* (laws) are not particularly child friendly.

Nevertheless, camping leaders embraced what was an obscure Jewish holy day in America with striking enthusiasm, citing the many benefits its somberness offered them as educators and transformers of American Jewish culture. Teaching and learning played a crucial role in these special days, as many campers learned the details of Jewish historical tragedies for the first time. Indeed, Tisha B'Av usefully offered a sanctioned moment in the summer schedule to pause from recreation and educate campers about horrific events of the Jewish past. But camp leaders concentrated more on making an emotional impact on campers than an educational one, harnessing the day's gravity and solemnity by way of moving, creative ceremonies. Seeing the advantage of such a day, Jewish leaders who described themselves as secular came to invent alternative memorial days that served similar ends, developing programs that taught campers about historical tragedies and allowed them to mourn the very recent Holocaust.[5] Punctuating the recreational highs of camp life with scheduled emotional lows, Tisha B'Av and its alternatives—such as Camp Hemshekh's Ghetto Day—emerged as some of the most highly anticipated and invested-in programs of the entire summer, essential in leaders' struggle for "cultural survival."

Contrary to the myth that Jews in the Holocaust's aftermath did not speak about the recent tragedy, the generations in postwar camps referenced, talked about, memorialized, and mourned the Holocaust openly and frequently. They built memorial statues and planted trees in dedication to the dead; they recalled the six million in their prayer services and inserted the Holocaust and other historical misfortunes into their role-plays and educational activities. Despite the heaviness of the topic and its incongruence with the summer camp's usual levity, most educators proved "eager to teach about the Holocaust," seeing that it proved a powerful tool in "contemporary Jewish indoctrination." As Eugene Borowitz, a Reform rabbi, professor, and philosopher, wrote, skipping the topic "for fear of traumatizing the children" not only undervalued their ability to handle upsetting information, but turned children into "co-conspirators in illusion which is unhealthy for them and treason to the Jewish people."[6]

And yet honoring the six million took its most overt and concentrated form on Tisha B'Av, with "every kind of Jewish organizational camp—Reform, Conservative, Zionist of every variant, Yiddish and Socialist,"

Hasia Diner explained, devoting "Ninth of Av programs to the memory of the slaughter of the six million."[7] Jewish leaders across this wide spectrum seemed to agree on two unique powers that Holocaust memorialization and other histories of Jewish persecution held within the camping context. In a moment marked by growing social mobility and affluence, the Holocaust functioned as a potent reminder of just how fragile personal and communal status and security can be and could take children "out of their ease in the non-Jewish world" and "strengthen their Jewish identity by letting them know what educated, cultured, and sophisticated gentiles have been known to do to Jews in modern times."[8] The traumas of Jewish history, in this sense, could be passed down from generation to generation, touching and affecting young people who had known only American comfort and relative social acceptance. As with many of the role-plays described in the previous chapter, however, Tisha B'Av programming also focused on stories of Jewish resistance and heroism within devastating circumstances. As educators worked to "inspire loyalty, self-esteem, and ethnic identity in the next generation of American Jews," wrote Rona Sheramy, the six million sometimes receded "into the background" of their memorial programs, with stories of how "Jews in Europe took control of their own fate and helped to defeat Nazism" and "acts of physical resistance and rescue" placed front and center instead.[9]

Seeking to find a balance between these two extremes, camp memorial days and commemorations appeared rather similar on the surface, often beginning with tragedy and sadness and ending with stories of resistance, heroism, and survival to encourage pride.[10] At the same time, their resemblances lay in the fact that Tisha B'Av's religious rites and laws provided camps a kind of how-to manual that they could build on and adapt to their young audience. At Zionist, Conservative, and Reform camps, Tisha B'Av observance always began at sunset with campers attending a solemn, candle-lit ceremony, where participants sang mournful songs (*Kinot*), listened to Eicha, and performed dramatic accounts of historical tragedies onstage. Depending on their age, many campers fasted or ate simpler meals until sunset the next day, which they spent attending low-energy activities like educational discussions and film screenings related to the day. Even as most eschewed the religious rites and rules of the holy day, Yiddish camps' rituals were also extremely similar, and the meaning-making rituals involved in these camps' memorial days offer a fascinating microcosm for rethinking the notion of Jewish secularism itself. Ardent secularists desired rituals too and developed within their rejection of Tisha B'Av a whole new set of customs that produced strikingly similar effects.

How camps' programs varied reveals not only their differing approaches to religion and secularism. Each camp's specific mission influenced its interpretations and uses of Tisha B'Av, the Holocaust, and Jewish history as well. As they placed their "particular ideological stamp[s]" on their programs and materials, camp leaders not only drove home their principles with urgency but came to instill Tisha B'Av and its alternatives with distinctive meanings and conclusions.[11] The Holocaust's recentness had an impact on Jews across the spectrum, but the moral of the story varied from camp to camp, inflected and redirected to answer to postwar anxieties and aims. Focusing on Tisha B'Av, then, provides an opportunity to see how different political and religious perspectives influenced how leaders used Jewish collective memory and grief. Without missing the irony of their shared lexicon, this chapter demonstrates how remembering those who died in one kind of "camp" inflected the lives of Jews within a wholly different one in the decades immediately following the end of the Holocaust.

## Tisha B'Av in Zionist, Reform, and Conservative Camps

While the rituals of Tisha B'Av shaped commemorations across the ideological spectrum, American Zionist educators embraced Tisha B'Av with nearly unanimous and zealous enthusiasm. To Zionists, Tisha B'Av reinforced the legitimacy of their cause, the Holocaust and other historical tragedies proof that Jews could never be truly safe in the diaspora. Performing a highly choreographed Tisha B'Av *tekes* (ceremony) each year, Zionist camps began Tisha B'Av with "the entire *machaneh* [camp]" gathering. A Habonim camper described the ceremony in summer 1944: "The *chaverim* [members of the movement] fell into the spirit of the day. Either the *sicha* [conversation] that day or the somber attitude of the older *chaverim* affected them." Dressed in white from head to toe, the campers marched slowly in double file alongside a "huge bonfire." After the camp choir sang "By the Rivers of Babylon," the camper explained how "the *chaverim*, without the smallest disturbance and in perfect silence, followed in line," a sight that "made a lasting impression." As they entered the cafeteria, the campers found that the usual posters had been taken down and that the room was pared down to a single "bench on which four *yarzeit licht* [memorial candles] burnt." After sitting on the floor listening to a reading of Lamentations in both the traditional Hebrew chanting and in English, a counselor stood up to describe a "Jewish extermination center in Poland," the campers in the room having "never came closer to the Ghettos of Poland than in that moment." The fact that Camp Habonim's ceremony evoked the Holocaust one year before the end of the war shows just how quickly the war entered the realm of Jewish education. But while the Holocaust played a role in the day, the main implication drawn from Habonim's Tisha B'Av observance centered on how nationalism "is ingrained in the very being of our people, in its traditions, ceremonies," with Tisha B'Av's presence in the Jewish calendar serving as "proof that Jewish nationalism is not a modern idea."[12]

Descriptions of postwar Tisha B'Av ceremonies at other Zionist camps show that most took on similar styles and themes, with the Zionist camp approach to Tisha B'Av becoming a tradition in and of itself. Zionist program guides used comparable source texts, schedules, and guidelines for evening ceremonies, with participants reciting dirges, poems, and essays describing Jewish tragedies, including such texts as Chaim Nachman Bialik's "City of Slaughter," and Yehudah HaLevi's "Ode to Zion." Opening and closing with melancholic songs as campers trickled in or out of the auditorium, social hall, or amphitheater, their observances tended to take place in dark spaces surrounded by candles, all in the effort to cultivate a solemn mood. The camp director often delivered a formal address setting the tone for the day, and additional songs, overtures, chants, and staged plays proved common, providing different ways for campers in the audience to connect with the day's significance.[13] After the solemn ceremonies on the eve of Tisha B'Av, Zionist camp participants rarely awoke in the morning to programs quite so solemn, with counselors screening relevant historical films, reading stories, and leading campers in arts and crafts projects that conveyed the themes of the day. The morning after Habonim's ceremony, for instance, counselors led campers back to the amphitheater for a reading of Josephus's description of the destruction of the Temple, as well as for a reading of the story "The Mayor of the Warsaw Ghetto."[14] At both Cejwin and Tel Yehudah, the day of Tisha B'Av also included further education, as well as time for reflective art projects and group discussions geared toward processing the information the day imparted and the emotions the evening ceremony may have stirred up.

In the years following Israel's establishment in 1948, "vigorous discussions," and "impromptu debates" took place among Zionists in Israel and the diaspora on whether Jews should continue to observe the holy day, since the establishment of the Jewish state was to many Zionists and new Israelis the conclusive fulfillment of Jewish yearning. And yet because Jewish educators and American Zionist leaders saw an educational use in Tisha B'Av, Zionist camps unanimously embraced it in the postwar decades, altering its themes to reflect these new historical circumstances.[15] Cejwin educator Samuel Dinsky explained that while the events of 1948 "fulfilled the prayer for a home," Tisha B'av should not be eradicated but rather refocused on "dedicat[ing] ourselves with renewed vigor and determination to reconstruct the lives of our people and to help rebuild the State of Israel." By focusing on the "rebuilding of the reborn State of Israel" instead of on mourning, Dinsky believed that the day would be more inspiring to campers.[16] That same year, staff member Etan Levine similarly warned that "if the sole emphasis [of Tisha B'Av] is upon the burning down of a building almost 2,000 years ago, no amount of verbal gymnastics will succeed in making its impact justify its observance." Focusing on the "work to be done" in Israel had much greater potential to intensify the day's relevance for campers.[17]

For all these reasons, Zionist camps similarly transitioned as the day progressed from a focus on tragedy to an emphasis on heroism and hope. Stories of resistance in the Holocaust, and in particular the Warsaw ghetto uprising, proved common starting points, but Zionists leaned even more heavily on the establishment of the State of Israel as a counterbalance to the heaviness of the day.[18] One educator from the American Zionist Youth Foundation explained that the heroism "of the Jews and Europe and the Warsaw Ghetto and in Israel" should be emphasized at the end of Tisha B'Av, with "all eyes . . . turn[ed] to the future and to Israel."[19] Massad's evening ceremony and early daytime activities similarly occurred "in the spirit of mourning, partaking in the sadness of our Brothers in Europe" while ending "with hope for the future rejuvenation of the people of Israel in our land."[20] Camp Habonim took the theme of hope even further, with counselors instructing campers "to dress in their holiday clothes" for the break-fast meal, where the "tables were set with tablecloths . . . the room was decorated, and a feeling of festivity prevailed." Within the twenty-five hours of Tisha B'Av, Zionist camps transitioned from mourning to celebrating how the "Zionist dream" became "a reality," the day's "sense of hope" ending with an "eruption of joy."[21]

The meanings and messages campers at Zionist camps derived from these programs were not static during this thirty-year period. As distance from the Holocaust, the massive social, political, and cultural changes of the 1960s, and Israel's trials and tribulations changed American Jewish identity and self-understanding, participants' experience and understanding of Tisha B'Av changed as well. Mourning the near-total destruction of Eastern European Jewry, for instance, transformed as Jewish youth embraced an emergent American culture in the 1960s of celebrating one's ethnic heritage and roots. While Habonim's 1944 ceremony mentioned a "Jewish extermination center in Poland," the camp did not yet have the vocabulary or the information to go into the kind of detail about the Holocaust that camps would as the postwar period progressed, when more research and testimony made such detail possible. These circumstances caused the meaning of Holocaust memorialization to change over time. As with so many other rituals of camp life, however, Tisha B'Av programs in most Zionist camps remained remarkably consistent throughout the postwar period. As program materials and somber ceremonies became ingrained camp traditions, educators and counselors recycled their performances and play scripts from year to year, typically making only minor changes. The events of the postwar period affected how campers and staff members interpreted Tisha B'Av but led to little variability within the day's programs within Zionist summer camps.

Certain changes did occur in educational Jewish camping's overall, sector-wide approach to Tisha B'Av, however, less so within Zionist camps than because of them. In the late 1940s and 1950s, Tisha B'Av at Ramah camps mainly reflected the Conservative organization's broader goal of producing future movement leadership, focusing on Jewish themes, traditions, and laws. Beginning with traditional sources such as the Shulchan Aruch, the Mishnah, and Sefer HaMoadim, Ramah's thorough Tisha B'Av program guides included the halakhot (religious laws) of the day, the full text of Lamentations, and a "Kinoh [dirge] in memory of the Six Million," as well as texts such as Jacob Neusner's "On the Question of Forgiveness" and Samuel Raphael Hirsch's "Why Is Tisha B'Av Observed with Fasting and by Observing the Law of Mourning?" In addition to running discussions about these texts, the Ramah camps used "written exercises" and an activity that taught campers the "Chronology of Tisha B'Av through the ages."[22]

Reform summer camps used Tisha B'Av "to teach about Jewish suffering throughout history" and to foster "identification with fellow Jews everywhere." As rabbi and former OSRUI staff member Donald Splansky explained, few of the young people in the Reform movement "ever experienced [Tisha B'Av] outside of the camp setting," and thus the day made "a big impression on campers." Without summer camps, Splansky argued, Tisha B'Av would have likely disappeared from the Reform movement completely.[23] Even as Reform camps seemingly emphasized the day less than Zionist and Yiddishist camps did, the ceremonies had meaningful implications for the Reform movement and reflected something crucial about Reform camping's educational mission: that life at camp should provide a complete Jewish experience, including rituals not usually found in other parts of the Reform movement.

Each Reform camp used Tisha B'Av to highlight different themes, demonstrating their independence from one another. At OSRUI, Tisha B'Av's ceremonies brought up questions as to why so much persecution befell Jews, and one source mentions that God "was questioned and criticized. A rather desolate feeling swept over the audience."[24] Staff members used theater to teach children about Jewish persecution, having campers perform plays like *The Wandering Jew*, which included Yiddish songs of persecution and resistance. At Goldman Union Camp Institute, Tisha B'Av activities focused primarily on ancient tragedies and the history of religious prescriptions for the day rather than on Israel and modern tragedies, while Camp Swig used the day to teach the value of *tzedakah*, or charity, by way of an "austerity meal" in which campers ate a simpler, smaller dinner to experience what it might feel like to be poor and undernourished.[25]

Rather than having one unified message, Reform camps' diverse programs and the Ramah camps more text-based, traditional approach show how camps molded Tisha B'Av to reflect multiple visions of Jewishness.

By the late 1960s, these diverse programs gave way to a more homogeneous message as educators highlighted the heroism of Zionist pioneers and Israeli soldiers, portraying Israel's foundation as the redemption of the Jewish people.[26] In the mid-1960s, for instance, OSRUI's ceremonies more directly focused on Israel while also broaching the subject of Jewish persecution in the Soviet Union.[27] Conservative and Reform Tisha B'Av observances never became identical to those of Zionist camps, keeping a broader range of themes, texts, and practices in their toolboxes. Israel's role in the day, however, increased over time, functioning as a useful symbol of hope and heroism in the Holocaust's wake. Using Israel in this way certainly reflected the growth of Zionist sentiment among American Jewry coming up to and after the Six-Day War and mirrored the rising roles of Israel and Hebrew culture within Jewish camps more broadly. In this way, their use of Israel reflected evolutions in mainstream Jewish politics. But educators also saw emotional benefits of ending Tisha B'Av with joy, redemption, and optimism, transitioning campers from sorrow and back into the recreational atmosphere of camp life. For children who emerged out of Tisha B'Av with fears of future anti-Semitic violence or a change in status in America, educators pointed to the nascent Jewish state, alleviating the anxieties of history by referencing the differences in their contemporary circumstance. Israel provided not only a symbol of hope but a relieving coda to the grief of the history for children absorbing its weight. This utilization of Israel, however, was not universal in Jewish camping. Within Yiddish camps, where the Holocaust meant the near-total destruction of the culture and language they encouraged and celebrated, many leaders saw Israel as providing a complicated challenge to the future of Yiddish in a post-Holocaust world rather than a simple, relieving finale.

### Memorialization at Yiddish Camps

Although only one Yiddish camp, Boiberik, marked Tisha B'Av itself, Yiddish camps' memorial programs shared some striking similarities with those of Reform, Conservative, and Zionist summer camps. Well known among Yiddish educators and cultural activists for his use of religious traditions at Boiberik, Leibush Lehrer had a particular and familiar order to Tisha B'Av.

On Tisha B'Av eve, Lehrer gave a speech on Jewish historical tragedies to an auditorium full of campers and presented a recitation of the traditional Eicha in Yiddish. At the end of the night, a *gelt zamlung*, or a charity collection, took place to raise funds in support of Holocaust refugees and new immigrants to Palestine and later Israel. Through these rituals, Lehrer hoped that Tisha B'Av would serve as an effective "antidote to forgetfulness," a forgetfulness he feared would set in as the authentic Jews—the survivors themselves—passed away.[28]

At the same time, the distinctive worldviews of Yiddish camps made their memorialization practices different from the rest in tone, content, and message. Yiddishists overwhelmingly focused their memorial programs on the Holocaust, mourning not only the death of millions of Yiddish speakers but the near-total decimation of Yiddish culture that their murders at the hands of the Nazis caused.[29] In Boiberik's case, the camp's focus on the Holocaust meant that its evening ceremony went in certain unique directions. Lehrer, for instance, led the camp through *Yizkor*, Judaism's synagogue mourning service that traditionally takes place on four specific holidays each year. Tisha B'Av is not one of those four holidays, and most synagogues invite congregants who have not lost close family to leave the sanctuary during the service. Nevertheless, Boiberik's campers prayed for the six million in this untraditional use of Jewish tradition, learning Judaism's mourning traditions by doing and identifying the loss of much of European Jewry as a personal one.[30]

While Lehrer exuded immense confidence in his program, he lamented the fact that the "dramatization of Jewish history and traditional life evoked no serious interest" from his fellow lay leaders at the Sholem Aleichem Folk Institute (SAFI). Indeed, the majority of his secular Yiddishist colleagues had little tolerance for religious ritual and staunchly opposed Lehrer's approach. None of his controversial engagements with Judaism, however, "evoked so much criticism, and so severely expressed" as his Tisha B'Av ceremony. "I attempted to enlighten some friends on the fact that we, Jews, are perhaps the only people who succeeded in turning physical defeats into psychological victories; that the very act of keeping alive the memory of all our catastrophes by highly dramatized methods had greatly enhanced our will to endure as a people," wrote Lehrer in 1959. But his passionate explanations failed to convince his fellow Yiddishists of the value of the day. During the years in which Tisha B'av happened to fall on Saturday evening, a time when guests stayed on the camp's adult side, Lehrer expected that many "will be angered and disappointed by our ritual observance," which, he concluded, "distressed me far more than I care to spell out." In the 1960s, for example, a "well-known Yiddish writer" who came to the camp as a weekend guest refused to enter Boiberik's theater on Tisha B'Av, "because he didn't want to witness a 'religious ceremony'" that "modern people don't need to observe."[31]

Some parents found Lehrer's ceremony objectionable as well, albeit for different reasons. One Boiberik camper's father, Lion Rosenthal, pointed out with "grave concern" in a 1962 letter to the camp's management that his daughter had "tearfully related to me what she had been told about the religious services to be held on Tisha Bov [sic]. She and the entire bunk have been informed by those girls who have had previous summers at Boiberik, that this is a complete day and evening of mourning. The older girls wear black . . . services are held in a room lighted with but a single candle." Mr. Rosenthal resented the idea that his daughter had experienced "but a single moment of anxiety about this whole matter," considering that she still had both "her parents and a good percentage of her grandparents." He argued that that the somber Tisha B'Av service should be optional, seeing "no reason for my children (age 10 and 14) to be present at any Kaddish services."[32] Such perspectives from parents are rarely found in archives. Given the recency of the war, however, and the fact that many Boiberik families included refugees or had lost close or distant relatives in the Holocaust, Rosenthal would have likely not been alone in thinking that Boiberik's Tisha B'Av practice was potentially unsuitable or overly upsetting for children.

Because other Yiddish camps were avowedly secular in character and sought to avoid the questions of religion that Tisha B'Av stirred up, Boiberik was the only Yiddish camp I encountered that observed Tisha B'Av itself. However, other Yiddish camps created moments in their schedules to memorialize the Holocaust too, reflecting how secular, Yiddish-oriented Jews created and desired rituals for dealing with trauma and grief. At Camp Kinder Ring, a Yiddishist summer camp operated by the Workmen's Circle, memorializing the Holocaust took a front and center role in camp programming: Mikhl Baran, one of the camp's head staff members (who later worked at Hemshekh), was a Holocaust survivor from Lithuania who had fought in the resistance, and his presence at Kinder Ring, sources explained, served as a "daily reminder" of the recent tragedy and the resistance as he told his story to campers. But the camp also similarly highlighted a yearly memorial ceremony they called "Yizkor" (the name did not, in this case, denote the mournful prayer service but rather the Yiddish and Hebrew word for "remember"). "Gedenk, remember!" read the script for one such ceremony. "May the Jewish people—and all men of good will remember, now and forever, the souls of all the upright and courageous men and women of the Warsaw ghetto and of all the ghettos, who gave their lives for the sanctification of Israel's name." Campers sang "Es Brent, Briderlekh" (It's Burning, Brothers), which describes a shtetl set aflame during a violent pogrom, and "Zog Nit Zayn Mol," the "Partisans Hymn," which recalls the Jewish resistance in the Holocaust.[33]

Camp Hemshekh took a more expansive approach than Kinder Ring, although their activities were similar in character. As the camp hoped to serve as a continuation of the Yiddish-speaking world of Europe and a camp that was founded for the children of many Holocaust refugees by Holocaust refugees, it embedded memorialization in its environment and interwove it into its everyday programming. The camp placed a memorial statue or a *denkmol* to the Warsaw ghetto uprising on its grounds (designed by teenager Daniel Libeskind, a now-famous architect who has designed many of the world's most striking Holocaust memorials and museums) as well as a banner above the stage that read *"Lomir Trogn Dem Gayst Vos Men Hot Undz Fartroyt"* (Let us carry the spirit that has been entrusted to us).[34] Staff members focused their scheduled educational programs on prewar Jewish culture, literature, and politics in Europe and recalled the Holocaust regularly. But while the *denkmol* "ensured that the Six Million were never far from our minds," as former camper Margie Newman wrote, "remembrance reached its peak" on the "third Sunday of every August," when campers and staff worked together to put on an elaborate Ghetto Night performance, followed by a set of mournful activities conducted beginning the next morning, on Ghetto Day.[35]

Hemshekh's invented, twenty-four-hour memorial day included elements reminiscent of other camps' Tisha B'Av practices. Ghetto Night

fostered an emotion-probing experience for campers through scripted recollections of the Holocaust, candle-lit spaces, and somber song. For children
of survivors, Ghetto Night proved particularly emotional as many campers
learned of what their parents had gone through in detail for the first time.
As at Camp Kinder Ring, however, the program was in great part "a tribute
to resistance," allowing campers "to think of Jews in the ghettos and camps
as heroes rather than victims, in control, brave and strong." For children like
Newman, whose parents were Holocaust survivors, "learning of [the resis-
tance] was a powerful antidote to the humiliation and shame I felt about my
father's travails."[36]

Ghetto Day not only functioned as a moment of commemoration and
mourning, but as an opportunity to emphasize the camp's ideological
cause. Hemshekh's ceremonies ended with campers exclaiming, "Long live
Yiddish!"—the message of the evening made explicit. By exalting resistance
fighters in the Holocaust, the ceremony implored campers to form their own
sort of resistance, confronting the temptations to abandon their language
and assimilate into mainstream American and American Jewish society.
Ghetto Day, then, was not only a form of what Jacob L. Moreno called "collective catharsis" for campers and counselors, as it presented an opportunity
to process the Holocaust's devastations with other second-generation survivors, but an integral part of Hemshekh's broader mission to prepare youth to
defend, preserve, and produce Yiddish culture. Just as the Jewish resistance
saved themselves and fellow Jews, the Ghetto Night scripts explained, so too
must Hemshekh's campers become a form of resistance, resisting temptations to assimilate, to forget their history, and to abandon their language.[37]

The message of Ghetto Day came through to campers loud and clear,
with one counselor reporting a huge shift in his campers' behavior and attitudes toward speaking Yiddish and Yiddish-related programming after
Ghetto Day. While campers already knew before the day that "at its best,
Hemshekh is a mainstay of Yiddishkayt's survival today," the counselors
complained that they littered the campgrounds and went to great lengths
to avoid attending Yiddish class, disrespecting the camp and its mission.
After Ghetto Day, however, campers reportedly headed to Yiddish class happily. One counselor suggested that the camp should schedule Ghetto Day

Campers at Hemshekh preparing their Holocaust monument,
or the *denkmol*, for the ghetto ceremony, August 1964.
Source: Photographed by Gabriel Ross. Printed with permission.

toward the beginning of the summer rather than the end, because then the
staff could remind them "for the next seven weeks, 'But you cried on ghetto
night, didn't you?'" recognizing that the transformative power of the day
for campers had not only educational but potentially practical applications.
Campers' essays, poems, and reviews from the *Hemshekh Weekly* also help
to provide a sense of how they experienced Ghetto Day. One camper's poem
described the somberness of the day and its message in rhyme:

*Today was a sad and quiet day,*
*Not for much laughing or bouncing around,*
*A day to remember the dead six million,*
*To remember what Hitler did to us,*
*To remember the ghettos that they put us in,*
*Dying of hunger, of illness, of frost,*
*And we hope that nothing as terrible will ever happen,*
*As what happened to our people then.*[38]

Another camper reported that his fellow campers fought on Ghetto Day about how sad they should feel, how they should behave, and what activities should cease for the day. And yet another camper described how meaningful the program was to her, explaining, "Ghetto Night means a lot to me and many others. I think that it is one of the most beautiful things to see. I know that I will never forget a Ghetto Night in Hemshekh, and therefore, I will never forget the horrors of the Nazi camps."[39] Their varied reactions demonstrate that campers did not respond to Ghetto Day uniformly but rather experienced the day and drew their own conclusions from it in deeply personal ways.

Zionist and Yiddishist memorial days undoubtedly shared certain tactics and programmatic structures, including the use of somber ceremonies, songs, readings, and skits. But whereas Zionist camps looked toward Israel as a sign of redemption after thousands of years of persecution, Yiddish-oriented camps rarely mentioned Israel. Instead of hope, Yiddish camps engaged with heroism, resistance, and survival as their themes, placing significant emphasis on moments of resistance like the Warsaw Ghetto uprising. Yiddish camps' memorial programs in the fifties and early sixties, then, left participants without an obvious optimistic note to help transition out of the twenty-four-hour mourning experience. Boiberik, however, became an exception to this rule beginning after the Six-Day War, marking Tisha B'Av in 1968 with a play titled *Survival*, which ushered the audience scene-by-scene through Jewish historical tragedies, covering thousands of years of history and ending with more recent times. In the barracks of a concentration camp, one scene involved a young boy penning a poem yearning for a peaceful time:

*Ikh vil azoy aleyn avek*
*Ahin vu s'voynen gute mentshn*
*Oif umbakante vegn—vayte;*
*Vu einer harget nisht kayn tsveytn;*

*Un efsher gor a sakh fun undz,*
*Un efsher toyznt shtark,*
*Veln dergreykhn yenem tsil*
*Eyder es vert tsu shpet.*

*I want to go*
*Where good people live*
*On unknown paths, distant,*
*Where no one murders another.*

*And maybe even many of us,*
*And even 1,000 strong,*
*Will reach that goal*
*Before it is too late.*

The notion of world peace, so integral to Lehrer's legacy, remained the main message of the poem. And yet the poem ended with a Zionist twist as Israel served as the end point of the characters' wandering. Lined up to join the reserves during the Six-Day War, two characters who survived the Holocaust and all of the other Jewish tragedies recalled in the play discuss their new situation:

*Uri:* So we're right back to where we started.
*Mar Cohen:* Yes, Uri, but this time it's different. Now we have a home and a country to defend.
*Uri:* I feel millions of martyred Jews are here with us. Will we survive this threat? That all Jews in Israel will be pushed into the sea?
*Mar Cohen:* We will! We will! No one will move us from here.
*Uri:* I wish they would let us live in peace.

The play concluded with one character touching the Wailing Wall in Jerusalem as he uttered the *Shehechiyanu*, the prayer recited when doing something for the first time.[40]

The Zionist message of Boiberik's 1968 ceremony marked a turning point for the camp that mirrored American Jewry's growing identification with Zionism and Israel in the years after the Six-Day War. And yet using Israel as a happy ending to a sad day proved an exception in Yiddish cultural camping rather than the rule. Instead, Yiddish camps more broadly used their memorial days to convey to campers that Yiddishists need to not only remember the dead but to become more like the resistance, defying tides of assimilation, resisting the decline of Yiddish, and never succumbing to the urge to forget.[41]

———

In 1966, education scholar Daniel Isaacman wrote an article for the *American Jewish Yearbook,* explaining the postwar growth of Jewish educational camping. As he exalted the power of summer camps overall, he specifically referenced Tisha B'Av, explaining that, "a [camp] Tish'ah be-Av program . . . can be an experience that no amount of formal study duplicates."[42] Dozens of postwar educators echoed Isaacman's praise for Tisha B'Av, embracing the day or an alternative to it as not only a part but the pinnacle of their educational programs. This ideologically diverse set of camp educators, counselors, and directors seized on Tisha B'Av and its alternatives as opportunities to prepare children in a struggle for "creative survival," refashioning the religious holy day and its secularized alternatives into an emotional and performative experience that displayed their ideologies and emphasized to campers why what they learned and how they lived during the rest of the summer mattered.

The notion that sadness, tragedy, and mourning had educational and transformational benefits ensured that the shadow of the Holocaust would cast itself over the summers of Jewish youth for decades. In their efforts to transform a generation of Jewish youth raised largely in comfort, safety, and affluence, educators molded Tisha B'Av to fit their various political, religious, and nationalistic missions, and similarly inserted stories of Jewish heroes to foster pride in the wake of the Holocaust. But even with messages of hope and heroism, camps' memorial ceremonies intentionally and effectively provoked sorrow in campers. As Margie Newman described her time as a camper at Hemshekh, the immediate aftermath of Ghetto Night left campers "weeping and sobbing." The camp mother, "a lovely woman with a number tattooed on her forearm," went from bunk to bunk, handing out cookies and candy and comforting the crying campers. Newman recalled that even as a child, she sensed "the dissonance of someone who had endured the [concentration] camps charged with soothing children who had led, for the most part, lives that were safe and comfortable."[43]

The dissonance Newman felt was not simply an accidental by-product of memorial days but rather the whole point. Jewish camps produced Tisha B'Av, Yizkor ceremonies, and Ghetto Day as emotion-probing experiences for "the comfortable American youth, that understand little about suffering." For Lehrer, Tisha B'Av proved that "a little suffering goes a long way" and that marking it "prepare[d] our children in their struggle for our own creative survival, a struggle which, incidentally . . . is rendered more acute in its severity in conditions of freedom."[44] In their commemorations of Tisha B'Av and Ghetto Day, the leaders of Jewish summer camps hoped not only to foster an "antidote to forgetfulness" but to ensure that Jewish youth carried the pains of the past and the lessons they brought to light into their brighter, safer American futures.[45]

# The Language Cure

## Embracing and Evolving
## Yiddishism and Hebraism

IN WINTER 1941, HAHISTADRUT HAIVRIT, an American organization dedicated to spreading passion for the Hebrew language, gathered its members in New York City to discuss their movement's next steps. Identifying youth as the key to their success, Shlomo and Rivkah Shulsinger, a young couple who met in Palestine, shared their vision with the group for an intensive summer camp, where "all activities ... including the recreational and educational program" would take place in Hebrew. In a matter of months, the organization founded a day camp program in Far Rockaway, New York, with a small cohort of just twenty-five campers, calling its program Camp Massad. In 1942, their vision expanded to a piloted sleepaway program on the grounds of an Orthodox summer camp, Machanaim. By 1943, they had acquired the funds and know-how to establish their own independent sleepaway camp, purchasing a site in Pennsylvania's Poconos. The camp expanded to an additional site in 1945 and again in 1966, the three locations all within an hour's drive of one another. The Shulsingers' vision of a Hebrew-speaking camp had become a reality, bringing the language into the lives of hundreds of American Jewish children and teenagers each summer.[1]

Massad was not the first Jewish summer camp to place language at the heart of its agenda. In the early years of camps like Kinder Ring and Boiberik, Yiddish operated as the everyday language for Yiddish-speaking immigrant participants and first-generation children and staff. Although Hebraically inclined camps "were not conceived of as Hebrew-speaking . . . and language proficiency was not identified as a goal," Hebrew played an important role in early camps like Achvah, Modin, and Cejwin, as well as in early Zionist summer camps, functioning "in tandem with other symbols to posit and reinforce a bond between the camp community and the new Hebrew society in Palestine."[2] The establishment of Camp Massad, however, marked the beginning of a new kind of relationship between Jewish summer camping and Jewish languages. Starting in the 1940s, educational Jewish camps increasingly emphasized the roles of Hebrew and Yiddish in their programs, placing Hebraism and Yiddishism at the heart of their missions.

The postwar period was a curious time for the growth of language-focused Jewish camping. Throughout much of history, Jews lived in multilingual societies, their speech divided into languages of Jewish learning and prayer (Hebrew and Aramaic), everyday Jewish vernaculars (Yiddish, Ladino, Judeo-Arabic), and the languages of the lands in which they lived.[3] But when they arrived in the United States, Jews embraced English, sending their children to public schools and rarely making the passing on of Yiddish a top priority. Yiddish declined in use from generation to generation, while only a small group of elites came to learn and advocate for spoken Hebrew. In a break from a diglossic and even triglossic Jewish past, the monolingual postwar context rendered Jewish language ideologies fringe, Yiddish becoming associated with an immigrant, poor, and largely socialist past many Jews wanted to distance themselves from and Hebraism remaining an elite enterprise for the learned few.

As fears of cultural decline intensified the urgency of educators' effort at camp, however, the potential and purpose of Hebrew and Yiddish education transformed. While Massad's leaders hoped campers would come to use the Hebrew they acquired for communicating and reading Hebrew, they aimed most pointedly toward "creat[ing] a Hebrew atmosphere, in which a child finds a complete culture." "The Jewish child in America," wrote Shlomo Shulsinger, does not live as "natural Jews, like the children in *Eretz-Yisrael*," nor is their world akin to "the world of the child in Europe before the war, in which the child grew up in a colorful, diverse Jewish atmosphere." Immersion in a Hebrew-speaking camp, Shulsinger asserted, was not merely an effort in language education, but a gateway toward a more "natural" and "complete" Jewish life.[4] Because of their fringe status, language ideologies like Hebraism and Yiddishism emerged as paths toward "fixing" American Jewish culture, as educators attempted to break through postwar Jewry's prevailing monolingualism to produce better, more "authentic" Jews.

American Jewry's English centeredness made camps' language plans both logistically and philosophically difficult. Not only did educators need to convince American-born children and teens that speaking Jewish languages was an attractive, worthwhile cause, a particularly uphill battle in the case of Yiddish, which most young Jews associated with their immigrant parents or grandparents; they also had to get their campers to learn the languages well enough to converse within the camp environment. Although Massad recruited campers from Jewish schools where Hebrew education was part of the curriculum, few campers could speak fluent Hebrew prior to their arrival. And although many campers at Yiddish camps arrived with Yiddish knowledge from the home earlier in the century, this proved less and less the case over each passing decade.

These challenges notwithstanding, camp leaders' fixations on Jewish languages did match other trends of the American and Jewish postwar moment. Although few American Jews pursued full fluency, Hebrew culture resurfaced in the postwar years as less of an elite enterprise of the few than a growing element of American Jewish culture, part and parcel of supporting and celebrating Israel itself. As the civil rights movement and the multiculturalism of the American 1960s and 1970s came to influence how American Jews understood their own identities through the lens of heritage, many young Jews came to see embracing Jewish languages as part of those efforts. Although they expressed their critiques of American Jewish culture in different ways, sixties' youth and their elders in communal leadership positions converged on the idea that language could play a crucial role in producing and embodying authentic Jewishness. Zionism's growing place in the American Jewish mainstream, particularly in the aftermath of the Six-Day War, bolstered the relevance of Hebrew, while mourning that the Holocaust inspired some Jews to revitalize and embrace Yiddish language and culture.

Camps emphasized different languages in accordance with their ideologies, and they did so at varying degrees of intensity. Zionist camps emphasized the blossoming of Hebrew culture in Israel, linking their efforts with Hebrew to their nationalism; Hebraist Camp Massad focused on cultural Zionism, envisioning the reconstruction of Jewish life around Hebrew more so than on a territory. Reform and Conservative camps began with the goal of expanding Hebrew knowledge for producing a learned laity but also came to focus more and more on Israel and Hebrew culture. Yiddish socialist and communist camps linked the language to the histories and cultures of their movements and heightened their rhetoric as many of their leaders came to see their camps as on the frontlines of a war against the decline of Yiddish. Some camps, like Massad, attempted something closer to full immersion, but most camps engaged with the languages more symbolically, using them to name sites, groups, and scheduled programs. These differences notwithstanding, all these camps shared a core belief: that language had a unique power to strengthen Jewish culture and shape youth, not despite but because of American Jewry's growing monolingualism. They shared this belief in large part due to the parallel origins of their ideologies, rooted in the history of language movements, nationalism, and the European Jewish enlightenment.

## Yiddishism and Hebraism from Europe to America

In the late nineteenth century, a variety of European nationalist movements intersected with a concurrent golden age of language ideologies that "utilized and championed vernaculars" toward attaining their "integrating and authenticating goals." Jewish lexicographers, grammarians, philologists, and writers proved highly influential in these developments, contributing to both the instrumentalization of language in nationalist movements and universal language movements like Esperanto, whose adherents held the cosmopolitan and antinationalist belief that a neutral language would lead to peace. Esperanto's popularity with Jews, and its Jewish founder, once Zionist and Yiddishist L. L. Zamenhof, reveals how invested European Jews were in the question of language and nationalism on both sides of the debate, elevating language "beyond the objective, instrumental" purpose of speech.[5]

While rooted in the Haskalah, the Jewish enlightenment that took place between the 1770s and the end of the 1800s, Hebrew and Yiddish became objects of Jewish nationalism during that same late nineteenth-century moment. Indeed, both Hebraists and Yiddishists shared the conviction that one "could not become a full-fledged, autonomous modern subject without a single, 'whole' language adequate to all domains of experience and self-expression" and believed in the "possibility of implanting a secularist, aestheticist intelligentsia culture in the whole of 'the nation.'"[6] Despite these similarities, however, Hebraism and Yiddishism "had been born out of almost inverted ideological commitments and sociological realities," developing in response, discourse, and competition with one another.[7] Hebraism began with a cohort of Jewish intellectuals in Europe who came to see Hebrew as a language of literary expression.[8] As *maskilim* (the Haskalah's activists) sought to distance themselves from rabbinic Judaism, they worked to transform Hebrew into a literary language, authoring journals and books in the language for their fellow intellectuals' consumption.[9]

Yiddishists emerged on the scene as a response to anti-Yiddish "assimilationists and Hebraists," wrote author and linguist Nochum Shtif, who "persecut[ed] Yiddish, wishing to uproot the language from its people."[10] Indeed, while the Jewish enlightenment movement mainly emphasized the revival of Hebrew, some of the Haskalah's adherents broke "with [the Haskalah's] sterile anti-Yiddish philosophy," particularly as the Haskalah spread from Western Europe to Eastern Europe. In the 1860s, for instance, author and lexicographer Yehoshua Mordechai Lifshitz appeared as an early ideologue of Yiddishism and Yiddish-language planning. In the same decade, Hebrew and Yiddish author Mendele Moykher Sforim penned an essay entitled "My Soul Desired Yiddish," describing his own revelation as he transitioned from writing in Hebrew to writing in Yiddish to reach the "Jewish masses." After he finished his first story in Yiddish, he wrote, "My soul desired only Yiddish, and I dedicated myself entirely to it."[11] With the flourishing of works by writers like Mendele, Yiddish literature blossomed in the intervening decades. The goals of Yiddishism as a linguistic movement, however, were officially outlined only at the Czernowitz Conference of 1908, when a group of writers, linguists, and intellectuals gathered to consider the question of how to raise the status of Yiddish and its authors by extension. The attendees declared Yiddish a national Jewish language of the Jewish people, seeking to assert its legitimacy through language planning and standardization, and through translating works of literature like Marx's *Das Kapital* and the Bible.[12]

Hebraism and Yiddishism continued to feed off one another as both became intertwined with Jewish nationalism. Not all Zionists believed Hebrew should be the language of a future state in Palestine, but cultural Zionists and Hebraists saw the Hebrew language as essential to a Jewish national revival, citing the longevity of the Hebrew language to link Jews to the Land of Israel.[13] Hebrew underwent dramatic linguistic revision in Palestine, exemplified in the work of lexicographer and Hebrew revivalist Eliezer Ben Yehudah, while cultural Zionist Asher Zvi Hirsch Ginsberg (better known by his pen name, Ahad Ha'am) aimed to build a Hebrew cultural center in Palestine rather than a state.[14] After battles involving both German and Yiddish, Hebrew won the language war, becoming the lingua franca of the Yishuv and ultimately the State of Israel.[15]

Although there were many streams of Zionism, Zionists shared a belief that the way to better the positions of the Jews of Europe was by leaving Europe and acquiring a territory or state of their own. But their form of nationalism was not the only one. Bundists sought out their own answers to the question of Jewish nationalism, taking on aspects of Yiddishism as they formulated their ideologies. Founded in 1897, the Jewish Labor Bund sought to defend and secure rights for Jewish workers in the lands where they already lived.[16] Operating under the principle of *doikayt* (hereness), a focus on self-liberation in the diaspora, the Bund stood in opposition to Zionism, advocating not for ethnic or religious separatism in the form of a state but for culture and socialism as bonds of Jewish nationhood. As it came to fight for the right of Jewish workers to assemble in Yiddish, the Bund would adopt a broader platform of "national-cultural autonomy on an extra-territorial basis," placing Yiddish at the center of its ideologies. While the Bund critiqued Yiddishists for their lack of attention to class and expressed "reservations about those nationalist trends which turn the struggle for Yiddish into an instrument with which to blunt the class consciousness of the proletariat," the movement aligned itself with Yiddishism in its "struggle against the assimilationists and the Hebraists," upholding the language as "the national language of the Jewish people." So too did many non-Zionist territorialists, who saw mass colonization as the best means to avoid the "assimilation and dispersion associated with individual immigration" and placed the continuation and strengthening of Yiddish culture at the center of their plans.[17]

As these different forms of Jewish nationalism took shape in Europe and Palestine, however, millions of Jews came to see immigration to the United States, not Zionism, as their preferred path out of poverty and anti-Semitic violence. Between 1881 and 1924, over 2.5 million Jews arrived on American shores, where both Yiddishism and Hebraism took on new meanings and forms.[18] Boosted by an increase in the rate of immigration of Yiddish speakers, Yiddish came to hold a place of great import in American Jewish culture. Yiddish newspapers increased in circulation, as did the number of theaters, films, book publishers, labor movements, and fraternal organizations that operated in the language.[19] Starting after 1900, a system of Jewish schools, the *folkshuln*, educated thousands of children in Yiddish, while camps like Boiberik, Kinderring, and Kinderland, established in the 1920s, occupied children's summers with Yiddish-speaking recreation.[20] In this growth period for Yiddish culture, prominent Yiddishist Chaim Zhitlovsky proclaimed that the future of Jewish "national" and "cultural existence" in America would center on Yiddish language, imagining American Jews "establishing [their] own educational institutions, from elementary schools to universities" that would constitute "the crown of Yiddish culture."[21] But despite the efforts of Yiddishists like Zhitlovsky, the language continuously declined in use as immigrants and their children came to learn English. The Immigration Act of 1924 ended a century of Jewish migration, putting a stop to the steady flow of new Yiddish-speaking immigrants into Jewish urban enclaves.[22] By the beginning of the postwar period, a potent combination of factors threatened the language's future on a national and global scale, including decades of linguistic assimilation into English, the murder of millions of Yiddish speakers in the Holocaust, and the systematic repression of the Yiddish language in the Yishuv and then Israel.[23] A handful of American Yiddish organizations continued to promote Yiddish education and cultural production during the postwar years, but mainstream Jews took few large-scale steps to preserve Yiddish culture.[24] At the onset of the postwar period, most American Jews had come to view the language as an object of humor and nostalgia.[25]

Zionism and Hebraism experienced a rather dissimilar trajectory on American shores. In the 1880s, small groups of European immigrants formed Hibbat Zion communities throughout New England.[26] A larger variety of Zionist groups, including the European movement Poale Zion, which entered the United States in 1905, and American movements like the Dr. Herzl Zion Club (which later became Young Judaea), founded in 1904, made inroads in cities with large Jewish populations. While, in the early twentieth century, American Zionist organizations had relatively small memberships, their leaders, such as Judah Magnes, Henrietta Szold, Abba Hillel Silver, and Louis Brandeis, wielded considerable influence in American Jewish life. A small American Hebrew movement, Tarbut Ivrit, developed beginning in the 1920s. Membership in Zionist organizations grew during and after World War II as word of the increasingly dismal plight of European Jewry reached American Jewry, and Zionist activism and philanthropy became more mainstream with each passing decade.

While American Hebraists wrote poetry and prose in American Hebrew journals, Tarbut Ivrit found its "most natural expression as a philosophy of higher Jewish education in the 1930s within the Hebrew colleges," and a later in summer camps.[27] Tarbut Ivrit viewed "the revival of Hebrew as a spoken language in Eretz Yisrael certainly served as a source of joy," but its adherents believed "its use and prestige should extend to the New World" too. The fact that the American Hebrew movement focused on making Hebrew the cultural language of the elite and not on "Hebraiz[ing] the masses of Jewish immigrants," however, eventually "spelled its end": the Hebrew movement did not successfully create consumers for its literature or establish a generation of "writers who would continue its work."[28]

The status of both Hebrew and Yiddish in America made educators' language-based missions formidable, uphill battles. And yet it was the battles themselves that provided the urgency and energy required to push these historical linguistic and nationalistic ideologies forward. There were many phenomena that created a perfect storm for language to rise to the top of the list of American Jewish camping's priorities, including the decline in

Yiddish, the Holocaust, the formation and decline of Tarbut Ivrit, the establishment of the State of Israel, the civil rights movement, ethnic revival, and the Jewish counterculture. Yiddish camps renewed, revamped, and reinforced their language-based missions in the postwar decades, as newer camping movements like Massad and Ramah placed American Hebraism at the forefront of their programs seeking to curb cultural decline.[29]

Whether a camp aimed for full language immersion or Hebrew infusion, certain essential efforts took shape across Jewish educational camps. Embedding Hebrew or Yiddish words into the environment and everyday vernacular of camp life proved a consistent first step, naming sites around camp, group names, and the periods on daily and monthly schedules. Symbolic engagements with language allowed campers to master approximately fifty borrowed words used daily at camp, which campers often embraced as fun, camp-specific lingo to use in otherwise English sentences. Hebraizing camp could happen, as one Ramah educator explained, through "flood[ing] the camp with attractive Hebrew signs for all objects, expressions," with "specialty area[s]" having "a master chart and single word labels spread out," and by placing an English-Hebrew dictionary in every bunk.[30] Yiddish camps took similar steps, calling their camper groups by the Yiddish words *Yingste*, *Mittele*, and *Elste* (youngest, middle, and eldest) and referring to sites around camp with terms such *es-zal* (cafeteria), *koytshbal-platz* (basketball court), and *khavershaft-platz* (the assembly space). By labeling camp time, groups, and physical spaces in Hebrew or Yiddish, camp educators believed that campers would not only acquire a new vocabulary through something like osmosis but would also come to see the languages as inextricable aspects of the Jewishness they acquired through their time at camp.

Many camps had more ambitious goals, aspiring to get campers to speak Hebrew or Yiddish to one degree or another. To reach these aims, they attempted an array of tactics that changed frequently, a failure with one method leading to a focus on another. And yet the most uncontrollable element camp leaders would ultimately face would be the youth in their midst, whose buy-in was the ultimate prerequisite to their success. Negotiations and tensions between campers and their leaders over language not only changed how individual camps engaged with their chosen language but would come to redefine the meanings and purposes of Hebraism and

Yiddishism in America for decades to come. The next sections look at the everyday uses of Hebrew and Yiddish in postwar summer camps and how camp life transformed Hebraism and Yiddishism for a new American age.

### "A Truly Hebraic Camp": Ramah, Massad, and the Quest for Spoken Hebrew

In 1955, writer Morris Freedman drove to Camp Ramah in Connecticut on an assignment with the magazine *Commentary*. His essay on Ramah covered a range of themes, including the camp's religious practices and educational programs. But more than any other element of camp life, the writer had a particular fascination with the camp's commitment to Hebrew. Observing the campers and staff over the course of a few days, Freedman notes in his essay how the staff shifted between Hebrew and English, that the camp's swimming sessions were "conducted entirely in Hebrew," and that both "the simplest announcements" and "the most advanced discussions" took place in the language. But while his description of Ramah reveals a hint of admiration, Freedman also expressed ambivalence about the camp's ideologies. When he interviewed the director, Morton Siegel, and pressed him to explain his "rationale for using the language" at camp, Siegel seemed perturbed by the question, as if the answer were obvious. "Well, how else are you going to get them to know their Jewish background?" Siegel asked Freedman. "They've got to live in the language before they can get its spirit, before they can grasp the meaning of the Holy Books. There's no substitute. Translation never does justice to a language. You can't get the spirit of a people in translation."[31]

On paper, Freedman and Siegel had a lot in common. American Jews born three years apart, both men were raised by immigrant parents in New York City in Yiddish-speaking homes, and both grew up to earn doctorates in their respective fields. Their conversation, however, revealed divergent approaches to questions surrounding Hebrew, Jewish practice, and Zionism, mirroring a split between Jewish intellectuals of their time. On one side were Jews like Siegel, first-generation Americans who embraced traditional Judaism, Hebraism, Zionism in the 1940s and 1950s—values their parents' generation had mostly rejected or overlooked in favor of assimilating into American culture. Jews like Freedman, more secular in their Jewishness, found the goals of men like Siegel, alongside the growing popularity of synagogues in suburbia and the expansion of Jewish education, curious developments of postwar Jewish life deserving of journalistic and analytic investigation.

The Siegels of the world constituted a minority within American Jewry but a majority of those who founded and ran educational and ideological Jewish camps, in particular within the Ramah network of camps. Through immersing campers in a Jewish lifestyle at camp, Ramah's educators believed that they would be able "to create an ideal Jew," imbued with the Hebrew language as "a means of identifying with his people."[32] As Judah Goldin, a professor at the Jewish Theological Seminary and lead educator at Ramah, expressed to Freedman, "We provide a setting where it is natural to speak Hebrew . . . [and] we hope everything else will follow. . . . But, of course," he continued, "the Hebrew is only a means to an end. It is almost incidental to our main aim, which is to develop a full consciousness of Jewishness. How without Hebrew, without the language of their people, can one get to love the tradition?"[33] To Ramah's leaders, the Hebrew language worked as a key that opened a treasure trove of broader beliefs, traditions, and ideas, producing ideal Jews through their own Ramah-based enlightenment.

Attempting to make Hebrew "the language of the ball-field, of the announcement in the dining hall, of the discussion groups" required ample forethought and planning.[34] In Ramah's first decade, the camping movement's first few locations aimed to accept only the best and brightest students of the Conservative movement's Hebrew schools, as leaders believed these campers would be best equipped to achieve much deeper fluency at camp. But even under these ideal circumstances, educators at Ramah found that they had had "entirely unrealistic" expectations of what these handpicked campers would and could do in regard to Hebrew. In large part, camp leaders cited the problems they faced as "social in nature." "While in prior summers," one educator explained in 1953, "the socially acceptable thing to do" at Ramah "was to speak Hebrew," six years into the camping network's existence, "even those [campers] who had very strong Hebraic backgrounds did not speak Hebrew, lest they become known as 'queers' or 'apple-polishers.'" Educators that summer aimed to "create an environment for the camper in which he felt a high degree of personal security" but failed to outline precisely how they intended to do so.[35] During Freedman's visit, he noted that campers conducted "animated discussions in Hebrew," but "equally often, in English," and that they rarely spoke Hebrew among themselves, particularly in situations that were culturally American, like on the baseball field.[36] When he observed a teenage girl attentively listening to a Hebrew announcement and asked her how much she understood, she "confessed" to Freedman "that it had been pretty much over her head." Even with such high admissions standards, many campers arrived without the level of prior knowledge required for being in a camp that, as one educator described, "literally lives in Hebrew."[37]

The situation worsened in the 1960s. As the Ramah network of camps grew to six sites across the Northeast, Midwest, and Canada, it changed the camps' admissions standards, opening the Ramah experience up to a wider audience of children. As one educator, Neal Lauder, put it in 1966, the side effect of this expansion meant that "no easy generalizations" could be made about campers' Hebrew backgrounds. The social issues of the fifties, moreover, began to mix with more complicated pedagogical ones, as camps attempted Hebrew immersion with children even less prepared for it than those of the previous decade. The camps had not found "adequate methods . . . [for] the proper transition between the fundamentals of modern Hebrew and the literary Hebrew of the classical sources," wrote Lauder, making Hebrew itself "the 'disease' of the curriculum," since students in the classroom all too often felt "embarrassed to try to formulate their ideas in broken Hebrew, and therefore choose to remain silent." "Until the conflict between language versus curriculum is resolved," Lauder concluded, the camp "has little hope for success in terms of beginning to create an intelligent laity for the Conservative Movement."[38]

Ramah's issues with language prompted staff members across the country to search for solutions and to debate whether formal or informal educational approaches better suited their Hebrew-teaching goals. Some of the Ramah camps in the sixties used audio-lingual programs like mass-market Hebrew learning programs such as *Shearim* and *B'Yad HaLashon*, putting their hopes in the systemized method of learning through listening and repeating.[39] But educator Steve Listfield of Camp Ramah in the Poconos found that the program presented the "major problem" of repetition. Campers of the previous few years, he explained in 1970, "[were] particularly unwilling to repeat sentence patterns, even when there is sufficient variety within the wording of the sentences themselves." While he believed that "constant and tireless repetition is the only way to develop a foundation in a foreign language," the formal and academic B'Yad Lashon program did not appeal to most campers, making it fundamentally ineffective. Listfield suggested that Ramah should instead present Hebrew with "creativity and variety, e.g. through games, simulation of real-life situations and pictures" instead. In the summer of 1970, he concluded, the camp "did not use *B'Yad HaLashon* at all. I think that this was the right decision, as the stories in the supplemental material present situations which the students identify with at camp, and the kind of vocabulary words which are reinforced in the bunk and at activities."[40] Focusing their Hebrew programs on the words campers needed to get by within the camp environment proved more effective and yielded more enthusiasm than their earlier formal approaches to Hebrew. Joseph Lukinsky came to a similar conclusion in the early 1970s, writing that the summer months "do not seem to be the time to learn Hebrew as a language formally" and that the camp should therefore teach it "informally, which means through the life of the bunk and through programming."[41]

From the late 1960s onward, educators largely followed a similar path as did Lukinsky and Listfield, working to bring Hebrew into daily life, recreational programs, and the arts curriculum. They prepared campers to perform plays entirely in Hebrew, including both Israeli originals and American popular plays and classics in translation, which could help inspire enthusiasm for Hebrew and teach new words to campers familiar with the plays in their English originals,[42] while camper newspapers provided creative opportunities for children and teens to use and learn Hebrew outside a formal, classroom setting.[43] Kallah, a Hebrew-immersion program, taught Hebrew to a smaller group of campers intensively over the course of a few weeks, bridging informal and formal education "to help the individual student make noticeable progress in his Hebrew speaking ability."[44]

But even as Ramah's professional staff tried these new methods as they continued to speak Hebrew "in the dining room and all places of public announcement," campers continued to resist the idea of speaking Hebrew among themselves. While young staff members often made "an attempt to speak Hebrew at the table, in cleanup, and several other routine areas," they rarely ran "cabin discussions, whether in the area of program, ideation or human relations" in Hebrew. Programs on the divisional level, such as committee meetings between staff or evening programs for campers, "paid tribute to Hebrew" but "more often break down into English." Even the camps' highest-level staff members, who supposedly conducted their business meetings in Hebrew, generally began their meetings in Hebrew but "converted to English within five minutes." Although new campers arrived with "fear of a really Hebraic camp," their fears were almost immediately dispelled: counselors began with hopes leading off their activities in Hebrew but "lost all resolve to do so" within "twenty-four hours of the campers' arrival." "The returning camper," wrote one educator, "has made peace with the pseudo-Hebraic environment of camp and is happy with it. He has, of course, made some Hebraic progress and been rewarded for it on his return to Hebrew School," but anything close to fluency proved a dream unfulfilled.[45]

By the late 1960s, most educators at Ramah camps had adjusted their language expectations from Hebrew proficiency to Hebrew exposure and engagement, moving their yardsticks of success as they struggled with campers' abilities and interests. As they reimagined the role of Hebrew in camp in negotiation with campers and young counselors, however, they also ultimately mirrored Hebrew's role in American Jewish life writ large. As Zionism became more mainstream, engaging with Israeli culture in ways that did not require full fluency—through dance, art, and music, for instance—supplanted the dwindling American Hebrew movement. To reach Hebrew fluency, one could go to Israel for a true immersive education. In America, however, symbolic use of the language had emerged as a tool for the upbuilding of identity or, as one Ramah educator put it, "an important instrument for immersing oneself in the ideal Jewish life."[46]

When the Ramah Commission formed in the late 1940s, a few years after the establishment of the first Massad Camp, its leaders aimed to create camps with a similar Hebrew immersion model as its predecessor. At the same time, Ramah also represented "a parting of ways" and a response to critiques that Massad "was too authoritarian, too Zionist, too focused on Hebrew, and somewhat hypocritical in its approach to religious practices."[47]

Ramah's formulation of itself as an alternative to Massad, as a "democrati-cally" imbued camp that was neither "too Zionist" nor ambiguous in its ap-proach to Jewish practice, contributed to its longer-term success as a camping movement. Such critiques of Massad, however, pointed to the camps' relative success when it came to fostering a Hebrew-speaking environment: Massad's lack of clarity about religious practice, a kind of ambivalent pluralism, meant that Massad not only recruited some of the Conservative movement's top afternoon Hebrew school students but also Orthodox day school students, campers who arrived with significant prior Hebrew knowledge. Since edu-cators did not fear failing to teach other Jewish topics, Massad's dedicated focus on Hebrew and Zionism helped keep camps' Hebrew immersion the central goal. Shlomo Shulsinger's notorious strictness, a total intolerance for the use of English in public announcements, songs, plays, classes, and even in discussions within earshot, were also essential ingredients. At Massad, all public speech took place in Hebrew as a matter of policy, giving campers and counselors alike a chance to put their school-year Hebrew into active use.

Nevertheless, Massad's staff struggled with Hebrew immersion when it came to private conversations between friends. In 1957, one anonymous writer addressed the camp's staff with a letter "intended to remind and awaken all to a well-known thing—the Hebrew language." "Today," the writer contin-ued, "with the rise of *Medinat Yisrael* and the ingathering of the exiles, there is no tool more important to bond brothers and bring us closer to our home-land than the Hebrew language." Announcing a campaign to improve the Hebrew spoken at Massad, the writer listed five objectives:

1) All of the conversations between the members of the head staff will be in Hebrew

2) To inspire friends to speak Hebrew.

3) To improve the language by the improvement of our linguistic form.

4) To read a Hebrew book.

5) To acquire new idioms and words.[48]

While most Zionist and Hebrew-centered camps focused on getting partic-ipants to construct a simple Hebrew sentence, Massad's unique characteris-tics allowed staff to focus their efforts toward speaking better Hebrew and even to read a book in Hebrew. But in practice, Massad's leaders found that counselors struggled to uphold the purportedly Hebrew-only atmosphere. Former campers described this dynamic in interviews as well. "The very young campers, of course, would talk English among themselves," explained Lawrence Kobrin in an oral history project, Massad Reminiscences, even as "the counselor tried to introduce as much Hebrew as possible in the bunk and at the dining room table."[49] Another former camper and counselor, Ira Spodek, noted that Massad Aleph fostered the most stringent Hebrew-only atmosphere among the three locations throughout the 1960s and early 1970s, but counselors and campers still spoke English in private.[50] Hebrew at Massad was more fluent than elsewhere, but still operated at a symbolic, performative level, not quite crossing into the natural, everyday vernacular of its campers or counselors.

Since Hebrew was Massad's central objective, evolving to match a declining interest in the Hebrew movement proved more difficult than it did for Ramah. Throughout the 1970s, as Massad's three camps struggled to find

Teenager at Hebraist Camp Massad, undated (likely 1949/1950).
Source: Photo courtesy of the American Jewish Historical Society. Printed with permission.

youth and families interested in Hebrew immersion, their declining registration numbers were leading to serious financial issues. Massad also faced challenges posed by new trends in American Judaism. Although it practiced something close to Orthodox Judaism in terms of its Sabbath observance and kosher adherence, it struggled to keep up with the evolution of American Orthodoxy as the Orthodox center became more socially conservative, halachically observant, and more closed off to other kinds of Jews. After the Shulsingers retired in 1977, the new leaders of Massad changed its rules and practices to keep up with changing trends, separating boys and girls more often and enforcing a dress code. But these changes were alienating for the camps' remaining Conservative families and proved a little too late for more strictly observant families, who had already left Massad in favor of new Modern Orthodox camps that better matched their lifestyles. Massad served thousands of kids over nearly forty years, raising a high-bar example for other Jewish camps when it came to language learning and engagement. But by 1981, all three camps had shut their gates, unable, or unwilling, to change alongside the communities they had once served.

Massad and Ramah each reflect the fantasies and the realities of the Hebrew-immersive camp, where the language became embedded in camp life as a vehicle toward a more ideal Jewishness. But while Jewish camps more broadly embraced a symbolic use of Hebrew from the outset, both Ramah and Massad fell short of getting campers and young counselors to speak Hebrew among themselves, facing both American monolingualism and the declining relevance of Tarbut Ivrit. Similar struggles with language, the next section shows, also took shape among a different set of linguistically minded Jews, Yiddishists, as they mitigated the decline of Yiddish as an everyday vernacular.

### Yiddishist Dreams and Realities at Hemshekh and Boiberik

Whereas few campers arrived at Hebrew culture camps already knowing fluent Hebrew, Yiddish camps began under extraordinarily different sociolinguistic circumstances. In the 1920s and 1930s, "speaking Yiddish," wrote Leibush Lehrer, was "a natural practice" at his Yiddish cultural camp, Boiberik.[51] As first-generation American children of immigrants, most campers at Kinder Ring, Kinderland, and Kindervelt also arrived with Yiddish fluency from the home; since most campers, furthermore, attended camps sponsored and founded by the Yiddish cultural or political organizations their parents were associated with, including various unions, the Farband, the Workmen's Circle, and in Boiberik's case the Sholem Aleichem Folk Institute, camp life largely mirrored the milieu of campers' home communities. When these camps provided Yiddish educational programs in their earliest decades, staff members primarily focused their efforts on improving campers' already fluent spoken Yiddish with an emphasis on grammar, reading, and writing. Before the 1940s, when Yiddish's naturalness made Yiddish less an ideological choice than a normal part of life, educators like Lehrer did not take issue with the casual use of English. Lehrer's 1928 essay, "Boiberik: The Development of an Idea," was written in Yiddish but barely mentioned the language, its use as an everyday vernacular of the camp so obvious as to not even require explanation. Boiberik's songbooks from its early decades included a handful of popular, patriotic American songs, along with a more extensive set of Yiddish folk tunes; staff members even held Hebrew classes for some years, assuming that at least for some particularly fluent and well-read children, Yiddish need not be the sole language objective of the camp. In this sense, Yiddish's role mirrored the prewar environment in which Yiddish coexisted with English, particularly for first-generation Americans who knew one language from the home and another from the school and street.

As the status of Yiddish in America shifted, so too did the role of the language within summer camps. During Boiberik's prewar decades, the handful of campers who came without prior Yiddish knowledge each year constituted a mere "small . . . often disgruntled minority," many of whom reportedly left camp early out of "sheer frustration."[32] This changed dramatically by the 1940s, however, as fewer and fewer campers arrived knowing fluent Yiddish. Corresponding with patterns of linguistic assimilation, director Leibush Lehrer reported that many of the youth he encountered in the forties not only did not speak Yiddish "but barely understood" it. With deep concern, he attempted to track the situation, inserting questionnaires geared to parents on camper registration forms, including questions such as, "Do you want us to correspond with you in Yiddish or English?" "Do you subscribe to Yiddish newspapers?" and "Do you have any Yiddish books in your household?" "By the end of the 40's," he wrote in retrospect, "only about 7% of parents asked for Yiddish" correspondence from the camp. By 1961, "even this small number" had shrunk, with every family asking for the camp to send them materials in English only.[53]

As Yiddish declined as a vernacular outside camp, Boiberik's staff struggled to ensure "the furtherance of Yiddish as the normal medium" inside it. While learning Yiddish in some way had a consistent place on the camp's weekly schedule from the 1920s onward, particularly for younger campers or those who did not receive supplementary Yiddish educations all year at the Sholem Aleichem Folkshul, the character of the Yiddish education changed substantially in the postwar decades, with what had once constituted grammar and writing sessions for Yiddish-speaking children becoming ever more basic. By 1951, Boiberik's education hour merely aimed for the youngest group in camp to "understand a few single words in Yiddish," or to name a few objects in the camp environment in Yiddish, while for the Mittele, those aged ten to twelve years old, Lehrer hoped to teach a more extensive vocabulary as well as the ability to write on a basic level.[54] That same year, each camper received a "mimeographed brochure on conversational Yiddish especially prepared for use during the Jewish Hour." Filled with English cognates, the brochure, which presented a basic set of "119 sentences, employing 301 different words, and a specially-invented game," displayed just how precipitously fluency levels had dropped.[55] This decline continued in the late 1950s and 1960s, when even Yiddish-speaking counselors proved increasingly difficult to find.[56] Former camper Marsha Kreizelman Singer recalled in an oral interview that she was interviewed on her first day at Boiberik in 1951 to see which class she belonged in for the Yiddish hour, which at the time took place nearly every day. But a few years later, she recalled that the Yiddish hour had transformed into the "Jewish culture hour," without an emphasis on Yiddish language, and it was no longer every day but just a few times a week.[57]

In 1962, Lehrer expressed how the camp's "conviction" that Yiddish served "as an important positive force in Jewish creative survival . . . never weakened," that their "work with Yiddish . . . as far as our opportunities and personnel permit, was unceasing . . . [and with] no compromise."[58] But in reality, Boiberik's staff compromised many times over, altering their programs and reducing their expectations of what kind of role Yiddish could have in camp. As Yiddish-speaking and culturally informed counselors became harder to find, Lehrer put more of an emphasis on all-camp festivals than on the educational "Jewish hour," since he and a few other knowledgeable staff members could implement such festivals with more oversight of their implementation and content. By delivering passionate speeches on Jewish heritage, Yiddish culture, and the beauty of Jewish traditions, as well as his daily announcements in Yiddish, Lehrer performed fluency for campers, hoping that they would absorb vernacular Yiddish to some degree. The camp also continued to use Yiddish in symbolic ways throughout the camp schedule and environment, particularly in the naming of groups, locations around camp, and periods of the day.

As Yiddish declined as an everyday vernacular outside camp, however, Boiberik became more overtly committed to Yiddish's future than it had been in its first few decades. English songs stopped being printed in the camp's songbook by the 1960s, and Hebrew classes were dropped too. This evolution continued even after Lehrer's death in 1964, when new camp directors like Perry Millbauer took the helm. In 1967, Millbauer explained how the camp he had attended as a camper eighteen years ago still managed an "excellent synthesis of camp life . . . and a cultural educational environment which is enhanced by an emphasis on Yiddish, both as a language and as part of our culture."[59] But he also noted that emphasizing Yiddish had come to taken on a different shape. While in the late 1950s and early 1960s, Yiddish teachers still attempted to teach Yiddish formally during the Jewish hour, teaching Yiddish toward any level of proficiency in the late 1960s and 1970s proved exceedingly difficult. One member of the education staff reported in the 1970s that the younger campers "resented being taught formal Yiddish for various reasons," including that "it mixes them up" with the Hebrew they learned from religious school at home and that "they prefer discussions instead of formal studies." The staff member did not "propose giving up Yiddish" but suggested that they explore other ways "to reach the group with Yiddish through Yiddish" and "create a little enthusiasm for Yiddish through various means."[60] As the staff of the 1970s sought to create this enthusiasm for Yiddish, they, like Lehrer, came to view camp-wide events as fruitful. Emphasizing language through special musical programs and plays, they added a new Yiddish-focused festival to their repertoire, a day devoted to the language through folk songs, explaining the language's roots, history, and culture to a generation of youth less familiar with it from home or school.

A spoken vernacular in the early twentieth century, Yiddish became an object of learning and cultural maintenance by midcentury. By the late 1960s, however, the camp reconstituted Yiddish once again, turning to the language as a path toward bringing campers "the more authentically Jewish of the older generation."[61] In this sense, struggling with Yiddish decline made its role in camp more central: the less it was spoken, the more meaningful Yiddish became.[62] Boiberik could not and would not produce proficient Yiddish speakers for a new post-vernacular era. But through folk festivals, music, and education, it did go on to produce a new kind of identity based around Yiddish, turning Yiddishism into an American Jewish project aimed at engendering a certain kind of Jewishness within children, one associated with the camp's values of cosmopolitanism, justice, and an appreciation for Jewish heritage.

Camp Hemshekh followed a similar trajectory as Boiberik, albeit on a different historical time line. Founded in 1959 for the first-generation American children of Holocaust survivors, the first *Hemshekhistn*, like the *Boiberikaners* of the twenties and thirties, often understood and even spoke some Yiddish from the home. Inserting the language into every aspect of the camp environment, staff members made announcements in Yiddish, sang Yiddish songs, and performed camp-wide events, plays, and skits in the language. Hemshekh's weekly "culture night" celebrated a revolving set of Yiddish authors and artists, and the staff even embedded Yiddish themes and personalities in their versions of color war.[63] Campers who arrived with Yiddish from the home attended special activities, including lectures in Yiddish from visitors from New York City (Bundists, Holocaust survivors, and Yiddish writers and performers), which went on into the wee hours of the night.[64] In 1966, for instance, older campers participated in a "literature seminar where they read and analyze works," as teachers born in Poland sat with campers on the porch leading Yiddish conversations and teaching reading and writing skills.[65] Younger children also learned Yiddish reading and writing, expanding their vocabularies according to their fluency levels.

Unlike Boiberik, Hemshekh never had a period of being a primarily Yiddish-speaking camp. In a sense, the camp faced a familiar set of challenges in its pursuit of spoken Yiddish as Ramah and Massad did with Hebrew: although select groups of campers were fluent from the home and even spoke Yiddish among themselves, the staff quickly figured out that they "couldn't impose Yiddish as the only language at camp."[66] When Hemshekh's long-time director, Mikhl Baran, started teaching in a school in the more affluent suburbs of New York in the late 1960s, he began to recruit his students, second- and third-generation Americans with no Yiddish background, to join him as campers and counselors. With this group of attendees came a new threat to the camp's ideology surrounding language, alum George Rothe explained in an oral history interview: campers complained about what remained of the Yiddish educational program, finding it dull.[67] The camp newspaper, originally a Yiddish-only publication, integrated an English section in the late 1960s, reflecting a reality in which a shrinking percentage of campers could or would write in Yiddish.

As the camp's Yiddish-speaking mission faced growing challenges in the late sixties and seventies, however, its dedication to Yiddishism was forced to become more explicit. The camp newspaper published passionate editorials, usually written by counselors, encouraging the camp to remain Yiddishist in character; the staff continuously pleaded in letters to parents "to help us in our struggle to continue Yiddishkayt" by supporting their children's Yiddish education beyond the two months of summer. Campers and staff members came to argue over the best ways to ensure a Yiddish-speaking future in America, even as they mostly refused to speak Yiddish among themselves. Counselor Sam Kazman wrote in the camp newspaper, *Di Hemshekh Vokh*,

> There is still the problem of learning and teaching Yiddish [at camp]. Singing may be wonderful, but it is not enough to be the *hemshekh* of a culture all by itself. We may all leave camp with a genuine feel for our Yiddish heritage, but what's going to happen in ten or fifteen years? ... If we can't learn Yiddish here, what's going to happen out THERE?

Kazman's editorial reflected frustrations around a passion for Yiddish and its culture bereft of an ability to speak it, and a fear that whatever Yiddish learning was going on at Hemshekh would not have an impact on the outside world. "The faces in the Hemshekh chorus," he wrote, "are beyond belief, let alone description," but he questioned whether campers' enjoyment of performing in Yiddish would prove enough to keep the culture afloat. "There are joys to be had in this camp," he concluded, "but no culture can survive solely in the smiling minds of people remembering their summer vacations." Keeping Yiddish alive, in other words, would require more than the production of nostalgia.[68]

Campers and counselors alike expressed similar concerns to Kazman in impassioned play scripts, skits, poems, and essays. *Di Hemshekh Vokh* published short articles from campers reflecting on their relationships to Yiddish and Yiddish culture; camper Sharon Cohn, for example, described what she saw as Hemshekh's role in the continuation of Yiddish language and culture. "Yiddish culture means a lot to me," she wrote. "I speak Yiddish a little, I sing a lot of Yiddish songs, and sometimes I go over my Yiddish at home. My parents speak a lot of Yiddish. . . . I like speaking Yiddish more than the other languages I know of." Sharon advocated that "it is a good idea that half of the people in camp are learning Yiddish" because "if half the camp won't learn Yiddish, then it wouldn't be such a Yiddish camp."[69] A play script, moreover, presented an imagined conversation between a counselor and a camper regarding Yiddish's decline, making a similar argument for Hemshekh's importance:

> *Counselor:* But why don't you want to learn Yiddish?
> *Camper:* I have too much to do already. Yiddish isn't important here. I'm American.
> *Counselor:* Yiddish is the language of our people. You're depriving yourself of a rich culture incomparable in the world.
> *Camper:* I don't care.
> *Narrator:* The children of Israel today are abandoning their culture as those who danced around the golden calf. The commandments become the building symbol for our growing and beautiful culture, which Hemshekh is preserving in the present world.[70]

The script framed Hemshekh as a place threatened by assimilation, where campers did not see the importance of Yiddish to their American lives. But it also aimed to give campers the feeling that Hemshekh was a place, perhaps the only place, where the Yiddish language could be preserved, revitalized, or "saved."

Like Massad, Ramah, and Boiberik, Hemshekh presented itself as fiercely ideological and unquestionably committed to Yiddish and Yiddish-ism. Nevertheless, the camp had to alter its expectations to match the interests and abilities of the youth in their midst. As in Boiberik, Hemshekh participants both young and old came to foster a new vision of Yiddishism for the postwar era, one in which the Yiddish language would serve not as an everyday vernacular and Yiddishism not as a linguistic ideology geared toward self-liberation, but as a tool toward fashioning American Jewishness. By turning Yiddish into a symbol of the Bund, secular Jewishness, and social justice, attendees of Camp Hemshekh reconstituted Yiddishism to fit a new American milieu.

———

In 1973, Sam Kazman published a story in the Hemshekh newspaper chronicling a magical "Yiddish pill" that would give campers the sudden ability to speak fluent Yiddish. "It is drawing towards the end of an extended free play, which means that it is getting dark," wrote Kazman. Mikhl Baran, the director, sat in front of the camp's office as a group of campers from one girl's bunk approached:

> Emily says, "*Farvos zitstu do alayn?*" (Why are you sitting here all alone?) Mikhl's interest picks up. . . . Laura says "*Di griln griltsn, di feygel zingt, ober Mikhl zitz alayn. Der dikhter Yehoyash hot amol gezogt. . . .*" (The crickets chirp, the birds sing, but Mikhl sits all alone. The poet Yehoyash once said . . .") Now Mikhl himself is up. For the next hour, they all speak in Yiddish. Mikhl tests the limits of their vocabulary and finds none. He speaks to other bunks. . . . They all speak Yiddish. They speak it fluently. How? No one knows. A few say they dreamt something the night before, that someone came and gave them a pill.[71]

In just a few sentences, Kazman's story perfectly conveyed the dream of the Hebrew and Yiddish-speaking summer camp. In the minds of educators like

Rivkah and Shlomo Shulsinger, Mikhl Baran, and Morton Siegel, camps would function as pills that could cure what they saw as American Jewish communal ills. Jewish educators flooded their camps with Hebrew and Yiddish, seeing language maintenance as integral to cultural maintenance, teaching children Hebrew or Yiddish on their paths toward different visions of Jewish authenticity.[72] Fighting tirelessly against linguistic trends, they embedded camp life with Hebrew and Yiddish vocabulary, performance, song, and learning to achieve their goals.

And yet camp life did not function like a fantastical fluency pill. While much of camps' scheduled programming aimed to produce "Jewish feeling" more so than knowledge, language education aimed to produce both. In day-to-day camp life, Hemshekh and Boiberik struggled with similar language issues as their Hebrew-centered counterparts did. Educators could not ignore the limitations of their success as campers struggled to express themselves in Hebrew or Yiddish. Compounding their pedagogical challenges were what educators called "social" ones—the fact that youth did not enthusiastically embrace, and even sometimes actively resisted, the language plans of their elders. While they ultimately moved their yardsticks of success, educators at Ramah, Boiberik, and Hemshekh often expressed disappointment over their apparent failures, grieving the impossibility of making their camps Yiddish or Hebrew speaking.

At the end of the 1970s, linguistic decline led to the decline of several Yiddish-focused summer camps, as well as all three of the Massad camps in the United States. After years of declining registration, Boiberik closed in 1979. A few weeks later, Hemshekh hoped to recruit Boiberik's former campers, sending a letter to their parents stating, "As we are deeply concerned with the preservation of Yiddish language and Jewish culture, we sincerely regret the closing of Camp Boiberik. We believe that you will be interested in learning of another camp with a similar orientation but with stronger emphasis on Yiddish language and culture."[73] In a twist of fate, however, Hemshekh itself would close only a few months later due to its own diminishing camper population and lack of funds. By the end of the 1970s, only a few original Yiddish camps remained. Kinder Ring and Kinderland continued to embed their programs with some songs and cultural touchstones of Yiddish culture. One former camper described his time at Kinder

Ring from the late 1960s through the mid-1970s: "There was a group of the teachers of Yiddish, and they would do something at the flagpole." However, it was not a major focus, and the "kids just went along with this as part of the camp."[74] In this way, Hemshekh and Boiberik's closures marked the end of the era of Yiddishist summer camping in America.

The closures of these camps, however, did not spell the end of language-oriented camping overall. Camps with more modest language goals, like Reform camps Swig and OSRUI and the formerly Yiddish-speaking camps Kinder Ring and Kinderland, adapted to these realities with markedly less agony. As Reform educators aimed to simply "stimulate interest" in Hebrew, their programs could more easily adjust to campers' interests and be deemed successful. This trend follows what sociolinguists Sarah Benor and Sharon Avni's describe in their work on Jewish summer camps: while camps that "historically identified as Hebrew-intensive" reported a drop in Hebrew use in the past several decades, engaging in a "discourse of Hebrew decline," Reform and independent Jewish camps "report an increase in their Hebrew use during that period."[75]

And yet perhaps fluency has always been beside the point. Camps' uses of language would not save Yiddish from its decline in speakers, nor would camps bring spoken Hebrew into the everyday lives of most American Jews. Nevertheless, engagements with language played a crucial role in educators' plans to bring campers closer to the lifestyles of Jews from other times and places and in marking camp life—and the Jews that campers became through it—as different from life on the outside. In this sense, postwar Jewish camps transitioned Hebrew and Yiddish from European linguistic nationalisms into American Jewish identity–building tools. Through life at camp, Yiddishism became a symbol and shorthand for social justice, secular Yiddish culture, and a nostalgia for prewar Europe, while engagements with Hebrew became a conduit toward fostering identification with Israel and Zionism. As they struggled to turn their Yiddish and Hebrew fantasies into realities, camp leaders not only altered their goals to match their capabilities; camp participants of all generations reconstituted Hebraism and Yiddishism for a new American moment, evolving these divergent nationalist ideologies into paths toward authentic Jewishness as campers, counselors, and educators each understood it.

Summer camps initiated their diverse language plans in hopes of changing the minds, habits, and priorities of Jewish children and teenagers. In the end, however, their strife surrounding language illuminated how those same children and teenagers could change the plans, goals, and dreams of their educators. The next chapters continue to examine the influence of campers in the lived experience of their camps through four additional lenses: power, democracy, romance, and sexuality.

# "Is This What You Call Being Free?"

## Power and Youth Culture in the Camper Republic

IN SUMMER 1967, A GROUP of campers at Swig Institute, a Reform Jewish summer camp in California, ran elections to see who would take part in Swig's camper council, serving as the camper body's representatives to the counselors and the higher-ups. One day, the council took on the question of how they and their fellow campers should observe the Sabbath and came to focus on a rule they took issue with: that swearing was not allowed on the Sabbath. But as they presented staff members with the issue, the members of the council quickly discovered the limits of their power. "SLAVES IS WHAT WE ARE: that's right!!!" wrote one teen in the camp's newspaper. As they proposed a bill allowing campers to curse on the Sabbath, they faced opposition from the counselor in charge, who explained that swearing went against the camp's rules more generally. "We're all little people to the counselors . . . but we can show them," the camper continued. Urging their fellow "freedom-loving" teens to gather on the stage for a protest, the writer pointed out the hypocrisy in Swig's so-called democracy. "If this is a government of our own, then there is no such thing as abiding to camp rules," the camper explained. "The counselors want us to have our freedom, BUT IS THIS WHAT YOU CALL BEING FREE?"[1]

Swig's struggle over cursing may seem a bit contrived or even a little tongue-in-cheek. Why would a group of campers fight for the right to curse, of all things, on the Sabbath, of all days? With so many other rules at camp and religious laws regarding Shabbat observance to question, why focus on swearing? Since the anonymous camper who penned this article cannot be reached for comment, the council's reasoning summons interpretation. In psychology, empathic inference refers to "everyday mind-reading," the moments in which we yield insights into the experiences of others through observation, knowledge, and reasoning.[2] In the field of the history of childhood and youth, empathic inference is the work of reading the minds and emotions of historical actors, or "the ability to imagine and to interpret historical events and sources from the point of view of young people."[3] In the case of Swig's camper council, one can consider either that the campers were earnest about their fight to curse or that the author ramped up their agitation for the sake of humor, a common feature of camper publications. But empathic inference allows for another option: the possibility that their aims sat somewhere in the fuzzy, teenage place between sincerity and irony. At a historical moment in which the young sought more freedom of expression, speech, and dress, Swig's campers likely saw protesting for their right to curse, and the satirical humor inherent in their issue of choice, as part and parcel of their broader desire to expand their autonomy at camp. Their proposed protest was less about the specific rule they sought to change than their strongly held belief that they should have the right to change it and that they could use irony and humor to do so.

Seen in this light, the campers' struggle for the right to curse says much about the states of education, American Jewry, and youth culture in the postwar period. In the 1950s and 1960s, young Americans emerged as a more powerful, political, controversial, and formidable force in American public life than ever before, bringing about new sets of behavioral, aesthetic, and relational norms.[4] Young Americans participated in and instigated a variety of social and political movements, fighting for their own rights as well as for the rights of others. As intergenerational tensions over civil rights and the Vietnam War took shape, conceptions of authority and power shifted, altering how children, teens, and adults related to and behaved with one another in homes, schools, universities, and, inevitably, summer camps. At a moment in which students sought their own freedom of expression, speech, and dress, Swig's campers likely saw fighting for their right to curse as a reasonable step forward, particularly since camps had fewer rules and lower stakes than schools did. As postwar youth became more visible and powerful as a cohort than those of previous generations, camp leaders of the 1960s saw a need to provide "greater allowances for a more self-directed youth culture" within their camps as not only a means of education but of control.[5] Just as schools of the 1940s and 1950s increasingly embraced student councils, proms, and student clubs to control and structure the youth culture developing in their halls, summer camps instilled forms of democracy, like Swig's camper council, into their camp programs, in hopes of directing the rebellious energies of older campers in more productive directions.[6]

While the events of the period made their mark on camps in all sorts of ways, notions of camps as miniature democracies had roots in the origins of American camping and in the entwined histories of democratic and progressive education. Starting in the 1920s, American camp leaders of all kinds organized camps as "children's republics" from the top down, using camper councils, camper newspapers, all-camp assemblies, and camper work to encourage democratic behavior for participation as adults. Jewish educational camps drew not only on the approaches used in public schools; their leaders took democratic education and infused it with particularly Jewish goals and ideas as they inserted their notions of Jewish authenticity into the camp schedule and environment. They shaped their democratic and labor practices according to their visions of Zionist movements in Europe and Palestine and the Jewish Labor Bund, but also emphasized Judaism's compatibility with American democracy and citizenship, particularly in moments of isolationism and rising anti-Semitism as in the 1920s.

Fashioning camps as camper republics, however, had one even more significant advantage for postwar Jewish educators. By bringing campers into the running of camp, and by associating camp life with freedom, allowance, and fun, camp leaders hoped that their campers would come away feeling that they transformed into the kinds of authentic Jews camps encouraged by their own volition. In this way, the right to curse exemplifies what anthropologist Randall K. Tillery calls "structured mayhem," the notion that "structure and anti-structure go hand in hand" in camps and that the "mayhem" that campers are allowed to stir up differentiates "the children's lives at home and their freedom to live differently at camp."[7] While a camp's influence on youth has to do with many rituals of daily life, this distinctive incorporation of leniency and recreation with ideology and control lay at the core of camps' "pseudo-religious" sensibilities.[8] The "freedom to live differently" at camp helped lead youth to believe that Jewish camps' cultural, political, and religious values were one and the same as their own.

This distinctive balance between freedom and ideological control is not simple to label as a form of brainwashing, although references to Jewish camps as "cults," some satirical and others less so, abound.[9] As in the case of camps' engagements with Jewish language, power, control, and influence flowed in multiple directions. As adult leaders sought their campers' buy-in, the responses of youth pushed their camps into new territory, shaping daily life from the bottom up. While summer camps have clear and defined boundaries for age cohorts, moreover, status and power blurred, shifted from year to year, and diverged from camp to camp. Counselors, as youth themselves, often participated in, egged on, and set the stage for campers' rebellions, working in cooperation to shift camp life to reflect the youth culture they shared, but they just as often defended the values of the older educators and leaders who managed their camps from the top down.

Camp leaders could never ensure that their campers would return home the kinds of Jews they wanted them to be, and the unity they worked to build did not win over every child or teen. Instead of revealing the absolute authority of adults or the surprising agency of the young, the story of postwar Jewish summer camps demonstrates what Gleason explained as the "messier 'in-between' of more nuanced and negotiated exchange[s] between and among children," and in this case, teens, counselors, and older staff members.[10] Age-based groups and generational cohorts created their Jewish summers not only in conflict but in tandem. Camps' engagements with freedom and democracy reveal both how children and teens direct their own experiences and the power adult leaders and educators wield to shape their thoughts, ideologies, and futures. Staff could lead their campers to water, but life at camp reflected their everyday decisions to drink or not to drink.

This paradox—that youth were empowered to lead, direct, question, and rebel but discouraged from thinking too far beyond the ideological bounds of their camps' missions—was a powerful force in transforming the hearts and minds of campers. Considering summer camps on opposite ends of the freedom, leniency, and democratic spectrum, this chapter explores how democratic education, intergenerational negotiation, and a broader focus on the teenager shaped life within, and reflected life outside, the Jewish summer camp.

## American Camping, Democratic Education, and the Teenage Camper

The connection between camp and democratic living found its footing within the earliest decades of American camping. In the late 1800s, camping leaders, typically clergymen or teachers, took groups of mainly boys to the country for a week or two, arriving at relatively or entirely undeveloped tracts of land. Such experiences necessitated a participatory atmosphere, offering campers and their one or two adult leaders the chance to build the camp environment and program from scratch. In the Progressive Era, camps became more permanent in their locales and larger in the size of their populations. Their programs also began to become much more structured and mission driven, with fresh air reformers, settlement house workers, clergymen, and private camping leaders of the 1910s and 1920s using camps for the Americanization of immigrants, building masculinity in boys, and improving the health and hygiene of urban children. Although the period's educational philosophies were influenced by notions of democracy, the practical consequences of larger camps meant that camping leaders of the era adopted more regimented styles of leadership and management, filling the day, awarding children badges and rewards for good behavior, or requiring uniforms, directing campers with a bugle's call and a preset schedule. At the same time, the camping sector's shift toward control reflected the period's more paternalistic approach toward children overall: a "fundamental mistrust of what children might do if left to their own devices."[11]

In the interwar years, camp directors shifted their approach to leadership and management once again, expressing a nostalgia for early pioneering camps and questioning their camps' regimentation. While some Progressive

Era camps sustained a more spontaneous, laissez-faire approach, Leslie Paris writes, Progressive Era and interwar camps' management styles were more similar than critics let on.[12] Nevertheless, interwar leaders' explicit rejection of the earlier child management approach and their romantic notions of early pioneer camps explains their more purposeful turn toward giving campers greater freedom and autonomy at camp.[13] Embracing progressive educational philosophies, many camp leaders came to support John Dewey's notion of democratic education in particular. Describing democracy as "more than a form of government . . . [but] primarily a mode of associated living, of conjoint communicated experience," Dewey's 1916 work, *Democracy in Education*, argued that classrooms should function as "miniature communities," preparing children "for better citizenship" by practicing on a small scale the roles they would assume as adults. Educators like William Kilpatrick popularized the idea that summer camps were even more ideal environments for putting democratic education into practice than schools due to their immersive natures.[14] Interwar camps across America, including Jewish ones, began to render their camps as miniature democracies with a new sense of intentionality.

Although many American camps embraced democratic education to one extent or another, this progressive mode of pedagogy held special currency in politically progressive communist and socialist summer camps, which were heavily attended, founded, and staffed by Jews. Pioneer Youth Camp (PYC) serves as a prime example. Affiliated with the communist youth movement, the Young Pioneers of America, PYC was founded in 1924 by Joshua Lieberman, a Jewish, former settlement house worker.[15] Lieberman's camp, to which Dewey himself served as an adviser, aimed "to create a living model of socialism for both the children and the adults in the camp." In the 1920s, children not only built up the camp environment alongside staff, but held the reins over what to do with their time, forming the camp program cooperatively.[16] Although few interwar leaders outside communist and socialist spaces "radically reorganized camp life" to the degree PYC's staff did, Lieberman's ideas, summed up in his 1931 book, *Creative Camping*, deeply influenced the sector, leading camp directors to make their camp environments freer and more democratic on a smaller, more manageable scale, including more free time, more one-off pioneering activities like building new structures, and creating modes of self-governance like camper councils.[17] In the same decade, books and articles by social workers and social scientists such as Hedley Dimock, Charles Hendry, and Louis Blumenthal furthered the idea that camps encourage "resourcefulness and self-direction, social responsibility in a democratic setting, and the ideals of progressive education," employing the social work notion of group work, which aimed to produce better individuals and more functional, constructive groups. Although camps remained hierarchical, interwar camp leaders used these theories and approaches to address the rights of children "to determine more of their own camp experience."[18]

Democratic education took on new significance as World War II began and Americans came to see themselves as worldwide defenders of democracy. In 1941, the US Office of Education and the Federal Security Agency published "Democracy in the Summer Camp," a pamphlet arguing for the importance of cultivating democratic "attitude[s] of the mind" by "inserting democratic tools and attitudes into the camp curriculum."[19] The pamphlet's author, educator Sterling Mason, laid out several paths toward doing so, including camper committees, promoting a "spirit of work," and engaging campers through discussions on American issues and world events.[20] Elbert Fretwell, Dewey-trained Columbia Teachers College professor and chief scout executive of the Boy Scouts of America from 1943 to 1948, had in fact proposed similar ideas in the 1930s. But heightened anxieties about the future of democracy made the uses of student councils, assemblies, clubs, newspapers, and magazines in schools and camps even more popular, securing their place in American education for the long haul.[21]

Although educational Jewish camps encompassed a sector of their own, they participated in camp director organizations and received training in the same education schools as leaders of other faiths and perspectives and found themselves embroiled in the same trends as those of other ethnic and religious groups, debating, embracing, and negotiating the opportunities and limits of camp democracy and progressive education. Furthermore, as educators, social workers, and social scientists, American Jews were often at the forefront of trends in progressive education, social work, and group work. And yet certain elements of their approaches to democratic education did prove somewhat unique to their Jewishness. In the moment of rising nativism in the twenties, democratic education helped Jewish communal leaders assert Judaism's fit with American life and values, using Dewey's philosophies to teach Jewish children how to be good participants in American democracy and how to defend their Americanness to the outside world. With the rise of McCarthyism in the early 1950s, this impulse became even more pronounced in socialist and communist camps. Although socialist and communist Jewish camps did not disavow their politics on the inside, their outward-facing documents, such as advertisements and promotional pamphlets, employed the language of progressive and democratic education in hopes of drawing in parents anxious about McCarthyism and to stave off government concern and inspections. (In the case of communist Camp Kinderland, these changes were not enough to shield the camp from investigation or from a tremendous drop in registration).²²

Jewish interpretations of democratic education gained an even more sweeping popularity in the 1950s and 1960s. As Zionist sentiments became more prevalent in mainstream Jewish institutions, reenactments of Jewish events like the World Zionist Congress or model Knesset (Israeli parliament) proceedings became commonplace, and educational camps increasingly linked their democratic purposes to their visions of real or ideal Jewishness. Camps' "Judaification" of democracy also appeared in their daily work hours (*arbet-sho* in Yiddish and *avodah* in Hebrew) in which leaders manufactured opportunities for campers to beautify, build, and take responsibility for the camp environment. American camps of all kinds included work and cleaning in their daily schedules, but educational Jewish camps specifically filtered labor at camp through the prisms of Labor Zionism or a Yiddish-imbued socialism or Bundism.

All of these examples show that democracy took on both broad American and Jewish educational purposes and that the place of democracy in Jewish camping was well established by the postwar decades. Nevertheless, the rhetoric and the character of the 1967 Swig campers' call to protest mirrored shifts in American youth culture and the growing presence of teenagers in the camper population, which transformed the purpose of democratic education in the summer camp once again. Older teen campers, ages fifteen through seventeen, were much more common in the postwar decades than they were in the early twentieth century. Although there were some excep-

Campers working the land at Massad's garden, 1949.
Source: Photo courtesy of the American Jewish Historical Society. Printed with permission.

tions, with some early camps including campers as young as four and as old as up to eighteen years old, the vast majority of those earlier camps served campers between ages eight at the youngest and fourteen at the oldest.[23] Having campers above age sixteen proved uncommon, as most older teens either wanted or needed to work for pay during the summer or did not want to spend their summers grouped in with and under rules made for younger children. Even as camp directors learned to mark age differences with group "names, special spaces, developmental needs, and rights," older teenagers proved difficult to recruit. To mitigate this problem, camps of the 1930s began to create counselors-in-training (CIT), junior counselors, and various kinds of work programs that offered older teen campers a chance to continue to return to camp while receiving more freedom and responsibility.[24] Although they varied by decade, camp type, and issues of pay, with some camps paying junior counselors and CITs and others charging tuition, keeping campers longer through CIT and work programs had similar financial benefits for camps, creating an uninterrupted pipeline for former campers to become full staff members later and offering camps a free or very inexpensive source of labor. For older campers, these programs offered independence, education, leadership development, and structure, a healthy balance for teens who felt too old to be campers but were legally too young to be full-fledged counselors.

Jewish camps maintained a vast array of work programs for teens in the 1950s and 1960s. However, they also began to create education-focused teen programs, infuse their preexisting work programs with more education, and create new camps entirely dedicated to high school–aged campers. These developments mirrored the growing understanding of the teenage years as a developmental stage of life, broad American anxieties over a more visible teen culture, and the nascent affluence of American Jewish families, many of whom could now afford to send their teens to camp rather than requiring them to get summer jobs. Some Zionist movements created small teen camping programs as early as the 1920s, but the peak years of creating Jewish summer camp programs specifically geared toward older teenagers took place in the 1950s and 1960s, when the Reform and Conservative movements and Yiddish camps Boiberik, Kinderland, and Hemshekh all took part in the trend.[25] By the 1960s, Jewish leaders were fully committed to the project of keeping teens as campers as long as possible, with hopes of making a lasting impact on them before they left the communal nest and went off to college.

The financial imperative to recruit campers to return the next summer meant that even very young campers had a hand in shaping what camp life contained and prioritized; they too could return home to their parents and influence their decision of whether to send the child back to camp the following year. However, postwar Jewish educators paid particular attention to their eldest campers, believing they had the most sway over their parents and the strongest likelihood of not returning due to the pull of summer jobs or other options. Bringing in older campers brought about new questions and issues regarding freedom and democracy. Camp Ramah director Walter Ackerman put it this way in 1966: "Anyone acquainted with camp life knows that there is a camper subculture which exists independently, sometimes in spite of and sometimes for spite, of the official camp programs and policies." While the "phenomenon" of youth culture "can be found in any school," Ackerman argued in the *Journal of Jewish Education*, it assumed "more significant" sway in camp life because of their "peculiar characteristics" as immersive environments with little authority over children's lives.[26] Social worker Solomon Green relayed similar ideas to an audience of dozens of camp leaders at the 1969 National Conference on Jewish Camping. The "problem facing camps," wrote Green, "is how to develop, interpret, and achieve acceptance by teenagers of both the structure and the standards"— how to convince them, in other words, to buy into the ideas and values their camps were selling.[27]

Seeing camps as having the ability to turn youth "inward or outward, off or on, [to] the Jewish dimension of their lives," achieving a balance between structure and antistructure proved a high-stakes endeavor.[28] Jewish educators, however, had quite a bit of confidence in their approach. By making campers feel like participants in a democracy rather than students, consumers, or customers and by structuring camp life to include mayhem and leniency, educators saw how children and teens would come to accept the ideologies their camps promoted as authentic elements of their own Jewish lives, chosen on their own accord.

While camp leaders agreed on this central notion, each camp had its own answers to the question of how much freedom campers should have and what camp democracy should aim to achieve. The camps of Hashomer Hatzair and Camp Hemshekh, for example, were both smaller than most of the other Jewish camps studied in this book, and their manageability and intimacy clearly made room for more experimentation and permissiveness. Camp Hemshekh's leaders, for instance, placed "extensive self-government" among its core values, aiming to make the camp "an exemplary children's society." A camper council, including one representative from each bunk, a weekly camp-wide forum in which all campers could "voice their opinions concerning all matters related to camp life, give suggestion, criticize," and a camper-run weekly newspaper made up the three major elements of Hemshekh's democratic program, which both staff and camper took quite seriously.[29] Counselors and older staff still had the power to turn down their requests, a fact that frustrated campers on several occasions over the 1960s and 1970s.[30] But in comparison to other camps, Hemshekh's adults gave a remarkable amount of power to campers because the camp's commitment to democratic socialism and its size allowed for such an arrangement. Hashomer Hatzair and Habonim's camps also operated with a high degree of freedom for campers and had very young staff members. In Hashomer Hatzair, campers became counselors at age sixteen, the camps creatively dealing with their states' health departments by hiring just enough staff over the age of eighteen to pass inspection. Tel Yehudah and Habonim's Tel Ari also kept campers as campers as long as possible by placing democracy at the center of their programs and creating total seclusion from their movements' younger campers. In Reform and Conservative camps, however, which were ran by rabbis and professional educators, a more top-down character prevailed. Engagements with democracy were less the central mainstays of their programs than experiments that changed from year to year.

The next two sections look more closely at Ramah, the most professionalized and top-down educational Jewish camps, and the Zionist youth movement camps of Young Judaea, Habonim, and Hashomer Hatzair, which occupy the more peer-led and democratic end of the spectrum. Their approaches to democracy were far from identical, shaped by their organiza-

Campers and counselors staging a satirical protest
at Camp Hemshekh, 1966.
Source: Photographed by Gabriel Ross. Printed with permission.

tional styles and their overall movement goals. And yet they shared a similar approach to the core purpose of camp democracy and structured mayhem. Instead of ignoring or squashing the rebelliousness that entered their camp, adult leaders tapped into those feelings of rebellion to "enhance and strengthen a Jewish identification and commitment," turning youth leaders into tools toward their own educational and ideological success.[31]

### Democracy and Power at Camp Ramah

When it came to the hierarchy of age and staffing, the summer camps ran by the National Ramah Commission occupied the furthest, most professionalized end of the spectrum of Jewish summer camps. Rabbis, teachers, and other leaders trained at the Jewish Theological Seminary not only populated the camps in significant numbers but exerted control over programs and educational curricula more so than in other camps, where young counselors often worked in tandem with older staff members to carry out the educational message. Ramah's archival documents reflect this level of professionalism, its folders filled with educational programs and internal correspondence but lacking in texts written by or about campers. When specific campers did come up in their writings, Ramah's leaders often described them either in idealistic terms, as successful incarnations of their educational fantasy to create ideal Conservative Jews, or as misbehaving obstacles standing in the way of that fantasy. Created to instill the values of Conservative Judaism in the next generations, the purpose of the Ramah camps as educators saw it was not to provide a democratic space for campers to debate the pros and cons of being Conservative Jews but to solidify and invigorate the movement's future through the experience of living Jewishly.

The Ramah camps' heavy sense of adult control influenced dynamics between staff and campers and their uses of democratic education in distinctive ways. In the late 1940s and early 1950s, as the Ramah Commission's leaders saw their camps as training grounds for a relatively small elite of future movement leaders, making camp function like a democracy took a backseat to the camps' other goals and purposes.[32] Instead of implementing consistent camper councils, newspapers, all-camp assemblies, or other means to give campers some power and voice as most other camps did, democratic education within Ramah camps generally took the shape of experiments in "democratic living," short and often one-off moments in which staff flipped camps' power structures by handing the campers limited reins.

The memories of former Ramah Connecticut camper Sarah described this dynamic from a camper's perspective. As a camper in the 1950s, she could not remember an instance in which the staff "asked for any feedback from kids about what they experienced." When campers had a question or complaint about something going on in the camp, "the answer" from staff "was always that just 'this is how it is.'" Occasionally, however, she noticed that the camp leadership "would change philosophies" for a period, with staff members realizing that "the kids could actually decide things." In one instance, a group of staff gave a group of campers she was part of control over casting that summer's play, which in prior years had been the role of the drama instructor. By the next summer, however, "the whole project" of letting campers choose how to cast the play "was dropped." In another democratic experiment in Sarah's time, the leadership announced that the camp was going to have "a 'lazy day'" in which campers could "do what [they] wanted." But the fact that educational programs remained mandatory on this supposedly free day bothered her. "If we were going to have a lazy day . . . we should be able to do what we wanted," Sarah recalled feeling at the time. In defiance, she led two bunks of girls "into the woods" beyond the camp's boundaries. When they got caught, the staff members identified her as "the ringleader" and told her promptly that they did not think she should come back to camp the next year. "I mean, they didn't really sit down with me and say, like, what possessed you to do this, or what was your point or what were you trying to do? They just looked at me and said, 'It was you, and you really should never come back.'" That was the "end of [her] career" as a Ramah camper. What she concluded from the experience is that the staff at her Camp Ramah "didn't really have a way of involving kids. It was either all or nothing."[33]

In the 1960s, Ramah's approach to democracy became more responsive to the desires and opinions of campers. As the camps expanded and changed their admissions standards and as staff faced a changing and more defiant youth culture, Ramah's educators increasingly gave children roles in planning the camp program, creating camper councils in charge of "recreational planning and limited areas of maintenance responsibility," and allowing campers to control more of their daily schedules.[34] Campers of the sixties had more opportunities to discuss their needs and desires with their counselors, with "weekly 'town hall' meeting or gripe sessions" appearing on camps' schedule. Their democratic "experiments" also became more frequent and pronounced. In 1967, for instance, a Ramah camp experimented in an intense practice of democratic living, giving campers near-total control over the entire camp program. "Our goal was to change a complete administrative structure, counselor work norms and camper behavior norms," wrote a Jewish Theological Seminary graduate student in a paper regarding Ramah's "experimental leadership summer." "We destroyed the scheduling structure by announcing to the campers that no activity was going to be scheduled," the student wrote. Yet changes did not occur immediately. It reportedly took "three days of testing to convince the counselors and campers that schedules would be built only about the campers' requests." To destroy previous hierarchical structures, furthermore, "uniforms for administrators were abolished," along with "special food privileges" provided to staff, including coffee and more appealing meat platters. The campers discussed their needs and desires with their counselors daily, and a structured "weekly 'town hall' meeting or gripe session" appeared on the schedule on top of the camper council, in charge of "recreational planning and limited areas of maintenance responsibility." Through these drastic shifts, the "leadership pattern changed." Among campers, "stars in sports and the arts lost status to planners and doers," while one-time "rebel" counselors replaced "passive 'good'" ones as leaders.[35]

While this experiment occurred as a one-off, other elements of Ramah's changing approach to power in the camp milieu proved more consistent and related to the specifically Jewish counterculture. Pointing out the contradictions they saw between the Judaism practiced at Ramah and the Judaism practiced within the Conservative movement in their hometowns, "the young people of Ramah," counselors and campers both, "joined the critique of adult society voiced by youth throughout the United States, direct[ing] themselves principally towards the liberal Jewish culture of their parents and towards the institutions of the Jewish community." The camps' separation from postwar synagogues "functioned as a pressure cooker" for religious experimentation. In 1969, experimentation reached a fever pitch as campers and young counselors attempted to "instigate radical changing of the religious order," hoping to "counter the culture of their parents in the name of what they perceived to be a full and compelling Judaism . . . unwilling to accept the discontinuity between camp and home, opt[ing] to restructure home and synagogue."[36] Campers and counselors embraced more traditional prayer styles and the daily wearing of yarmulkes, while also pushing Conservative Judaism in more egalitarian directions regarding women's roles in prayer leading.

Such "rebellions," however, were targeted against adults outside camps more so than the staff within them. Indeed, campers' interests in traditional Jewish practice matched in some ways their adult leaders' beliefs about the inauthenticity of postwar synagogues. Critiquing suburban, mainstream Judaism became an all-camp endeavor, demonstrating how giving campers the power to lead and space to rebel helped make camps' transformational missions more possible. As sociologist Marshall Sklare put it in 1974, Ramahniks in the late 1960s "demonstrated an unerring ability to utilize age-old Jewish symbols and practices in a way that gave them an anti-establishment tone." But while wearing a *kippah* (yarmulke) became "a kind of provocation, directed against the 'uptight' Jewish establishment with its excessive fear of seeming too out of place in American life, or too 'different,' " it represented a victory for Ramah's staff members, for whom this "rebellion" was a sign that they had succeeded in inspiring campers to live Jewishly.[37] Conservative leaders of the cities and suburbs questioned if Ramah was making good on its promise of "providing the synagogues with an indigenous leadership" or if "it was separating itself from the movement and cultivating a feeling of alienation from, and superiority toward, the local synagogues." But the adults within the camp felt they had successfully channeled these provocations to fit their educational goals.[38]

Even as Ramah's leadership found ways to converge with campers on religious practice, some campers of the 1960s behaved outside the bounds of what camp leadership saw as acceptable behavior. Each summer, the leaders of Camp Ramah in the Poconos compiled a list of campers who, they believed, like Sarah, should not be allowed to return to camp the following year. In the 1960s, one camper made it on the list due to her "negative attitude

toward Judaism," for having a Catholic boyfriend "and . . . not seeing a problem in it," "hating and talking constantly during class and *tfillot* [prayers],"
and for not being "concerned much at all with keeping kosher and Shabbat."
Another camper similarly had "a very negative attitude toward religion and
Hebrew," despising "classes, prayers, and even the speaking of Hebrew" and
influencing other campers to feel the same. A boy who acted like a "wise
guy" regularly cut activities, refused to speak Hebrew, criticized the camp
program, and acted as a "detriment to the group."[39] Writer Morris Freedman noticed similar issues in his 1955 *Commentary* article, as he described
how Ramah's administration "was not happy about backsliding campers."
When Freedman met a teenage guest who had driven up to camp to see
some friends from the year prior, he found out from the director that the
teenager chose not to return due to lack of interest "in continuing the regimen." The staff felt they had "made a mistake" when they admitted him in
1954. "We can't afford to invest our effort and time indiscriminately. . . . I'm
surprised we took someone that old who had such little promise in the first
place."[40] Such campers may have been extreme cases; many campers fit into
the camps' regimen as staff had hoped. But educators worried tremendously
about the influence of some campers, noting how one "bad camper" could
easily influence dozens of others to behave poorly.

In 1969, the issue of misbehaving campers came to a head at Ramah
Palmer in Massachusetts. On top of normalized marijuana consumption,
campers "absented themselves from daily services," "the cutting of classes was
common," and "there were charges that the observance of kashrut was lax."
Against the camp's language program, Sklare described how the "time honored Ramah tradition—the presentation in Hebrew of a successful Broadway musical—was also observed in a peculiar fashion, with older campers
selecting 'Hair' and then proceeding to present it in English." When Ramah
Palmer did not open in summer 1971, some blamed low enrollments. But
Sklare, as well as several of the former campers I spoke with, interpreted
the decline of Palmer differently. "This," wrote Sklare, "the first closing in
Ramah's history—was widely interpreted as a sign that eclecticism had its
limits."[41] Palmer presented an extreme case, and yet other Ramah sites faced
similar resistance that changed educators' goals and approaches to the youth.
Ramah's leadership reduced the amount of formal teaching from the early

years through the 1970s, embracing more informal and experiential methods to satisfy and better engage campers. Just like Ramah's decreasing use of spoken Hebrew, the camps' growing commitment to informal educational methods over the 1960s and into the 1970s showed that the behaviors of campers forced staff to change their methods and plans.[42]

While the campers of Ramah spurred changes in their camps, and by extension the Conservative movement, Ramah remained among the more controlled and professionalized within the Jewish camping sector. Even counselors had less control over the camp program than in most other camps; one former camper and counselor noted, "These were rabbis. These were schoolteachers of long standing. They were generally middle aged. And they set the tone [and] certainly set the curriculum," with counselors having "no role in setting any of that up."[43] Nevertheless, Ramah leaders mostly found ways to meet youth—campers and counselors both—in the middle, integrating and reimagining camper rebellions as part and parcel of the camps' transformational processes. "Given the proclivity of Conservative Judaism to reject or disregard in regard those aspects of Jewish law or custom it finds unacceptable," wrote Sklare, "there were few developments in the past decades in the realm of personal behavior which Ramah felt it necessary, doctrinally, to dismiss outright." Instead, Ramah's educators were able to use most of the "potentially challenging developments" for their own "purposes," even claiming "authentic Jewish precedent for them."[44] Ackerman shared this perspective. "No matter what the camp officialdom does," he wrote, "the campers will develop a 'life of their own' which provides much of the fun in camp and makes even the worst of them tolerable." But "wise camp directors," he continued, "will permit that [camper] sub-culture to flourish and will even use it as base upon which to develop their programs."[45] While Zionist camps, as the next section shows, occupied the opposite end of the democracy spectrum, they were similarly adept at using campers' wills, rebellions, and desires toward their own purposes, creating a milieu of convergence, and making the case for maximum freedom.

## Democracy and Leadership in the Zionist Movement Camp

In summer 1971, Susan, a fifteen-year-old from the Midwest, attended her first session at Camp Tel Yehudah (TY). The program she participated in that summer was typical of most other American sleepaway camps: she lived in a cabin with other girls, and the days and programs were organized by counselors according to a preset schedule. When she came back in 1972 at the age of sixteen, however, she took part in a very different kind of program: Machane Avodah (literally "work camp"), also known as M.A. During M.A, she and dozens of other campers lived in a separate part of TY's 150-acre campsite, sleeping in tents without counselors, cooking their own food, and working in various capacities at the camp. Envisioned as simulating early Jewish immigration to British Mandate Palestine, the program placed kibbutz-style communitarianism at the center of the educational experience. But while Susan remembered that educational programming occurred during M.A., she could not recall the details. What she remembered instead were the parts of the experience she described as "random and ridiculous." "Honestly," she continued, "I think you did kind of what you wanted. I know we had chickens. There were some animals we had to take care of, the big deal with *shmira* [guard duty] at night, stay up all night 'til like 5:00 in the morning, just walking around with a flashlight and drinking coffee."[46] Machane Avodah's structure provided an educational model based on a vision of authentic Jewish living. What remained of the experience years later, though, was its "antistructure": the permissiveness, late nights, and laughter.

Susan's experience of freedom in MA in the 1970s was not the product of a lazy curriculum but an intentional reflection of how TY's leaders merged the American youth culture of the period with the democratic ethos of the kibbutzim they aimed to emulate. As early as the 1920s, Zionist camps filtered democratic education through a Jewish lens, simulating the kibbutz by functioning with a communal pot of money called the *kupah*, centering work in the camp program, and holding assemblies called *asephot*. In the very first session of Tel Yehudah in 1948, the director praised the camper council as "perhaps the outstanding part of the TY camp program," boasting how camp life functioned "along democratic lines," as staff and campers "joined with the camp administration in planning, managing, and executing the camp program." Elected by the entire camper body, the *Moetza* (camper council) held meetings on "policy, procedures, self-discipline, and the program," while the staff encouraged "freedom of expression" and made opportunities for youth to assume leadership. The campers themselves even determined who would run flag raising, *shmira*, *toranut*, or kitchen duty, for the day.[47] At Habonim's Camp Kvutzah, the asepha and kupah similarly proved fundamental to the camp program, forging camp as "an authentic Jewish atmosphere."[48] With year-round movements led by high school–aged peers, moreover, Young Judaea's Tel Yehudah, Habonim's Camp Habonim, and Hashomer Hatzair's Shomria shared a strong emphasis on teaching leadership by giving campers a high degree of freedom and power within the camp environment. As Zionist educator Avraham Shenker explained, self-government was "a basic principle of Zionist camping," even as certain elements varied according to the traditions of different movements and camps."[49]

For all these reasons, Zionist summer camps occupied the other end of the mayhem-and-leniency spectrum from the Ramah camps, filling the summer with opportunities for campers to shape the camp experience according to their wills. But while these Zionist-imbued democratic methods and traditions predated the 1960s, they took on new weight when the wider youth revolts of the period mixed with power dynamics inside camps. A former Habonim camper named Dan had an experience similar to that of Susan at his movement's leadership camp, Machane Bonim. In the 1970s, Habonim's rising seniors attended the camp from across the country, experiencing a high degree of freedom in a kibbutz-like program nearly identical to that of Tel Yehudah. "I mean, you know, looking back, your parents really had to believe in you as a leader to send you these to do these things. I mean, most kids my age were probably getting summer jobs . . . and here I am, like, wasting more of my parents' money," Dan explained to me in an interview. But while he mostly remembered how he and his fellow campers used self-government to their own ends, creating, for instance, a *Vaa'd Mesiba*, (a party committee), which requested that part of their communal pot of money be used to buy alcohol, he also felt that he "learned something that summer" through the experience of self-government and gained leadership skills that stuck with him in adulthood.[50]

Zionist camps' focus on leadership and self-government also led to the creation of orienteering exercises, such as Hashomer Hatzair's "Survival Day." As a former camper named Judith explained, the counselors at Moshava dropped the seventeen-year-old campers off "somewhere" in the wilderness, giving them a few days to find their way back to camp.[51] Recalling the same exercise, another former Shomria camper, Efrat, remembered that she and her fellow campers were "woken up early in the morning and taken about 10, 15 miles away from the camp." A staff member gave one camper ten dollars, and they had a "little bit of drinking water, but nothing else." Survival Day, which the camp included in its program for at least a decade, quickly devolved: instead of learning how to brave the wild, a camper came up with the idea of going to a Catskills resort and "danc[ing] for our suppers," earning enough money to take "taxis back to camp after having stuffed their face in town."[52] Nevertheless, the notion of leaving campers in the forest to find their ways back to camp reflected the Zionist camp's intense approach to freedom, independence, and leadership.

For campers younger than seventeen, Zionist camps provided opportunities for self-government and leadership development through camper councils, mock Knesset proceedings, newspapers, and negotiations over how to use the kupah. In the cases of Hashomer Hatzair and Habonim, campers at the age of fourteen or fifteen even had a chance to run the camp each year on days called Revolution or Topsy Turvy Day. As former camper Judith recalled of her time at Camp Moshava in the 1960s, "There would be a day when all of the counselors left and a camper would be assigned to be, you know, *Rosh Moshava* [head of camp] for the day." At age fourteen, she got her chance, awakening to a note under her pillow that she recalled stating, "'Congratulations, Yehudit! We are gone. You have been chosen. Here are the things you need to do during the day. And the cooks are your backup.'"[53] Dan recalled a similar day at Camp Tavor, in which "the counselors in training ... would take over," kicking the actual counselors and head staff out of camp for the day. "That was their chance to try to act like my *madrichim* [counselors]," and "for us it was the revolution."[54]

Revolution Day, Survival, and Machane Avodah all demonstrate the unique ways by which Zionist camps created a great sense of autonomy for their oldest campers. Zionist leaders provided structure through modes of self-governance, labor, and outdoor adventures. But the freedom campers were allowed and even encouraged to express—to try to procure alcohol, dance for suppers, aimlessly wander the campgrounds until dawn—played a crucial role in the educational picture too. Leniency provided the stuff of camp life that helped camps foster the most commitment and buy-in from campers. Freedom within Zionist camps had limits. Most campers were aware that self-governance could run up against camp rules, and even in the most left-wing of camps, questioning Israel's right to exist or its policies toward Palestinians was not welcome, nor were the sharing of views considered too right-wing. Katherine, a former camper, recalled that camp leadership "had a really strong ideological hold on everything": there was a sense of freedom, but it was "the freedom to be exactly the same kind of differentness"—different from mainstream American society or mainstream Jewry, but not different from one another. And yet this understanding of her camp became clear to her only in retrospect.[55] As teens, campers within Zionist movement camps generally believed that their camps were in many ways spaces of a rather radical and unusual degree of freedom and came to associate the freedom they felt at camp with their feelings for Israel and Zionism. Like the Ramah camps, Zionist camping leaders succeeded at using methods like self-governance not only to teach democratic behaviors but to have youth see the transformations they underwent at camp as wholly and utterly their own.

————

When considering youth-serving institutions like summer camp, it can be tempting to think of their adult leaders and founders as having an all-encompassing power, shaping every element of the lived experience of those in their care. Camp directors certainly held tremendous authority over what camp life contained, their visions and missions reflecting Jewish communal priorities and concerns that extended well beyond their gates. To most educational practitioners and scholars of Jewish camping, the "power of camp" owed itself to its totalizing essence and the capacity it gives adult educators for structuring the living experience of the children over a period of weeks or months. And yet the very elements that educators hoped would make these camps ideal sites for transforming the next generations—their isolation from broader society, their 24/7 immersive environments—also provided youth opportunities to pursue their own desires and push back against adult plans in ways they could not in synagogues and schools. Camps' democratic components gave campers a time and place for critiquing their camps' programs and plans and an escape valve for their tendencies to rebel; without parents around and the issue of grades to worry about, campers had little to concern them as they challenged authority through rolled eyes, protests, and misbehavior. Because staff members aimed to make camp inspiring, relevant, and enticing, moreover, youth's responses to their plans altered their programmatic and ideological priorities. As the adults in charge sought their buy-in, campers of all ages held remarkable sway over what leaders included and hoped to achieve within and through their summer camps.

Since camp leaders directed the freedom youth experienced to match their own goals, the notion of children and teenagers having autonomy and power in the camp environment is in many ways a contradiction in terms. By making their camps spaces of relative freedom and leniency, educators believed that campers would come to see themselves as partners in the creation of the total experience rather than subjects of it, and thereby would see their camp ideologies, and the identities their camps sought to instill within them through those ideologies, as natural and inseparable parts of themselves. As much as campers felt free as they roamed the grounds, procured alcohol, directed for the day, and hiked alone in the woods, they were subject to the rules and oversight of counselors, unit heads, directors, and rabbis, who watched and intervened from a distance. Most Jewish camp leaders encouraged challenging and questioning ideas presented during educational programs, but they ultimately discouraged campers from embracing ideas outside the ideological boundaries of their movements. The feeling of freedom many campers described felt real to them, but staff members used the freedom, allowance, and leniency of camp life toward their own ends. Revisiting the words of the Swig camper in 1967, "Is this"—the controlled and instrumentalized version of freedom camp leaders generated—"what you call being free?"

While the freedom of campers was far from complete, however, the choices youth could make to accept or not to accept, to transform or not to transform, afforded them the power to change their camps' trajectories, and the trajectories of American Jewishness by extension. In the blurry space between allowance and control, postwar camps emerged as spaces for Jewish Americans of different ages and stages to produce Jewish cultures and identities that fit their needs, dreams, and desires. Looking beyond autonomy, power, and agency and toward intergenerational negotiation and nuanced exchanges between youth and adults, how children and teens influence the institutions that order their lives comes to the fore. As romance and sexuality emerged as a particularly central avenue for campers to push camps toward more permissiveness, staff found a new point of convergence with youth, redirecting campers' interests in the opposite sex toward the aim of curbing growing rates of interfaith marriage. In the next chapter, the issue of youth culture continues to take center stage as we turn to romance and sexuality within the postwar Jewish camp.

# Summer Flings and Fuzzy Rings

## Camper Romance, Erotic Zionism, and Intermarriage Anxiety

IN SUMMER 1962, A TWELVE-YEAR-OLD named Josh began a six-year journey at Habonim's Camp Tavor, first as a camper, then as a counselor-in-training (CIT), and then, in his last year, as a full-fledged counselor. As Josh reflected on his romantic experiences at camp, a number of scenarios came to his mind, representing each of these ages and stages: big bonfires each Saturday night with "skits and singing" in which boy campers "would invite girls to sit on their blanket with them" for "a little bit of making out"; how counselors went around with big flashlights they called "Zug Busters" ("couple busters"), embarrassing campers who were off canoodling instead of participating in activities; a more experienced friend teaching him how to hold the hand of the girl camper he was "going out" with. At sixteen, he advanced from holding hands to "kissing and fondling" his girlfriend behind the *chadar ochel* (dining hall), and as a seventeen-year-old CIT, he recalled the romantic energy when the group held singing circles and deep conversations in a room at night, lit by a single candle. "Well, in the dark," Josh explained, "a lot of things would happen." In Josh's case, he remembered "holding a girl, and holding her breasts," with coupled-off CITs around him taking part in similar acts of cuddling, petting, and kissing.[1]

Sarah, a camper at Ramah in the 1950s, explained that a feeling that "everyone needed a boyfriend or girlfriend" permeated the camp atmosphere, with campers divided into "two classes of people: those who had successfully coupled off, and those who had not."[2] A Camp Hemshekh alumna of the 1960s recalled a similar feeling : "If you were going with someone, there was a certain status attached to it. . . . You'd come back to the bunk. 'Oh, what did he do? What did you say? How did he do it?'" After experiencing such attention on a personal level one summer, she moved through the rest of her years at camp believing that "the camp season was only successful if you were able to go with someone for at least part of the time."[3]

Real and metaphorical Zug Busters did not need to flash their lights at every camper. Of the thirty former campers I spoke with, eight said they never had a boyfriend, girlfriend, or summer fling in their many years as campers, deeming camp romance as the domain of "cool kids," older campers, counselors, or, in the case of campers who came out as gay or lesbian later in life, straight kids. And while the romantic atmospheres of camps presented opportunity for discovery, they also had the potential to perpetuate peer pressure, group hierarchies, and social anxiety. Since sexuality permeated the camp environment through public displays of affection, spin-the-bottle games, public and in-bunk sexual humor, sexual graffiti on bunk walls, and late-night gossip, no camper was completely impervious to its significance within the everyday life of their camps. Those who did not couple off often left feeling that they had missed out on a crucial part of the camp experience.

For campers who did engage in romantic or sexual exploration, their experiences contributed to the overall ability of camp to heighten emotions and bend time. Since campers spent nearly every hour of every day together, former campers described their relationships—even those that lasted only a few days—as somehow epic, playing more significant roles in their lives than dating may have during the school year. Although such relationships were rare, camper romances that lasted beyond the summer proved even more meaningful within the life histories of the former campers. While their memories of everyday camp activities often came with a disclaimer of uncertainty, their stories of dating, romance, and sexual relationships left some of the most indelible traces on the memories of the former campers I spoke with, recalled with a unique degree of confidence and clarity.

When I asked the alumni if they could recall times when their camps' rules or their counselors' oversight curbed their relationships, few to none could. But while laissez-faire approaches toward romantic and sexual expression gave campers a feeling of freedom and autonomy, camp leaders played crucial roles in shaping the camp sexual and romantic cultures from the top down. Counselors cheered or egged on their campers, participating in or overhearing the before-bedtime who-kissed-who discussions, encouraging campers to make moves, and doling out advice. From camp dances to dating games, moreover, staff members scheduled moments for heterosexual romance to bloom, educated campers about puberty and sexuality in educational and informal activities, and emphasized Jewish marriage as an ideal through role modeling, education, and simulated wedding ceremonies.[4] Observing the behavior of counselors as their older and cooler role models also affected how children and teens understood their camp's norms and expectations around dating and sexuality. Sarah noted that impressions of what counselors were up to in their own romantic relationships "set a tone" for the entire camper body: campers aspired toward their more advanced relationships, gossiped about their potential sexual escapades, and developed crushes on them.[5] In some cases, teenage campers even ended up dating staff members, their small age differences blurring the disparity of their roles and power dynamics during the summer.[6]

Despite this relative openness, camp sexual cultures did operate with certain limits. During and after the sexual revolution, the prospect of campers advancing to sexual intercourse raised more concerns than the kissing and petting of earlier decades; camp directors began to try to control camper sexuality to some degree, lest campers become "too advanced" for their ages. Camp leaders and camper culture, moreover, encouraged only heterosexual coupling. To borrow a term from feminist scholar Adrienne Rich, camps of the postwar period promoted compulsory heterosexuality—romantic and sexual exploration modeled only through a heteronormative lens.[7] While campers who later came out as gay or lesbian noted a whole range of feelings stemming from their experiences at camps, none experienced the kinds of sexual liberty that straight participants reflected on with nostalgia.

At the same time, Jewish camping leaders focused less on limiting sexual contact than on guiding its inevitability toward their own evolving objectives. Dating and sexuality emerged as central to the camp experience because campers sought those exciting firsts, but also because camp leaders saw benefits in allowing these romantic cultures to flourish. Logistically, giving campers the ability to pursue the opposite sex helped foster the association of camp life with freedom essential to receiving buy-in from campers, much like democracy, permissiveness, and "structured mayhem."[8] From an ideological angle, however, romance at camp also helped shape campers' values surrounding marrying fellow Jews, as staff responded to rising rates of intermarriage from the 1960s onward. Zionist leaders also found ways to fuse camper culture with notions of Zionism's "promised erotic revolution," their laxness surrounding sexuality adding to camps' emulation of Israeliness.[9] Dating and sexuality became core to camp life not only because campers arrived curious, pre-, mid-, and postpubescent, and desiring, but because adult leaders figured out how to harness the behavior of their teens and preteens to their own evolving missions and interests.

## Gender and Sexuality in Prewar American Camps

While rising rates of intermarriage began to deeply influence Jewish camps' approaches to camper dating from the 1960s onward, these dynamics started developing only in the 1920s, when Jewish organizations began to embrace coeducational camping for adolescents with a particular kind of enthusiasm. In the early twentieth century, most American summer camps operated as single-sex environments. As both progressive reformers and proponents of muscular Christianity problematized the impacts of industrialization and urbanization on children, most early camps focused on "masculinizing boys" or producing healthy urban girls in camps segregated by sex. At the turn of the century, many private camps for well-established Jews and philanthropic camps for the children of immigrants followed a similar single-sex trajectory, serving Jewish boys and Jewish girls separately.[10]

This early norm of single-sex camping came into question beginning in the 1920s, as psychologists such as Sigmund Freud and G. Stanley Hall advocated for the importance of heterosocial development to counter the development of homosexuality. In response, some boys-only camps integrated girls in the 1920s or 1930s, while others built or associated themselves with a "sister" or "brother" camp nearby, so that campers of both sexes could occasionally interact.[11] But while most camp leaders came to support coeducation in principle, "the degree to which children had the right to be sexually exploratory was controversial," leading most camps that served adolescents to remain single sex. Through the 1930s, wrote Leslie Paris, coeducational camps largely operated for preadolescent children, who, most camp leaders and parents believed, "were too young to create sexually charged environments."[12]

Although they initially followed a similar trajectory, Jewish organizations embraced coeducational camping for adolescent youth more quickly than many of their counterparts in the American camping sector writ large. Jewish fresh air camps founded at the turn of the century, like Camps Tamarack and Wise, were coed from the outset; so too were "radical and progressive interwar camps" like Kinderland, Wo-Chi-Ca, and Pioneer Youth Camp.[13] Historian Abigail Van Slyck further confirms that Jews took on coeducational teen camping earlier and more vociferously than other groups. "Like other camps organized around ethnic or religious affiliations," Van Slyck explained, Jewish camps "were typically coeducational" as they "encouraged young people to marry one of their own."[14] Progressive politics and an interest in encouraging marriages between Jews of similar backgrounds and political affiliations made coeducational camping a norm within Jewish organizational camping except for a few camps for children from Orthodox families. When camps with more explicitly Jewish educational purposes opened in the 1940s and 1950s, they emerged out of this tradition of the ethnic, progressive, and nonprofit Jewish camp, separating campers into girl and boy bunks, but otherwise combining the sexes in most activities from dawn to dusk.

While the prevalence of coeducational Jewish camping is relatively clear, it is more difficult to decipher whether the sexual cultures of Jewish summer camps were substantially more lenient than those that proliferated in other kinds of postwar American camps: a lack of secondary source research on the sexual cultures of other kinds of postwar camps makes such sweeping generalizations impossible. Although most religious Christian camps had policies discouraging sexual contact or kept their programs single sex, a scholar of Christian camping, Jacob Sorensen, confirmed for me that many campers at religiously Christian camps met their spouses as campers.[15] There is also plenty of evidence in popular culture to suggest that romance and sexuality permeate American camps of all kinds. If popular culture holds a mirror up to real life, however, it is worth noting that most movies and TV shows that relate to romance and sexuality at camp correlate to experiences their creators had at Jewish camps of various kinds. The cult-classic *Wet Hot American Summer* reflects director David Wain's experience at the Jewish camp, Camp Wise; the creator of the Nickelodeon show *Salute Your Shorts* attended a historically Jewish camp with Friday night services, Camp Weequahic; in the HBO series *Girls*, a Jewish character, Shoshanna, reconnects with a boy from Camp Ramah on the streets of Manhattan; *Gorp*, starring Fran Drescher, was set at a Jewish summer camp in 1980 and "focuse[d] its energy on the important things: sex, poop, and rabbis." More recently, Netflix's *Big Mouth* had a camp-based puberty- and sexuality-focused episode based on creator Nick Kroll's experiences at a "Jew-ish" summer camp, and included comedian Seth Rogen, who attended a Habonim camp in Canada.[16] In the pop culture landscape, the majority of references to sex and dating at camp turn out to be drawn from experiences at Jewish camps or camps with majority Jewish populations.

What makes Jewish camps' romantic and sexual cultures distinctly free, well known, and widespread relates to how and why camping leaders have managed, directed, and encouraged them from the top down. That adolescent campers arrived interested in dating and sexuality was all but inevitable and obvious; that camp leaders would fuse those inevitable interests with communal and ideological goals was Jewish specific. Mingling like campers at the social, the generations at camps fostered these sexual cultures together, less through discourse than through everyday decisions that sought to balance leniency, ideology, and control.

### Romance, Gender, and Sexual Behavior in the Postwar Jewish Camp

Marsha Singer's love of Camp Boiberik related to many elements of camp life: the yiddishkayt, the friends, the shabbes rituals, and the songs, to name just a few. But her love of Boiberik also had a lot to do with romance. Arriving in 1951 as a ten-year-old, she continued on through 1958, and with the exception of just one year, had "at least one boyfriend" each summer. "Boiberik and boys; Jewish culture and boys; sex and boys, it was all there," Singer explained. "That was Boiberik." As I listened to Singer describe her memories of dating culture at camp, I was surprised by one anecdote: that she and her fellow girl campers used to sneak into the bunks of the opposite sex at night with impunity and that the boys would sneak into the girls' bunks too.

Why did the staff of Boiberik, I thought aloud, permit campers to enter the bunks of the opposite sex at night? That seemed to run counter to the idea of the 1950s as a more sexually conservative time than the decades that followed. "My friends and I were not even allowed to do that in the early 2000s!" I explained. Despite the coupling off that occurred among her peer

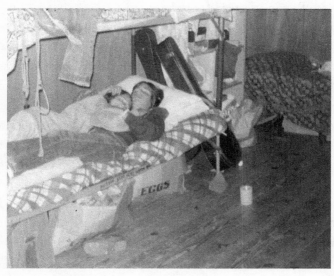

Hemshekh campers cuddling in the bunk, 1977.
Source: Adrian Shrek. Printed with permission.

group, Singer replied, the fifties were a "different time." Unlike teens of future decades, most of her friends waited until marriage to have sexual intercourse. Boiberik allowed "sneak-outs" in the 1950s, she intuited, because staff assumed nothing too "promiscuous" went on once campers reached the bunks of the opposite sex.[17]

As I spoke to other former campers, I noticed that what Singer pointed to was something of a trend: campers of the 1950s experienced fewer rules around dating, and much less supervision overall, than campers of later decades. As the sexual revolution brought camper sexuality to new levels of openness in terms of discourse and as reports of rising rates of teen pregnancy entered the public consciousness through the press, camp leaders worried more and more about what sexual behaviors campers might engage in if left to their own devices for too long or with too much privacy. The camping sector also faced increasing forms of regulation from the states they were in, the insurance they were compelled to purchase, and the rules of the American Camping Association, all of which raised requirements for camper supervision over the course of the 1960s and 1970s. By the time Singer's children attended Boiberik in the 1970s, she noticed that her children did not get the chance to sneak out: the staff had banned it as the changing times on the outside of camp affected life on the inside.[18]

Surprisingly, however, the sexual and romantic behaviors campers took part in were more consistent between the 1950s and the 1970s than adult staff seemed to fear. The dozens of former campers I spoke with from across the decades described their paths and paces with the opposite sex as campers and counselors in strikingly similar ways, often using the long-standing baseball metaphor of the four bases to describe their and their friends' romantic and sexual acts and practices at camp. As if in unison, one after another described how under-the-clothes ("third base" activities) proved uncommon among campers younger than sixteen or seventeen, although rumors of more advanced behaviors occurring at those ages proliferated. Dancing, holding hands, cuddling, kissing, and over-the-clothes petting encapsulated the typical trajectory of their experiences as campers from the ages of ten to sixteen. Former campers who attended as high school juniors and seniors recalled having friends who advanced to more advanced sexual acts, and those who attended in the 1970s were indeed more likely to believe that some of their peers were having intercourse than those of earlier decades. But while some of the campers of the 1950s progressed to touching under the clothes, others of the 1960s and 1970s remained at first base. Their experiences varied less by decade than by their own personalities, statuses within camp social hierarchies, and personal development.

Speaking about crushes and sexual experiences between friends also played a consistent role over the course of the postwar decades. Singer and her friends of the fifties, for example, talked about their crushes and boyfriends in the bunk after lights out, listening with particular focus on the girls "who didn't pay attention" to the youth culture's rules of the four bases. Listening to the "sexy girls" (those who went beyond kissing and light petting), Singer recalled, was like hearing from "celebrities."[19] Campers of the 1960s and 1970s pointed out a similar dynamic, particularly in that time between the end of the day's activity and lights out. While discussing boys bonded some girl campers, however, it also created an atmosphere of pressure and a possibility of feeling left out. "If the girls were giggling and talking about whatever was happening with their boyfriends," one former Hashomer Hatzair camper of the 1960s told me, "and you were not part of that? Then you're just not part of it."[20] As a former camper recalled her time at Tel Yehudah in the 1970s, conversations about "who's hooking up with who" were quite often "socially stressful," leading her to feel less attractive than those who had a hook-up to report to the rest of the cabin.[21]

As they changed and showered in close quarters, the single-sex space of the bunk also became a site for campers to note and compare their developing bodies. Some camps had communal shower houses, which provided little privacy. This arrangement made nudity between kids of the same sex a communal norm in many camps. Whether a function of culture or design, however, being nude around one's fellow campers stirred up both positive and negative feelings, functioning as a kind of bonding ritual at best and making campers feel bad about their development through puberty at worst. A former camper from Camp Kinderland of the 1940s and early 1950s recalled that she felt very bad at age eleven when "all the girls in my bunk," some of whom were a year older, "were much more advanced physically and sexually than I was.... They had breasts.... They had boyfriends."[22] Pressures surrounding looks came up when clothed too. Photographs of female campers of the 1950s wearing curlers, having neat and blow-dried hair, and wearing well-fitted and fashionable outfits indicate that girls spent significant time getting ready each morning. Most female campers who attended in the 1960s and 1970s mentioned that being considered sexy at camp did not have to do with looking particularly "girly," since the hippy styles of Birkenstocks and denim overalls dominated the fashion trends of the period. Still, looking good to the boys and to the other girls remained on campers' minds. "I was overweight. I had facial hair," one TY camper explained. "I just wanted to be accepted and liked."[23]

Former male campers revealed a somewhat similar culture within their bunks. Boys spent a significant amount of time nude together, "hanging naked from the rafters," showering, and changing clothes in the same spaces. At the same time, boys sometimes compared their bodies through "penis measurement contests," and talked about sexual desire and experience frequently. "There was a lot of masturbation humor, you know, circle jerks, that kind of thing," explained one former Ramah camper of the early 1970s. He also recalled boys taking part in what was called a "'cookie jerk,' where everybody masturbates on to a cookie." While he reflected on these memories with a laugh, he remembered "feeling quite uncomfortable" when the subject of masturbation came up in the cabin at the time because he had not yet had his first orgasm.[24]

Boys also spent significant time in the bunk discussing the opposite sex. While he never went further than second base while at camp, Josh of Habonim recalled that there were always "other campers" and CITs rumored to have progressed to third base or full intercourse. Dan, a seventeen-year-old at Habonim's Camp Galil, recalled a similar dynamic among the boys in his group in the late 1970s. "It was a big deal talking about sex and wondering who had and who hadn't," Dan explained. As a "closeted gay kid," he had "no desire to do anything that people were talking about." But like his straight peers, he "kept a tally of who was and who wasn't a virgin." Staying in touch with members of his Habonim cohort into his adulthood, Dan later found out that a lot of his peers "were just blustering." Although he remains sure that some fellow campers advanced to penetrative sex, he now realizes that at least some were just trying to keep up with appearances, pretending to move from base to base at the same imagined pace as other campers their age. The notion that most or even many campers were having full sexual intercourse in camps of the sixties and seventies was speculative at best.[25] Nevertheless, the bogus reality such rumors and blustering created turned sex into the goal for many boys, and any boy believed to have reached that goal became "an object of much envy."[26]

It may come as a surprise that campers of the 1950s through the 1970s had similar experiences. And yet the stability of their sexual progressions matches scholarship correcting popular understandings of the decades before the sexual revolution. Like American teens more broadly, campers of the 1950s took "control of their sexuality" through "dating, going steady, necking, [and] petting."[27] The advent of the birth control pill in 1960 certainly changed options for women, giving them the freedom to explore sex before marriage. But while divisions between "sexual suggestion" and "license," wrote historian Alan Petigny, have allowed historians to depict the sixties "as a morally tumultuous decade" and the 1950s as a conservative one, popular culture actually lagged behind "a sharp, though unacknowledged, surge in illicit sexual behavior."[28] Campers of the 1950 and 1960s behaved similarly; those of the 1950s simply talked about that behavior less frequently and less publicly.

Whereas camper-made documents of the 1950s rarely mentioned a camp's dating cultures, references to campers' romantic and sexual exploits were commonplace in the pages of camp newspapers by the late 1960s.[29] Camp Hemshekh's "Dear Trish" and Camp Shomria's "Dear Avi" columns, for instance, which both appeared in newspapers ran by campers but edited by counselors, portrayed fictional stories of camp love gone awry, poking fun at the idea of camps as places of crushes and awkward romantic encounters;[30] a 1961 Tel Yehudah newspaper, *Kol Yehudah*, published a story on one camper who had "assorted boyfriends and Israelis, sometimes intermixed."[31] Comparable jokes also appeared in "last will and testaments," which campers wrote to honor and celebrate inside jokes between one another. In one such document from TY, for example, a camper named Steve "left his lips to Mike because his are getting worn out."[32] Camp Cejwin's newspaper for CITs specifically highlighted gossip surrounding couples and potential couples among the group in a section called "The Dustpan." Since the group-specific newspaper likely offered more privacy and less counselor interference, the author of "The Dustpan" wrote about campers' relationships and sexual interests with striking candor. "With broom in one hand and dustpan in the other, we begin to sweep," explained the anonymous writer. "Is friendship the only reason behind Barry S. Giving Joyce F. a cute stuffed animal? . . . What's this sudden affinity that Gloria G. has taken to Israeli dancing? Could it be a certain Israeli dancer?" In coded language, the CIT also alluded to one camper's masturbation habits, asking "What happened when Barbie B. rubbed her magic lamp?"[33] By the 1970s, TY campers and counselors even made sexual jokes on the camp's public address system. The first time one former camper overheard an announcement for "Jack Meoff to come to the office," she didn't understand why it brought about such laughter among her fellow campers. As she came to understand the joke, however, she also came to see sexual humor as an inextricable part of the teen camp's internal culture.[34]

### "A Lessening of Tension": Staff Directing Camper Romance

Examples of sexual and romantic humor in Jewish camps of the 1960s and 1970s are infinite and reflect how the sexual revolution entered camps through speech. But while these public documents reveal the leniency of the camp counselors and higher-ups who permitted such writings to go to print, the effects of the sexual revolution also raised leaders' concerns over teen sexuality to some degree. As American psychologists, parents, and teachers expressed dismay at increased public displays of affection between teens and worried greatly over increasing rates of teenage premarital sex, Jewish camp leaders could not help but be influenced to some degree by this growing panic.[35] And yet adults both within and outside camps responded to these shifting norms with both "condemnation and celebration." Some adults wanted to control teenagers' sexual expression, while others supported the youth culture's embrace of sexual liberation.[36]

How camp leaders attempted to shape, direct, supervise, and control camper romance and sexuality in the 1960s and 1970s provides a window into that very ambivalence. While camps separated campers in gendered bunk areas for sleeping and showering, almost all camps prohibited campers from entering the bunks of the opposite sex.[37] In terms of their schedules, however, Jewish campers spent most of their days and nights in coeducational activities, providing ample opportunity for romance or desire to blossom. Staff also cultivated specific moments in the weekly and monthly schedules, such as camper socials, for relationships to begin and thrive. Regularly scheduled camp dances not only gave campers an excuse to pursue their crushes; they also provided staff with a chance to control and supervise those romantic engagements.

Two examples surrounding socials at Camp Boiberik elucidate how these events ordinarily functioned and why camp staff placed them in their schedules in the first place. While staff attempted to direct and supervise dating culture at Camp Boiberik in both the 1950s and the 1970s, they did so for rather different reasons. As one Boiberik staff member bemoaned in the 1950s, the socials that staff planned presented "a serious problem" among the oldest campers, because they made the girls "live only for their late nights," spending hours a day "washing, ironing, and primping," detracting "from their interest in the daily activities." After all that preparation, the girls often found themselves disappointed when the boys sat around on benches, initiating "very little social dancing." As a reaction, girl campers often "left the late-night programs before they were over," complaining that the boys their age did not know how to dance. Seeking romance with older waiters and counselors instead, they also expressed disappointment and frustration when the waiters did not show up and reportedly started "minor riots on the hill after curfew" to share their frustrations with their counselors. When camp leaders tried to fix the problems caused by the late nights with "creative and constructive" activities, however, the eldest boys "deliberately sabotaged any attempts" by the staff, as such programs "would interfere with their efforts to 'make out' with the girls."[38]

As Boiberik's late-night issue shows, striking a balance between permitting and controlling while satisfying campers' curiosities and desires proved challenging for staff members. But what is notable in this example is that the author's issue with the dances was not that girl campers wanted to mix with male staff members or that the girls were absorbed in the desire to date more generally. Rather, the problem had to do with making late-night activities satisfying for all campers, to prevent "riots" or other forms of camper "sabotage." By 1972, however, a different head staff member at Boiberik pointed out the problems of camp dances and late nights in an entirely different light. In a training guide for counselors, the staff member explained that while it "may seem 'cute' for an eight-year-old girl to speak of her 'boyfriend,'" counselors should not encourage it, nor should staff create a situation in which "youngsters imitate their elders by walk[ing] their girls to the line dividing the boys' and girls'" bunk areas and feel subsequent pressure to kiss them goodnight. The sexual revolution may have made talk of sexuality more open at camp, but it also made adult leaders more sensitive to the pressure that socials and other scheduled date-like events could place on campers and how such pressure could "unwittingly create or accentuate coed problems."[39]

Whether to include a period of free time before bed proved a similar source of debate and contention. Between the last activity and lights out, Jewish camp leaders generally permitted older campers to walk themselves back to the bunks, creating a window of opportunity for couples to find privacy somewhere around camp in an unlit and unoccupied room or outdoor area. Former campers recalled that Friday nights emerged as the most popular night of the week for coupling off and seeking out some privacy, as later wake-up times on Saturday meant later bedtimes and dressing up for a formal Sabbath dinner intensified the sense of romantic possibility. The time between the end of the evening activity and curfew, which some Ramah camps called *otzar*, the Hebrew word for treasure, could last anywhere from ten to twenty minutes, enough time for campers to have some kind of sexual interaction. Anything resembling full privacy, however, proved difficult to come by, and the environment's inherent limits assured leaders that time spent in the dark together would remain relatively innocent, typically remaining in the realm of kissing and petting.

In the early 1960s, correspondence between Camp Ramah Wisconsin's head staff regarding their "late nights" or the otzar period demonstrated how complicated balancing romantic and sexual opportunity for campers with supervision and safety could become. In these internal memos following summer 1961, three division directors put forth their ideas of what had constituted acceptable behavior during the "post-evening activity period" according to the needs and maturity levels of his campers.[40] The division director for ten- to twelve-year-old campers, for instance, believed that his staff had kept "boy girl problems ... to an absolute minimum" by "establishing a policy of no *otzar* time after the evening program, and discouraging all physical contact between the boys and girls . . . as it should be at this age."[41] Regarding relationships between twelve- to fourteen-year-olds, however, the leader for Adah Bet expressed more ambivalence. Reducing social pressures "toward pairing off" proved difficult, but the group's staff worked "to help create a more healthy social climate."[42] They attempted to replace "the custom of allowing the boys to walk the girls home after the evening program" with more controlled, supervised events, including "a full program of mixers and entertainment . . . so that even the perpetual wallflowers might enjoy themselves."[43] After taking such measures, however, the group still had "about six or seven more or less steady couples," and some switching of partners occurred. Having a boyfriend or girlfriend remained "a prestige symbol," campers talked about the opposite sex incessantly, and the boys "boasted of great sexual conquest." Nevertheless, the division director was comforted by a belief that little physical contact took place between the boys and girls in that tender age between preadolescence and teendom.[44]

In step with these age-based notions surrounding sexual progression, the division director for Machon, a group of campers ages fifteen and sixteen, advocated for more permissiveness. Understanding that the period before curfew could cause "considerable tension" for campers who were not ready to "accompany or be accompanied back to their bunks by campers of the opposite sex," the leader, Mark Elovitz, ensured that the volleyball and basketball facilities would be open and lit for kids with who had not coupled off to socialize with one another.[45] But rather than limiting the possibilities for campers who had coupled off, staff made it easier for them to find privacy, putting out all of the lights in the area around the girls' cabins, and flickering the lights at the end of otzar as one would to signal the end of a play's intermission, eliminating the issue of their inveterate lateness.

Elovitz's solutions generated some criticism from a staff member who argued that the camp had made a policy "of encouraging intimate and frankly sexual relationships among children who are not prepared for it." But the director defended his decisions, arguing that the camp was not "encouraging anything inherently immoral," had "provided legitimate activity for campers" who did not want to engage with the opposite sex, and had successfully "set bounds on boy-girl relationships in a manner much more effective and more acceptable to campers than has ever been the case." His solutions also yielded what he saw as an important benefit: "a lessening of tension" between campers and staff, since attempts to "limit opportunities for boy-girl relationships" in the past had led to a "severe reaction" that "drain[ed] away energy" from the rest of the camp program. The leader argued, in other words, that giving campers the freedom to explore relationships at night made camp life better, more efficient, and ultimately better able to pursue its goals.[46] While few expressed it quite as concisely as did Elovitz, camp leaders across the spectrum operated under a similar set of assumptions: that sexual experimentation, within "age-appropriate" limits, could be healthy and safe within the camp setting and that permitting that experimentation satisfied campers' desires for autonomy, smoothing intergenerational tensions in the process. Much like camper democracy and other forms of sanctioned freedom, allowing some campers to explore relationships and sexuality improved camp life and made bringing campers into the ideological fold of camps' broader movements easier. An openness toward sexuality reveals the changing norms of midcentury America, and perhaps even the progressive approach of postwar Jews to sexuality more generally. But it also underscores how camp leaders transmuted the desires of campers into means to their own ends.

By the mid-1960s, offering campers the freedom to explore romantic and sexual relationships began to serve one such emergent communal mission: curbing rates of intermarriage, which were on a steady rise. In 1964, a group of Jewish adults gathered in Long Beach, Long Island, for a conference on intermarriage and the future of the American Jew. Among the rabbis, community leaders, and social scientists in attendance that weekend was the National Ramah Commission's director, Bernard Resnikoff, and Graenum Berger, the consultant on community centers and camps for the Federation of Jewish Philanthropies of New York. Gathering to "urge that synagogues and social agencies cooperate to assure 'the creative survival of the Jewish people,'" Berger's speech included an anecdote he heard from a rabbi: "A Jewish girl, away at college, was keeping company with a Gentile boy." Concerned, her parents brought her back from college and immediately arranged for her to work at a Jewish summer camp. Their plan fell apart, however, when the young woman "fell in love and married the waterfront man, who was a Gentile. I am not citing this because of its humor" or its "tragedy," Berger concluded, but "to accent the policy that we have to display as lay people and professionals. How do we counteract these influences to provide survival?"[47] Although lessening tensions between campers and staff remained an important objective, directing and encouraging camper romance took on new purposes as the subject of intermarriage climbed toward the top of Jewish communal agendas.

## When the Continuity Crisis Met Camper Culture

When Jewish organizations embraced coeducational adolescent camping in the 1920s, they did so in part because they saw camps as ideal sites for young people to meet future husbands and wives.[48] At a time in which few early Jews married outside the faith, however, camps of the early twentieth century mainly sought to guide youth toward marrying Jews of their same specific ideological stripe. Camps' usefulness as sites for matchmaking was less based in concerns over interfaith marriage than in the interest in bringing together politically and religiously aligned couples from the same geographic area. In the decades following World War II, the use of camps as sites for Jewish matchmaking shifted under vastly different conditions as demographic studies began to imply that "the once-assumed stability of Jewish endogamy (or in-marriage) was in danger."[49] While in the interwar years, Lila Corwin Berman wrote that Jewish social scientists and communal leaders had frequently focused on how " 'despite Jews' tendency to marry other Jews, they could still integrate into and enrich American life," social scientists and leaders of the early postwar period did not see "the midcentury indicators of increased Jewish exogamy as a sign of Jews' successful integration." Instead, they framed rising rates of intermarriage as cause for "rising alarm," worrying "that these patterns foretold an enfeebled Jewish future."[50] In 1953, Milton Himmelfarb, the editor of the *American Jewish Year Book*, published an article in *Commentary* suggesting that the low American Jewish birthrate threatened the American Jewish future.[51] In 1961, social scientist Erich Rosenthal published an article in the *American Jewish Year Book* revealing data comparing the relatively low birthrate of Jews with those of Protestants and Catholics. In 1963, he published yet another article reporting statistics indicating that the intermarriage rate had doubled from just six or seven years before, with a rate in Washington, DC, at "13.1 percent," and in Iowa, an estimated "rate of 42.2 percent." When compared with numbers from the 1920s and 1930s, which put the rate of Jewish intermarriage about 1 or 2 percent, "these numbers appeared striking."[32] Comparing numbers from 1920s' New York with 1960s' Iowa, as Berman pointed out, had methodological flaws, considering that New York's Jewish population density made marrying fellow Jews easier. Nevertheless, Rosenthal concluded with alarm that the numbers "cast doubt on the doctrine of the persistence of religious endogamy in American life."[33]

This doubt swiftly entered Jewish public discourse. In April 1964, sociologist Marshall Sklare warned in *Commentary* that intermarriage was becoming "a matter more crucial to Jewish survival than any other."[34] Just one month later, an article entitled "The Vanishing American Jew" appeared in *Look* magazine, explaining to a broad American readership how "young Jewish men and women are threatening the future of Judaism with their ever-increasing tendency to marry and raise their children outside the faith. And slowly, imperceptibly, the American Jew is vanishing."[35] That same year, the *American Jewish Year Book* announced that intermarriage had become "the major preoccupation of American Jewry."[36] This preoccupation began to penetrate American Jewish education as communal leaders saw the use in trying to guide the future marriage choices of young Jews from childhood onward.[37] Camps' long-standing recognition as sites for the blossoming of young Jewish romance readied them to be at the leading edge of this anti-intermarriage education, as leaders harnessed their camps' romantic cultures toward new, more urgent aims. "The Jewish teenager represents the Jewish community's future," explained social worker Solomon H. Green to a conference of camp directors in 1969. Citing a study of New Orleans teenagers, 40 percent of whom "were involved in interfaith dating" by the twelfth grade, Mogilner believed that statistics were "illustrative of the need camps can meet for the Jewish community to help engage teens in a dialogue about their own happiness and their relatedness to the Jewish community being expressed concretely, not only feelingly." "Our task," he concluded, is to help Jewish teenagers "move easily from identifying as a Jew to a commitment of living as a Jew," including in the realm of dating and marriage.[38]

As leaders identified the potential in camps to shape values surrounding dating and marriage, campers' preexisting dating and sexual behaviors became enmeshed with this urgent sense of purpose. In some camps, this focus on limiting intermarriage was far from subtle: speeches and guided discussions about the perceived problems and dangers of marrying out, both to the individual and to the Jewish community, appeared as a blatant expression of intermarriage anxiety within camps' educational programs. At Reform camp GUCI, educators led conversations with campers, asking, "What makes this ceremony distinctly Jewish?" and "How does Judaism view marriage?" to educate campers about the value of marrying within the faith. In a simulation activity in 1972, moreover, a group of GUCI participants were instructed to write up a platform on the issue of intermarriage. Working with staff to construct it, the group proclaimed in their platform that marrying a non-Jew went against the tenets of Reform Judaism.[59] At Reform camp Swig, programs for CITs included lectures and conversations on, for example, "The Jewish Attitude to Sex and Marriage" and "The Jewish Attitude to Birth Control." At a Bnai Brith camp, staff gave campers a study guide that included a reading titled "A Jewish View of Love and Marriage" alongside "Ritual in Jewish Life" and "Judaism and Ethics."[60] At Ramah, a camper's essay on how "dating out of our faith" as "one of the biggest problems" in the Jewish community reveals the degree to which campers could internalize these messages. "The communities in which most of us live now usually consists of people with different religions," wrote the camper. While socializing with a diverse group of friends had potentially positive benefits, the camper understood that friendships between teenagers of different religious backgrounds "could very well lead to dating and even to marriage."[61]

Messaging surrounding Jewish marriage was also pervasive in the more implicit or "hidden curriculum" of camp culture.[62] A male camp director and his wife, for instance, provided a Jewish family structure for the entire camp to observe and internalize. Typically, the husband—a director, Israeli *shaliach*, a rabbi—played a patriarchal role as teacher, adviser, and rule maker. Wives generally worked in gendered roles as social workers, parent liaisons, and arbiters of bunk cleanliness. Marriages need not be official, moreover, to make an impact on campers. Camps across the ideological spectrum held fake Jewish wedding ceremonies, with campers or counselors in full costume under the *huppah* (a Jewish wedding canopy). Such activities hearkened back to Catskill traditions of fake wedding ceremonies as fodder for creating celebratory parties set to klezmer music. But at camp, simulated weddings also functioned as forms of experiential education that taught marriage rituals and asked campers to consider "the importance of each part of the ceremony" as they watched and participated.[63] Campers pretended to be brides and grooms at camp carnivals and festivals too, where "marriage booths" allowed them to "marry" friends or summer flings. As Josh recalled, his Habonim camp's Sadie Hawkins Day merged romance, play, and the performance of a "wedding" together: as the boys went off to "try and hide," the girls would search for them and "bring them back to get married," the marriage ceremony being the ultimate "culmination of the day."[64] Mixed with camps' sexual and romantic allowances, these make-believe weddings played a role in promoting Jewish marriages. Receiving photocopied "marriage certificates" and rings made of strings or fuzzy pipe cleaners, this common activity implied that a camper's crush, camp boyfriend, or camp girlfriend could be more than just that with time, an official recognition of camps' roles in bringing couples together.

Simulated marriage ceremony at Camp Cejwin, 1976.
Source: Jeffrey Young. Printed with permission.

Although the 1960s would prove to be the tip of the iceberg, the intermarriage anxiety that began to permeate the Jewish community expanded
the purpose and legitimacy of leaders' encouragement of camper romance,
allowing these implicit and explicit messages to become fused with camps'
preexisting atmospheres of romantic and sexual experimentation. Still, a
movement's ideologies, the social and class milieu of a camp's clientele, and
their geographic locations influenced the way different camps broached the
issue of marriage and to what degree. Ramah and UAHC leaders, for instance, conveyed their values surrounding marriage in more direct and urgent
ways than did Zionist or Yiddishist camps, reflecting how their movements
grappled with the issue. Ramah's postwar staff focused more on directing
camps' romantic cultures toward relationships that could lead to marriage
and remarked on camps' usefulness in guiding the future marriage choices
of youth, both campers and counselors. Reform leaders addressed the issue
of intermarriage much more overtly through direct conversation and education. The Reform movement would not accept interfaith marriage until
decades later, but its more common occurrence within Reform communities
of the 1960s gave the issue greater immediacy earlier than in other camps.

At Yiddish camps, interfaith marriage factored into the messaging much
less. One former Camp Hemshekh camper joked in our interview that intermarriage at Hemshekh meant "marrying outside the Bund": the camp's
focus on fostering a continuation of Yiddishism and Bundism took precedent over more mainstream American Jewish goals.[65] Since many of the
campers were first-generation Americans from the New York City area,
whose parents' involvement in the Bund, Yiddish cultural institutions, or
groups of Holocaust survivors shaped their children's worldviews and their
social circles, intermarriage was less of an issue for children and teenagers
than it might have been for campers from other movements and other places
in the country. Still, romantic relationships at Hemshekh did intersect with
the camp's ideologies: like Jewish camps earlier in the century, encouraging
marriages within the relatively small community of Yiddishists had important implications for the future of the language and its culture. While
the camp's leaders never quite put it as such, Hemshekh's leniency toward
boy-girl relationships—reflected in camper newspapers and oral histories—
likely stemmed from both an interest in making camp feel free and a desire

to build a sustainable future for the Yiddish language through relationships, marriage, and eventually, the raising of Yiddish-speaking children.

## American Zionist Camping and the Promise of Erotic Zionism

Although not yet a central issue within their movements, Zionist leaders were not exempt from the intermarriage anxiety that had just begun to shape mainstream American Jewish youth work in the 1960s and 1970s. Young Judaea, the most centrist and religiously pluralistic of the Zionist youth movements, tended to be more involved in broader American Jewish communal affairs than the young leaders of the socialist Zionist youth movements, and there are signs that concerns over endogamy influenced Young Judaea's educators early on. By the 1990s, Young Judaea would come to take part in studies that used high in-marriage rates to prove Jewish camps' educational success, revealing that an interest in curbing intermarriage had become one of the organization's goals with youth.[66]

A whole set of other ideas, however, shaped the sexual cultures of Zionist movement camps in unique ways. While intermarriage anxiety likely lurked in the background, looking toward Israel took precedent over other American Jewish issues. Zionist camps, such as those of Habonim and Hashomer Hatzair, fashioned themselves as simulations of pioneer life, modeling their programs to match their understandings of how young *halutzim*, *kibbutzniks*, and Israelis lived, worked, spoke, and governed. A similar dynamic emerged surrounding dating and sexuality, as elements of Zionist history and contemporary Israeli culture comingled with the youth culture inside camps to produce unique sexual mores and gender norms.

Zionism's history regarding gender and sexuality was far from straightforward, and yet what American campers and counselors understood about Zionist and Israeli culture was more impressionistic than factual. Since Habonim and Hashomer Hatzair identified with labor or socialist Zionism and Young Judaea also drew on imagery of the kibbutz, they all rather similarly idealized the lifestyles of the Jews of the Yishuv and Israel as "New Jews" whose masculinity, experiences as soldiers, and connections to the land opposed visions of neurotic and weak Jews of the diaspora. They also believed that moving to Israel, where they could become New Jews them-

Boys' bunk at Camp Tel Yehudah, 1974.
Source: Judy Schwartz Rodenstein. Printed with permission.

selves, stood as the ultimate fulfillment of their movements' values.[67] For the young men of Zionist movements, this meant embracing a new form of Jewish masculinity within their camp's imitations of life in Israel; for women, it meant believing that Zionism was a radically egalitarian movement that had aimed for "full equality between the sexes" decades before second-wave feminism.[68] For both genders, Zionism's history also related to questions of sexual repression and liberation.[69] Such ideas took a particularly blatant form in Hashomer Hatzair's history, which, in its early European years, fused "small-town reactionary and conservative attitudes" toward the cosmopolitan sexuality of Vienna with "an advanced, sophisticated urban stance" shaped by psychoanalysis. When they arrived to the Yishuv, many Hashomer Hatzair members left behind repressive ideas in favor of a more sex-affirmative stance, connecting nineteenth-century notions of sexual vitality with Freudian ideas surrounding libido. But this new stance did not transform into "free love." Instead, movement members sought to redirect their sexual desires for the sake of building community. One early leader,

Meir Yaari, promoted a belief that halutzim should not repress but rather sublimate their libidos to make work "an erotically charged act" and to build erotically charged communities.[70]

The most enduring image of this trend in Zionist history is the Bitania experiment of 1920, a commune in Palestine consisting of twenty male and four female Hashomer Hatzair members from Poland. With Yaari as its leader, the Bitania group "devoted their nights to rituals intended to help them achieve catharsis," writes Ofer Nordheimer Nur, public confessionals in which Bitania members were required "to reveal their innermost secrets to one another."[71] These practices resembled the sicha, which, as other chapters have shown, became a mainstay of Zionist movement work and camping in the diaspora. But Yaari's methods made the confessionals different and more manipulative. When several members experienced trauma from the practice, the group came to understand Yaari's practices as abusive, exiling him from Bitania. After only eight months, the commune dissolved. This short-lived experiment, however, came to hold a particularly prominent place in the Zionist imagination, giving "birth to a powerful myth among Jewish youth in Palestine and in Eastern and Western Europe."[72]

How exactly the idea of Zionism as a utopian movement in pursuit of erotic liberation arrived in the American branches of its movements is unclear. It is likely that both Israeli shlichim and American members who traveled to Israel brought such stories and notions back to their American branches, as they did other elements of culture in the Yishuv and Israel. The former Hashomer Hatzair campers I spoke with recalled learning about Yaari and the movement's Freudian roots in educational activities about the movement's history, and this background helped them make independent connections between their own sexual and gendered experiences at camp with Hashomer Hatzair's history.[73] An openness to speaking about sexuality at camp, for example, stood out to them as particularly radical for the time, as did the fact that older counselors and Israeli shlichim "provided us with very good education about safety and, you know, healthy sexuality in terms of birth control, in terms of avoiding abuse and stuff like that." They also understood that their camps' radical approaches to coeducation related to the movement's past. Not only did the eldest campers of both sexes sleep and change clothes in the same room or tent; many former campers noted that sleeping in beds with campers of the opposite sex was considered normal, acceptable behavior. The intimacy of their living arrangements did not lead to sexualizing the opposite sex: instead, it yielded quite the opposite, fostering what one former camper named Efrat called a "sibling dynamic." The staff encouraged campers not to "see each other only as sexual beings," but to be able to have friends of the opposite sex and "to have a group identity regardless of gender."[74] While different from the Bitania experiment, this approach to the opposite sex recalls some of the tensions between sublimation and sexual repression that Hashomer Hatzair members toggled between earlier in the century and the notion that the "new youth" of Zionism "should not be afraid of the body, not even the naked body."[75]

Although the New Jew ideal centered itself on men and masculinity, socialist Zionists in Palestine also aimed to create a "new sexual ethic" that "opposed bourgeois marriage and affirmed a healthy sexuality."[76] The rejection of bourgeois marriage was not quite relevant to preteens and teens, but campers found a more age-appropriate target to reject as a distraction to their goals. "We were very serious, and any sort of relationship was supposed to be one of integrity . . . we weren't supposed to just screw around," Efrat continued. Short-term, "unserious" relationships were frowned on. But "the atmosphere and the mores of the youth movement" could be contradictory and confusing for campers. "I remember that there were young women who were sexually active or who were planning to be, and it wasn't suppressed. We weren't told that it was a bad thing," Efrat explained. Yet the Marxist and psychoanalytic elements of the movement's history created a sense of rigidity that she believed affected her ability to connect romantically with men even in her twenties and early thirties.[77] In this way, Hashomer Hatzair's American camps mirrored the movement's broader trajectory, in which principles of " 'free love and 'puritanism,' " explains David Biale, often "coexisted in a peculiar dialectic."[78]

Habonim and Young Judaea members could not draw a direct line of ideological lineage to movement leaders of the past as easily as Hashomer Hatzair's could. Still, broader understandings of Zionism's approach to gender and sexuality similarly influenced the internal cultures of their camps, emerging more from impressions of 1960s' Israel than Zionism's early twentieth-century history. Indeed, former campers from both movements recalled internalizing the idea that the kibbutz movement held exciting sexual promise for youth, as well as an impression that Israelis had less prudish attitudes surrounding sex and sexuality than Americans at the time. As in other aspects of daily life, campers and staff wanted their camp life to reflect this assumed Israeli approach, which engendered a lenient approach to dating and sexuality from the top down and a sense of experimentation and freedom from the bottom up. "I think it's also a spillover from Israel," explained a former Habonim camper named Katherine. Israelis "were much more sexually open and they don't have the Victorian past that we have in America, like being Americans were particularly sexually hung up and Israelis were not. They were much more natural, especially kibbutzniks." The idea of Israeli youth as more sexually free influenced campers' behaviors as well as the handling of those behaviors by counselors and leaders. Katherine also noted that many campers and counselors started smoking at camp to embrace "Israeliness," since they associated smoking with their "cool" Israeli counselors.[79]

An anecdote from another Habonim camper, Dan, further illuminated this dynamic. In the 1970s, he and his fellow seventeen-year-old leadership program campers voted to buy condoms with their collective fund. Given the camp's commitment to self-government, the counselors agreed to the decision and even saw the condoms as a sign of the campers' sense of responsibility. When the condoms arrived, the campers placed them in a public place, a popular spot for couples they dubbed "*Cheder* F**k" ("F**k Room").[80] Such a story cannot and should not be removed from the context of the American sexual revolution, which undoubtedly influenced Zionist camper culture and the ideas young staff members had regarding what was appropriate or inappropriate sexual behavior. In the cases of Ramah and Boiberik, however, staff members of the sixties and seventies became more concerned about the possibility of intercourse than those of the past, not less. While based largely on impressionistic stereotypes of Israeli culture, ideas surrounding sexual norms in Israel and in the longer history of Zionist youth mixed with the American sexual revolution to shape the behaviors and values of campers and counselors within Zionist movements in unique ways.

While Zionism "had sought a radical break with the Jewish past," Zionist movements "often ended up returning unwittingly to traditional patterns" in regard to gender.[81] Women of the kibbutzim, for instance, experienced a kind of "conditional equality" but were often relegated to housework and "expected to embrace the male ethos and compete with men" on men's terms.[82] The dream of labor Zionist communities as egalitarian societies, however, influenced Zionist camps all the same. Many former female campers described having formative experiences as leaders in the camp and in the movement, being surrounded by "strong women" and being deeply "serious" about carrying out their movement's missions.[83] At the same time, Zionism's perceived progressivism regarding gender roles often blinded camp leaders to problematic dynamics and inequalities within their movements. When Judith was a teen at Hashomer Hatzair's Camp Moshava in the mid-1960s, for instance, the head of her local chapter brought all the boys and girls in her group together to give them "a talk in one of the cabins." " 'So, girls,' " Judith remembered him saying, " 'I just want to let you know that the reason you're here is to service the boys now.' " When I asked her to expound on what she thinks he meant by that, Judith said, "Well, to kiss them, to take care of any looming adolescent needs, so that they wouldn't stray—out of the movement, perhaps." This message, which stuck with her a full six decades later, undermined the feeling that her devotion to and leadership in the movement mattered. She also recalled tensions between the girls and the boys over perceived differences between the sexes, with boys arguing that they were better "logical" leaders and that girls were too "emotional." This idea was reinforced as campers learned about male leaders of the Zionist movement and observed the gendered roles of their staff members. The shaliach, Judith explained, "was always the 'husband,' " and only he led educational conversations, guiding the messages campers received. His wife was almost always relegated to the role of nurse or dancing teacher. "It wasn't until I was in college, and I actually took a logic class and aced it" that she realized how harmful this idea of women as irrational and illogical had been to her sense of self. " 'We have logic too,' " she realized after her years at camp. "It's just that we come from the heart."[84]

Gender issues also extended into romantic dynamics between female

campers and male staff members. Because of the smaller age differences between staff and campers, Zionist camps seemed to have more instances of
camper-staff relationships. "There were all these seventeen-, eighteen-year-
old male counselors who were involved with the thirteen, fourteen-year-old
girls," former Habonim camper Naomi recalled, with few efforts made to
keep such relationships a secret within camp.[85] Campers from across the
ideological spectrum described having crushes on counselors in interviews,
as did anonymous campers in camp newspapers from the time. As role
models, counselor sexuality contributed to an environment of sexual possibility and pressure. Zionist camps were not alone in facing the problem of
camper-staff relationships. But such relationships, rumored and actualized,
blurred the boundaries between age-based groups at camp even further, and
made room for potential abuse.

The theoretical openness of Zionist camps' sexual cultures did not make
it easier for campers to come out of the closet. Of the four former campers
I spoke with who identified as gay and lesbian as adults, none were out of
the closet during their years at camp, and they did not know anyone who
was. Despite the postwar camp environment's compulsory heterosexuality,
they reported having formative experiences at camp as they discovered their
sexualities through crushes and intimate friendships. One former Habonim
camper explained,

> What happened was these incredibly intense friendships between the
> girls. Including what it was in hindsight, very obviously, my first crush,
> my first relationship, even though there are things we just never even
> thought about. . . . the girls could walk around with their arms around
> each other, you know, just like boyfriend girlfriend kind of thing. . . . I
> could take long walks with this woman who we will call Sally and [we]
> were holding hands and we shared a bed, totally dressed and hugged.
> And that was it, there was nothing—we didn't think of it as sexual.
> There were lots of these relationships.

The overall intimacy of the camper culture in which girls cuddled and held
hands with other girls provided space to have such "intense friendships."[86]
Nevertheless, that intimacy did not make it easier for the two gay and lesbian

former Habonim campers I spoke with to come out as campers or as counselors. In fact, one alumna believed that these dynamics delayed her discovering her own sexuality. Two other gay former campers I spoke with, one from Boiberik and the other from Ramah, recalled similar experiences, but the case of the two Habonim campers was more striking due to the movement's open, intimate, and liberated character. While the situation for LGBTQ+ campers has improved dramatically in more recent decades, the sexual openness and freedom of the postwar Zionist summer camp was not open and free for all.

————

For postwar Jewish youth, crushes, love, and sexual experimentation became core parts of camp life. In many ways, their evolving norms and behaviors within camps mirrored the youth culture outside them. Although sexual behaviors remained largely similar from the 1950s through the 1970s, the sexual revolution made camps more open in terms of discourse and humor. But what set Jewish camps apart from broader American camps was the mix of motivations that camp leaders had for allowing and encouraging dating and sexual experimentation. Adults did little to stop campers from seeking out sexual and romantic experiences, knowing that any attempt to do so would take their energies away from fostering camper buy-in. Instead, they attempted to shape their camp's dating cultures to better fit their camps' ideological goals, promoting in-marriage and infusing camp life with ideas of erotic Zionism. Romance became central to life in the Jewish summer camp not merely because youth desired and pursued sexual and romantic experience, but because camp leaders saw ways to merge campers' interests with their own practical, communal, and ideological goals.

As I listened to former campers recall their camp memories, it became clear that the freedom to explore one's sexuality amounted to a largely positive experience. Feeling free in the summertime allowed campers to forge close friendships with peers of both sexes and prepared them with sexual experiences and educations they took with them into college or their movement's gap-year programs in Israel. And yet former campers also understood their camps as places where age-based boundaries blurred; where they could feel awkward, undesirable, and ostracized for not being part of the dating scene; where women were promised equality but were not treated equally; and where gay and lesbian campers felt their acceptance was conditioned on their silence. It has taken decades for the downsides of Jewish camps' sexual cultures to begin to be considered, but both the pros and the cons of camps' romantic environments made their mark on Jewish camping for the long haul. As rates of intermarriage continued to rise and as camps evolved to meet the needs, anxieties, and beliefs of new generations of American Jews, many of these issues continued to shape camps in the 1970s and beyond, the subject of the next, and final, chapter.

# Jewish Camping Post-Postwar

IN THE IMMEDIATE POSTWAR DECADES, Zionist, Yiddishist, Conservative, and Reform movements made very similar cases to American Jewry: that camping not only had the power to produce healthy young Jews in body and spirit, but to transform them, ensuring the next generation would carry Jewishness into the future. As the revolutions of the 1960s wound down, these camps faced new challenges, causing many to close. Even those that remained open, however, came to reflect several evolutions in American Jewish life. No longer new to suburbia, Jews of the 1970s and 1980s found themselves more comfortable and assimilated into middle-class life than in the early years of the postwar period, and never before "so secure, successful, and integrated." They expressed pride in their Jewishness more publicly, thanks to the identity politics and multiculturalist messages of the period, and due to rising Zionist feeling following Israel's victory in the Six-Day War. This comfort expressed itself through more inward-looking causes, as many Jewish organizations set their focus on Soviet Jewry, growing concerns over intermarriage, and Israel. But while the organized Jewish community represented a certain subset of Jews who identified strongly with their Jewish identities, the comfort and acceptance Jews faced in American society led many others to feel that their Jewishness was "a matter of minor significance, a mere fact of parentage, perhaps a curiosity, but devoid of personal meaning and making no difference in how they led their lives."[1] For communal leaders, perceptions of ever-rising assimilation, and rising rates of intermarriage they saw as mirrors of it, became consuming causes. By the 1990s, sociological and demographic research typically painted the present and future of American Jewish life as bleaker than ever before. "At a time when there are few tangible penalties attached to Jewish identification," wrote Sylvia Barack Fishman, disturbingly small proportions of the American Jewish community are choosing to demonstrate their Jewish ties."[2] American Judaism had come to represent what Jack Wertheimer called a "bipolar model," with "a large population of Jews moving toward religious minimalism and a minority gravitating toward greater participation and deepened concern with religion."[3]

With this new moment in American Jewish history came a new paradigm of Jewish camping. In stark contrast to the crucial decade of Jewish camping, when many camps were founded, however, this era began with a series of conclusions. Cejwin, Massad, Boiberik, and Hemshekh all closed in the late 1970s and early 1980s as struggles with recruitment, the lingering effects of the 1973–1975 recession, a declining Jewish birthrate, higher operating and insurance costs, and greater competition from travel programs and other camps plagued the sector. Many camp leaders of the time, however, believed that financial and demographic forces were only partly to blame for these closures. As American Jewry evolved culturally, socioeconomically, and religiously, the leaders of Massad, Boiberik, Cejwin, and Hemshekh recognized that the specific ideologies their programs promoted had entered a moment of decreasing relevance. The stringent Hebraism of Massad, the passionate Yiddishism of Boiberik and Hemshekh, and the Jewish pluralism modeled by Cejwin all crumbled in a time of denominationalism, the decline of the Hebrew movement in America, and severe Yiddish cultural, institutional, and linguistic decline.[4] That most Jewish educational camps outlasted the financial difficulties of the 1970s demonstrated certain logistical advantages, like strong parent organizations whose funds helped them weather the storm. Denominational camps, which recruited campers and raised money from congregation members and received funds from their broader movements, had financial stability that these other camps lacked; most communal camps, sponsored by local Jewish Federations and the Jewish Welfare Board, also managed to survive. But their survival also revealed their willingness and capacity to adapt to a changing cultural milieu. Yiddish-cultural and left-wing camps Kinderland and Kinder Ring, for instance, survived the 1970s bust not only because of their ties to the still-existing Worker's Circle or Arbeter Ring, but because they had begun the process of decreasing their emphasis on Yiddish decades before.

As many of these original camps began to close, however, the reputation of immersive, educational, and ideological Jewish camping as an entirety and as a concept rose dramatically. In the postwar decades, Jewish educational camping was the purview of a few thousand campers each summer. In the 1970s and 1980s, however, a much larger assortment of Jewish camps intensified their Jewish and Zionist educational commitments, utilizing Ramah, Reform camps, and Zionist camps as models. As Jewish continuity became an ever more ingrained goal in communal life, camps garnered more investment and attention from communal leaders, philanthropists, and educators. Concerns over assimilation drove Jewish demographic and educational research to gain significant steam in the 1980s, 1990s, and 2000s. Under these conditions, camping became a frequent subject of inquiry for sociologists and educational researchers, who reached the near-unanimous conclusion that Jewish camps "work," leading kids to identify with Jewishness for the long haul and making impacts on their future marriage choices. The growing consensus over the power of camp that this research engendered became a recurring topic in the Jewish press and brought about a new era of advocacy, funding, and professionalization for and within the Jewish camping sector. In the postwar era, the promise of the educational Jewish summer camp became clear to Jews motivated by certain nationalist, linguistic, and religious ideologies. By the 1990s, the case for intensive Jewish education within camps had been made to a much wider audience of camping and communal leaders, as well as parents and other Jews who shared their concerns.

A single chapter cannot do justice to the complex dynamics of the past five decades. As more time passes, the history of camping and Jewish youth in the post-postwar era will undeniably deserve a book of its own. In pointing to some of the issues, themes, and trends of the more recent past, however, this chapter focuses on the issues that place the formative decades of

Jewish camping into bold relief. Considering American Jewish camping's evolution as an educational model and a cultural object, this chapter contemplates what Jewish camping's more recent developments tell us about its more distant past and what its past tells us about its present. Using four thematic lenses—Jewish education and the continuity crisis, gender and sexuality, the expansion of Orthodox camping, and the evolution of American Zionism—the following sections chart how Jewish camping has continued to adapt to communal anxieties, politics, and religious developments.

## Jewish Education and the Continuity Crisis

In the late 1960s, Jewish education entered a contradictory moment. On the one hand, the number of Jewish children receiving education was on the decline, with fewer Jewish children attending supplementary Hebrew schools that had not only reduced the number of hours they met per week but allegedly declined in rigor. As they bemoaned these falloffs, Jewish educators and communal leaders sought to understand what had gone wrong and how to move in a better direction. On the other hand, this crisis mentality began to drive up the amount of communal funds spent on Jewish education. A certain subset of committed Jewish families, moreover, sent their children to full-day Jewish schools in larger numbers than ever before.[5] For one group of Jews, American Jewish education had never been so paltry in quality and quantity, while for another, it was more intense and absorbing than ever.

Jewish camping's changing status reflected this paradoxical state. Many Jewish educational camps struggled to recruit families in the 1970s and 1980s and to secure the kinds of funds that would help them weather the impacts of the 1970s' recession. And yet the educational potential of Jewish camping emerged more and more salient as attitudes toward afternoon Hebrew schools reached new lows. The mid-1960s began a new era of investment in educational camping, which dovetailed with a rise in educational and demographic studies centered on camping. In his 1966 study of sixty-one Jewish summer camps, Daniel Isaacman explained how "Jewish educators have been considering every medium of education which may further the efforts of the American Jewish community to imbue youth with creative Jewish values."

Under these circumstances, the Jewish summer camp, "whose potentialities as an important instrument for Jewish education have long been recognized," Isaacman wrote, was "now receiving increasing attention." Assessing the results of a questionnaire he created under the auspices of the American Association for Jewish Education directed toward camping leaders, Isaacman concluded that when "properly organized, financed, programmed, and staffed," camps "can advance Jewish educational aims." But he was disappointed to find that few Jewish camps of the period prioritized Jewish education: while "Cejwin, Ramah, Massad, and some of the Zionist camps" filled both an "educational and emotional void between June and September," the over one hundred communal and private camps that peppered the United States had not yet embraced their methods.[6] "The vast majority of American Jewish campers," concluded Isaacman, attended camps "where there is little, if any, stress on Jewish living."[7]

Leaders of the Jewish Welfare Board (JWB), which sponsored communal camps across the country, responded defensively to Isaacman's study, describing his questionnaire as poorly worded and disorganized. Indeed, several camps the JWB sponsored steadily increased their Jewish content over the course of the postwar decades, guided by the visions of a handful of uniquely qualified and passionate directors. But they agreed with Isaacman that summer camps were "the most natural and most effective way" to teach children how to be Jewish and acknowledged that the full potential of their camps on a national scale had not yet been realized. One leader in the Jewish Community Center movement, Arthur Brodkin, had raised similar ideas one year prior to the study, noting that "the expansion of the denominational camps has excited the interest of a number of communities" and predicting that in the coming years, "much more critical looks are going to be taken at resident camp programs and what they are contributing," with more "importance attached to educational camping than does exist at the present time."[8] Miriam Ephraim, an influential leader within the JCC movement, came to a similar conclusion in 1966, arguing that "the time had come for Jewish educational sponsored camps and Jewish communal camp leadership to sit down together to pool their experiences."[9]

In the years following Isaacman's study, Ephraim's idea came to fruition: Jewish camping leaders across the spectrum increasingly came together for conferences, sharing their program ideas and educational methods, while the JWB began to issue its own internal recommendations and program manuals for their camps, urging more engagement with Israel, Tisha B'Av, and Hebrew. Jewish communal camps did not change overnight, and the degree to which a camp emphasized Jewish education continued to vary from camp to camp, region to region, and director to director. But as Edward Robbins, director of a communal camp in Missouri, Camp Sabra, put it in 1972, Jewish communal camps, as well as those that see "themselves as social work or character development-oriented camps," had come "a long way" from where they were ten years earlier in regard to Jewish education.[10] Similar trends in the expansion of Jewish education took place in the Jewish Federation as well, a powerful nationwide organization that increased spending on Jewish education from $7 million to $20 million between 1966 and 1974.[11] The steady expansion of Jewish educational camping mirrors trends in American education more broadly too, as teachers and educators of all kinds became increasingly interested in informal and affective forms of education.[12]

As the financial recession of the 1970s, the "aging out of camp" by baby boomers, increasing operational and insurance costs, and growing competition from travel programs challenged American camping writ large, many Jewish leaders also saw an economic rationale behind making camps more educational. As many as "twenty-five hundred camps nationwide, or about one in five" American camps went out of business from the 1970s through the 1990s.[13] As Christian camping scholar Jacob Sorensen explains, this dire period in camping history proved one of "consolidation" as support for camps waned among Christian groups.[14] The Jewish camping sector faced similar difficulties. As camp advocate and educator Asher Meltzer explained in the 1980s, "some of our oldest, better-known [Jewish] camps have closed down and others show drops in enrollment," while even camps "in large urban areas seem to be having difficulties filling beds and places."[15]

Jewish camping leaders did not see their problems as merely about numbers. There were enough Jewish children "to fill each one of our places and camper beds." What truly held camps back, according to Meltzer, was the "poor quality" of their programs and facilities, caused by years of limited funds. Jewish educators had not successfully convinced enough parents, or the leaders of major Jewish organizations, "that camping is a vital service, a priority service, an effective service, a necessary service," that with the right amount of fundraising "can aid in the continuity and the strengthening of the Jewish community." Jerry Shapiro, director of Camp Young Judaea in California, concurred and argued that camp professionals should work "as lobbyists on behalf of camping," presenting "to the organized community" the data that showed the value of camp for bringing children into "contact with Judaism."[16] If they could better convey the power of camp to the powers that be, camp leaders believed, the problem of empty beds would disappear.

Jewish educators and camp directors had already entered a period of convincing starting in the 1970s, aiming to save declining Jewish camps by arguing for their crucial role in deterring intermarriage and assimilation. But the stakes of camping only seemed to get higher and higher in their minds as rates of intermarriage rose. While worries over youth and intermarriage began in the mid-1960s, the 1970 National Jewish Population Survey proved a turning point in the history of this particular communal panic: although only 9.5 percent of married American Jews at the time had non-Jewish spouses, the survey reported that the "proportion of Jewish persons intermarrying in the period 1966–72 is much greater than corresponding proportions in earlier periods," as "31.7% of Jewish persons marrying in this recent time span chose a non-Jewish spouse."[17] In the aftermath of the survey, youth-serving Jewish organizations of all kinds came to put markedly more emphasis on their role in stopping the trend. In the camping world, the Jewish continuity crisis spurred more Jewish camps to embrace the kinds of identity-building, experiential educational programs that had been commonplace in Zionist and denominational camps for decades and to harness communal concerns over intermarriage to argue for more financial support from American Jewish organizations.

An emphasis on continuity expanded in the 1980s and 1990s, especially in the wake of the 1990 National Jewish Population Surveys sponsored by the Jewish Federations of North America (no survey took place in 1980). In 1982, the Jewish Welfare Board, the federation's Jewish Education Service of North America (JESNA), and a new organization centered on Jewish education, the Mandel Foundation, established the Commission on Jewish Education of North America (CJENA), which issued a landmark report in 1984 "urging a dramatic shift in the mission" of Jewish Community Centers "in ways that would signal enhanced attention to Jewish education, culture, identity, and continuity."[18] Several other philanthropic foundations also made Jewish continuity their focus in the eighties. Mirroring "a more general malaise within the Jewish community about the effects of rapid integration on Jewish ethnic and religious survival,"[19] writes Jonathan Krasner, CJENA's 1990 report, "A Time to Act," argued that the

> fervently Orthodox community aside, North American Jewry, basking in an unprecedented level of social acceptance, was facing a continuity crisis as it struggled to come to terms with high rates of assimilation and interfaith marriage. Long-term survival could only be ensured through a strong, versatile, and adequately resourced education system, sustained through a professionalized force of teachers and administrators, and driven by research-informed policy and program development.[20]

While "A Time to Act" had an important impact, however, the release of the 1990 National Jewish Population Survey, which found that "fifty-two percent of all Jews married since 1985 had entered unions with non-Jews," doubling the intermarriage figures of the 1980 survey, was what historian Jonathan Krasner has called American Jewry's "Sputnik moment."[21] Demographers interpreted the survey to mean that American Jewry essentially existed in two subcommunities, "one that related to Judaism as a central force in Jews' lives, and another that considered Jewishness to be peripheral." The survey also reported a major decline in the percentage of Jewish children receiving a formal Jewish education since 1970. Combined with the fact that "seventy-two percent of children in intermarried families continued to be raised with no religion or a religion other than Judaism, hopes for a robust American Jewish future seemed, at best, imperiled."[22]

Jewish communal leaders increasingly saw Jewish education as their best way to stem the tide of intermarriage and assimilation, a perception that shaped not only Jewish educational and denominational camps but communal camps too. In contrast to Isaacman's 1965 study, for instance, which reported paltry Jewish educational offerings among communal camps, a survey conducted in 1994 found that 97 percent of JCC camps "celebrate the Sabbath in some way" and that 94 percent included Jewish songs in their music programs. Over two-thirds of such camps also reported training their counselors in Jewish education, "and nearly as many" claimed that they hired a Jewish education specialist for a "significant part of the summer." The survey, the authors wrote, revealed "the metamorphosis of Jewish education in Jewish Community Centers," demonstrating an "almost universal intensification of levels of Jewish education" over the course of decades.[23] The years following the publication of the 1990 NJPS proved a period of expansion in other areas of Jewish education as well, witnessing "the creation of multi-foundation initiatives, such as the Partnership for Excellence in Jewish Education (PEJE), the Foundation for Jewish Camp, and Taglit-Birthright Israel."[24] After over a decade of "convincing" the Jewish community that camping mattered, the Foundation for Jewish Camp's establishment in 1998 in particular ushered in a moment of greater funding for camp infrastructure, camper scholarships, and staff professionalization.

Throughout the 1990s and early 2000s, furthermore, Jewish sociologists and demographers continued to study camps with urgency, using data surrounding the marriage patterns of former campers to quantify camps' influential powers. The work of sociologists such as Steven M. Cohen and Sylvia Barack Fishman crossed over into Jewish communal discourse regarding youth work and "Jewish continuity." In 1998, for instance, the Jewish Telegraphic Agency reported on a recent study of Jewish summer camps, concurring that camps were "vital to maintaining commitment" to Judaism and signified "nothing less than the survival of American Jewry." Dozens of similar articles praising camps' importance in the fight for Jewish continuity appeared in the Jewish press in the 1990s, and indeed continue to appear up through the current day. [25] The project of encouraging in-marriage remains a continued focus in Jewish education and in camping.

Several programs of the past two decades represent a natural extension of this discourse of camp's success and reflect how CJENA "heralded the entry of mega-donors into the Jewish education field."[26] Founded in 1999, Birthright, a ten-day, all-expense paid trip to Israel, represented a new direction in Jewish educational and philanthropic priorities of shaping youth into their "emergent adulthood." The program was initially geared toward youth ages eighteen to twenty-six but expanded to age thirty-two in 2017.[27] Even more recently, camp experiences for Jews in their twenties and thirties,

namely Camp Nai Nai Nai and Trybal Gatherings, essentially recreate the
Jewish camp experience over long weekends for the postcollege, premarriage
set, in hopes that romantic sparks will fly between participants.[28] Like the
dozens of other philanthropically funded programs geared toward millen-
nials, including Moishe House, Adamah, One Table, Honeymoon Israel,
Base Hillel, and Birthright, both Trybal Gatherings and Nai Nai Nai show
how today's funders of the Jewish community hope to foster the magic of
camp-like socialization for young Jews not only through high school but all
the way up through the point of marriage.[29] The power of camping has not
only become a widely accepted fact among American Jewish leaders, but an
essence that Jewish organizations seek to replicate in other settings and for
older constituencies.

### Intermarriage, Gender, and Sexuality

As the fixation with fighting intermarriage grew, the impact of it on Jewish
camps, youth movements, and camp-like, episodic programs became more
pronounced. The presence of sexuality in Jewish summer camps has been reflected not only in communal discourse and the Jewish press, but in popular
culture. In 2010, the Jewish educational website MyJewishLearning hired
comedian Amir Blumenthal to promote summer camps, which he described
as "just learning about touching the opposite sex, with a little garnish of
Jewish."[30] While Blumenthal was aiming to be humorous, he had sourced
the joke in his real perceptions of the ways his friends talked about sexuality
at camp as they returned at the end of summer. As the *Forward* reported in
2012, "Administrators at Jewish sleep-away camps say they discourage campers from getting frisky with each other," and yet "former campers" of the
1980s, 1990s, and early 2000s "tell a different story, of counselors who turned
a blind eye or even gently egged their campers on. The unspoken subtext,
they say, is Jewish continuity," making "hooking up at camp . . . a hallmark
of the American Jewish youth experience."[31] The director of Surprise Lake,
the longest-running Jewish summer camp in the United States, put it similarly in 2002: "If intermarriage is the problem, one solution is giving young
people the chance to become romantically connected to other Jews" while at
camp.[32] Intermarriage anxiety has even prompted Ramah to create marriage-

encouraging programs for its alumni. Ramah collects the stories of married couples who met at a Ramah camp as campers or as staff from the 1950s on to exhibit on their website in the "Ramah Marriages" section, and individual Ramah camps honor their alumni couples by creating things like a "Shidduch Wall" in the cafeteria of Camp Ramah in the Berkshires, covered with plaques inscribing the names of couples who met at camp, or a similar Gazebo Zugot (Couples' Gazebo) at Ramah in the Poconos (*shidduch* is the Hebrew and Yiddish word for matchmaking). In 2014, Ramah made its most direct move in the realm of marriage, beginning a partnership with the Jewish online dating platform JDate to create "RamahDate," a "dating site for Jewish singles affiliated with Ramah.' "[33]

Even more recently, the reflections of former campers regarding their camps' romantic and sexual atmospheres have begun to change from mostly lighthearted to increasingly critical. In 2016, a former Habonim camper published an article in the left-wing online magazine *Mondoweiss* critiquing her camp's "nationalism born of the fusion of sexuality and Zionism." With the provocative headline, "How Many More Orgasms Will Be Had for Zionism?" the camper of the eighties described her camp's sexual culture as politically manipulative.[34] And yet the cultural shifts brought on by the #MeToo movement have transformed the issue of camp hookup culture and sexuality into a much more open, mainstream, and urgent Jewish communal conversation in both the press and on social media.[35] In a 2017 *Forward* article, Josh Nathan-Kazis described contemporary hookup culture and power dynamics in Jewish summer camps and youth movements, bringing to light how camps and movements have turned a blind eye to problematic hookup games and point systems, in which youth movement leaders of different ranks are assigned more points, which other teens collect by making out with them. Since point systems are a long-standing tradition in many movements and their camps, with some alumni attesting to their existence as far back as the 1980s, Nathan-Kazis blurred past and the present when he asserted that "Jewish youth group leaders and summer camp directors have generally been more permissive in allowing teens to pursue sexual relationships than with other notionally forbidden activities, like taking illegal drugs."[36] Sociologist Steven M. Cohen agreed with Nathan-Kazis's assessment of the situation, reporting to the journalist that camp and youth group leaders "are very happy if their young people form romantic relation-ships that they carry forward into life."[37] Steven Cohen put this idea in sim-ilar terms in a 2015 interview with national Ramah director Mitch Cohen. "Ramah and such camps are among the best ways to assure that our young Jews meet and marry other Jews," Steven Cohen explained, "especially now that intermarriage is being undertaken so widely. Because of their Ramah friendships, they marry fellow campers, or they participate in strong Jewish social networks that make romantic referrals."[38]

Steven M. Cohen's longtime research focus on Jewish marriage patterns, youth programming, and fertility rates came under a microscope when he became a subject of a Jewish communal #MeToo moment after several alle-gations of sexual harassment came to light. Prominent Jewish philanthropist Michael Steinhardt, who has devoted much of his fortune to Jewish educa-tion geared toward curbing intermarriage, was also accused of sexual harass-ment by several women who worked with him.[39] In both cases, scholars have made connections between their intense interests in encouraging "Jewish babies" on the one hand and their treatment of Jewish women on the other.[40] "What we know is that the Jewish communal world, even to this day, is led primarily by men," wrote Jewish academics Kate Rosenblatt, Lila Corwin Berman, and Ronit Stahl in the *Forward*,

> and that these men have tended to hire other men, including Steven M. Cohen, to survey American Jews. This large and expensive social research apparatus, driven by male leadership and sustained by aggres-sive boundary policing, has placed Jewish continuity at its center and defined Jewish continuity in extraordinarily troubling ways. . . . Jewish communal leaders, in turn, learn that the continuity crisis—and its pre-scriptions about how to regulate primarily women, their bodies, and their sexuality—has its own productive energy that can be harnessed to convince donors to open their pocketbooks and support the very re-search and programs that prove that the crisis exists.[41]

While their assertions regarding how Cohen's harassment relates to his scholarship received pushback from some Jewish sociologists and demog-raphers, the debate surrounding what to do with Cohen's work in light of the allegations against him has undoubtedly made its mark on the field of Jewish studies.[42] How it will shape the continuity-related goals of communal organizations, including youth groups and summer camps that previously worked with Cohen, is still an open question.

The #MeToo movement has also led to transformations in the field of camping regarding gender, sexuality, and relationships between campers. Jewish Teens for Empowered Consent (JTEC), a movement led by young alumni of Jewish youth groups, has called out the "hypersexualization" in Jewish youth spaces that is often encouraged from the top down. "Overwhelmed by the precarious state of our continuity," write the leaders of the JTEC, Jewish leaders do not understand "the consequences of imposing components of rape culture onto teens." "Hypersexualization" in Jewish youth group spaces "is upheld as a means to that end." JTEC's Instagram account features dozens of stories from anonymous camp and youth group alumni about how this hypersexualization influences the consent issues and peer pressure young Jews faced in their own experiences at camp or youth movement weekends.[43] Prompted by these conversations, the Foundation for Jewish Camp cited the #MeToo movement's influence in its new program, the Shmirah Initiative, which seeks to "to prevent sexual harassment and abuse" through "staff trainings at Jewish camps about sex, gender and consent."[44] Moving Traditions, an organization whose mission is to "embolden youth by fostering self-discovery, challenging sexism, and inspiring a commitment to Jewish life and learning," launched their Culture Shift program in 2019, which works to train camp leaders about how to "communicate clear policy" and "work with staff to address some of the most challenging, often hidden, social dynamics of camp." "Pressure to say who you have a 'crush' on, to act in a sexual manner or even to engage in sexual activity are commonplace at camp and are too often ignored or even encouraged by junior staff," explains the Culture Shift project's web page. "While camp is a safe place for many adolescents to explore emerging desires and romantic interest, for others the camp environment can reinforce harmful pressure to hook up for reasons of status and fitting in."[45] Embracing Moving Traditions and the Shmirah Initiative show how camping leaders increasingly recognize the negative role that continuity as a mission has played in creating their camps' sexual cultures. "I think that once you're starting to make your camp's goal—

secretly or underlying—the continuity of Jewish children," explained Sheira Director-Nowack, director of Camp Havaya in Pennsylvania, to the *Times of Israel*, in 2021, "then hookup culture is something you're intrinsically accidentally doing."[46]

Finally, making camps safe for lesbian, gay, bisexual, and transgender children has emerged as a much more significant priority in the past decade. The experiences of these campers have improved over the years in step with changes in American culture writ large: more and more campers are open about their sexualities at earlier ages, making it possible for the romantic cultures of camps to reflect and include a wider range of experiences. Transgender and gender-nonconforming campers, however, face challenges in camps, since campers generally reside in bunks separated by gender. After some of the difficult experiences of transgender children at Jewish camps came to light in 2013, both the Foundation for Jewish Camp and Keshet, a national Jewish LGBTQ advocacy organization in Boston, began to train camp staff members toward better inclusivity of trans and gender-nonbinary campers.[47] Some camps have created mixed-gender bunks or accommodated transgender campers with private bathrooms and changing areas. Beyond these logistical accommodations, however, Keshet has encouraged camps to change their internal cultures so that children feel welcomed on an interpersonal level. At Habonim's summer camps, Hebrew language practices have changed as part of their efforts to include transgender campers, with the camps "pioneering a new gender-neutral form of Hebrew."[48] This story is very much ongoing, but these evolutions point to how the values and needs of new generations of young Jews shape the trajectory of camps in directions earlier generations never thought possible.

### Modern Orthodox Camping

Less affected by continuity concerns and the crisis mentality over Jewish education, the trajectory of Orthodox camping diverged from that of the broader Jewish summer camping sector in several ways. At the beginning of the 1950s, the Orthodox movement proved "the only Jewish religious group without a major denominational youth movement under its wing," its lack of an organized youth program reflecting the state of Orthodoxy itself at the time, which was less structured, without a singular institutional body, and smaller than the other movements of Judaism. While there were some camps for Orthodox children in the interwar and early postwar period, they were largely private and with no institutional Orthodox affiliation. But Orthodox Judaism of the late 1960s signified a "new phenomenon in American and Jewish history."[49] The centrist Orthodox Jewish community, increasingly known as the Modern Orthodox, began to take what Etan Diamond has described as a "distinct and decided shift . . . rightward," increasing "standards of religious adherence," with younger Orthodox Jews tending to observe Jewish law more strictly than their parents. Meanwhile, Orthodox Jewry splintered into several different groups, with the more right-wing Ultra-Orthodox challenging Modern Orthodox Jews, "who hoped to partake of middle-class American culture."[50]

Orthodoxy's shift to the right affected relations between different kinds of Orthodox Jews, as well as between the Orthodox and more liberal Jews. While ultra-Orthodox Jews rarely worked alongside non-Orthodox Jews, centrist Orthodox communities have "historically maintained more open lines of communication with Reform and Conservative organizations and institutions." In the past several decades, however, "such communication became less and less frequent, as centrist Orthodox Jewish leaders felt the pressure of Haredi Orthodox Jewish rabbis to limit interdenominational contacts."[51] As Modern Orthodox Jews became clearer about their differences from both Conservative Jews and the ultra-Orthodox, moreover, creating youth groups and summer camps for their children became a much bigger priority.

Camps for more right-wing ultra-Orthodox, Haredi, or *misnagdic* Jews slowly developed beginning in the 1940s. Yeshiva University endorsed camps as far back as the 1920s, practicing traditional Judaism with daily prayers and kosher facilities but otherwise providing primarily recreational rather than educational programs. Some Orthodox Zionist camps sponsored by Bnei Akiva, such as Camp Moshava, also predate the 1960s, while Orthodox families of the 1940s and 1950s had embraced camps like Massad. But while Massad had practiced Judaism in an Orthodox fashion, the hardening of lines between the liberal denominations and the various streams of Orthodoxy reduced the remaining Orthodox presence in pluralist, nondenominational camps. A more unified Modern Orthodoxy, in other words, began to seek camps that catered to their specific tastes and practices.[52]

Camp Moshava, a Zionist, Bnei Akiva–affiliated Orthodox camp with two locations in the United States, followed the patterns of other Zionist, kibbutz-style camps in the 1930s; some private camps catering to Orthodox families also bloomed in the interwar decades. Reflecting both Orthodox Jewry's new confidence and middle-class status, however, Orthodox camping expanded dramatically in the late 1960s and 1970s. New camps such as Camp Morasha and Camp Stone (of Bnei Akiva), both established in 1969, and Camp Lavi, established in 1977, proliferated.[53] Camp Moshava in Pennsylvania moved to its present facility with "attractive building and ample facilities" in 1969, and in its twelve years under the direction of Rabbi Yitzchak Pessin, it expanded considerably, adding to its "usual Torah study a focus on experiential learning through monthly themes and an extensive repertoire of special activities and simulations," adopting many of the approaches long associated with other Zionist and denominational summer camps.[54] Sephardic Adventure Camp, located near Seattle, has also expanded in more recent decades, from a smaller communal camp to a national camp emphasizing Sephardic ritual and traditional Judaism.[55] Modern Orthodox camping continued to expand beyond the New York City area to regions across the United States and Canada throughout the 1970s, 1980s, and 1990s and often brought campers together from different states and both countries, a trend that mirrors what Diamond calls the "continental socialization" of Orthodox youth.[56] Today, there are five Bnei Akiva overnight camps in the United States, and Canadian camps serving Hasidic Jewish children have grown dramatically in number and in size in recent decades as well.[57]

Each Orthodox camp has its own values and mission, the sector much less unified than the Reform and Conservative camping networks. And yet Orthodox Jewry's growing embrace of camping reveals the influence postwar educational camps had on the sector as it entered a new period. Orthodox Jews do not share the same kinds of concerns over assimilation and continuity that have motivated changes in Jewish camps more broadly, but their growing catalog of camps demonstrates how the notion of camp's educational and transformational potential crosses denominational lines.

## Zionism, Israel, and Emerging Diasporism

Another transformation in Jewish camping involves tensions between Jewish youth and camp leadership over Israel and the meaning of Zionism. In the late 1960s, Zionism reached a new peak of popularity among America's Jews, the "roller-coaster of seemingly imminent destruction followed by the joy of victory and salvation" leaving "its mark on American Jews and their cultural practices."[58] Denominational and communal camps reflected the broader Israelification of American Jewish culture, becoming ever more similar to their Zionist predecessors as they sang Hebrew songs, infused camp life with Hebrew words, and created kibbutz-style programs. The Jewish Agency for Israel began to send more Israeli shlichim, or emissaries, to Jewish summer camps, aided by declining costs of air travel.[59] Starting in 1973, Jewish camps embraced the Israeli scouting movement's Tsofim Friendship Caravan program, which brings singing troupes of Israeli teenage boys and girls to visit camps across the country to perform Israeli songs and dances and to deliver positive visions of Israeli life, particularly of the *halutzic* New Jew.[60] Beginning in the late 1960s and increasing dramatically in the 1970s and 1980s, moreover, Jewish camps, schools, and youth movements also began to integrate youth pilgrimages to Israel into their offerings for teens and college students, making travel to Israel a fairly common American Jewish experience for youth and allowing "what can only be simulated" at camps in America to be experienced as "the 'real thing' in Israel."[61] In 1986, for instance, "as many as 400 different Israel educational programs" were in operation, including "educational tours, year-long university and yeshiva programs, high school semesters and work programs on Kibbutzim."[62]

Zionism's intensifying role in Jewish youth work did not arise without some tension. As teens and college-aged counselors in the late 1960s and early 1970s received different messages in colleges and in civil rights, antiwar, and feminist movement circles about Israel than they did at their summer camps, counselors could find themselves torn in two different directions. Still, in the years following the 1973 Yom Kippur War, Israel's growing impression on American Jewish life paralleled a "stifling of dissent within American Jewry," with criticism of Israel becoming taboo. When, in 1973, a group of "highly committed Jews" came to believe that "the time had come for a public discussion about Israel" founded the movement Breira (meaning "choice" in Hebrew), they argued for "involved dialogue and compromise with the Palestinians rather than violence and occupation."[63] But the Jewish press vilified Breira's members "as self-haters and enemies of Israel," and leaders of Jewish institutions would not meet with them to discuss their goals. It is not terribly surprising, then, that none of the alumni I spoke with recalled hearing criticisms of Israel or questioning their Zionism while attending camp as campers or staff members under these conditions, nor did I find a single written source alluding to such criticisms or internal conflicts (although it is possible, if not likely, that such conversations occurred without leaving a record). Even at Yiddish-oriented camps, where leaders did not place Israel in or even near the center of their programming, Israel's existence, politics, or policies were not questioned in any official capacity. Many of the alumni I spoke with, however, recalled questioning Zionism years after they stopped attending or working at camp, during college, while on a movement gap year program living in Israel, or decades into adulthood. Former Habonim camper Dan reflected,

> You know, we had learned a certain history [at camp]. . . . We had turned the desert into green. . . . And it's like, oh, yeah, awesome, you know? And then when the first intifada happened, and the truth started coming out, you know, about how people actually lived there for thousands of years . . . I was like, OK, I didn't hear any of this stuff . . . and that was a real eye opener . . . as an adult. . . . I do remember there were some progressive things that were going on in the movement, but Israeli politics was not one of them.[64]

A former camper from a different socialist Zionist camp recalled a similar realization, also noting the disappointment she experienced when she visited Israel in the late 1970s in the midst of its turn away from the Labor party and its evolution away from socialism and toward capitalism.[65]

These former campers' relationships to Israel follow broader trends of the past several decades. For many American Jews, particularly for those who are liberal or left-wing Jews, Zionism and Israel have become more complex and sensitive subjects. Jewish public discourse surrounding Israel began to shift most markedly during and after the second intifada (a roughly five-year long period of Palestinian rebellion that started in September 2000), when "Israel was criticized for its armed responses to terrorism and failure to make peace with the Palestinians," writes the *Forward*'s Aiden Pink, "and Jewish communal leaders grew concerned that a small but growing number of young Jews were not following the party line."[66] Indeed, as Israeli politics has moved toward the right with settlement expansion, the growth of ultra-Orthodox political parties, and the near-total dissolution of the peace camp, how Jewish youth view and react to Israel has changed. "Among American Jews today, there are a great many Zionists, especially in the Orthodox world, people deeply devoted to the State of Israel," wrote Peter Beinart in 2010, "And there are a great many liberals . . . people deeply devoted to human rights for all people, Palestinians included." But these two groups are ever more distinct, especially among younger Jews, in part because "the leading institutions of American Jewry have refused to foster—indeed, have actively opposed—a Zionism that challenges Israel's behavior in the West Bank and Gaza Strip and toward its own Arab citizens."[67]

Reflecting these trends, how Jewish educators address Israel in camps, schools, and youth movements has changed too. The field of Israel education emerged in part as a response to the fact that as education researcher Bethamie Horowitz put it, "The socialization of young American Jews into a deep and meaningful connection with present-day Israel is not as self-evident or as—natural as it was 40–60 years ago."[68] Since 2000, "at least 15 new organizations were founded to address what and how younger American Jews should be learning about Israel." Israel advocacy, or *hasbara*, has been part of that expansion, with training for teenage Jewish leaders in how to defend Israel against teachers, professors, and friends they might encounter in high school and college. Horowitz's interviewees in the field of Jewish education placed building a "personal connection between the student and Israel as lying at the heart" of what they do. Although there is consensus among her interviewees about the importance of an education that allows "the learner to explore and investigate," Horowitz found that disagreement and tough questions about Israel concerned educators. They did not want their programs to indoctrinate youth, but many feared the potential reactions of donors, parents, and board members should they enter more political territory. Because of these dynamics, most educators Horowitz spoke with "take a neutered, disconnected approach . . . teaching only what is safe or expected."[69]

Calls for better, deeper Israel education have come from advocates across the political spectrum. As Gil Troy, a professor of American history whose Israel politics leans toward the right, explained in 2003, "I have seen graduates of the best Jewish day schools in the Diaspora emotionally, intellectually, and ideologically unprepared to defend Israel or to withstand the intense pro-Palestinian onslaught from Arabs, academics, and their fellow students. Jewish educators must take stock of this failure" and create a "true education and real ownership by our students of the facts and ideas, not a 'line' we peddle to them to pass on to others."[70] Peter Beinart has pointed to a similar problem from the liberal Zionist perspective. "For several decades," he wrote, "the Jewish establishment has asked American Jews to check their liberalism at Zionism's door, and now, to their horror, they are finding that many young Jews have checked their Zionism instead." Saving liberal Zionism, according to Beinart, starts with "talking frankly about Israel's current government" and "by no longer averting our eyes."[71] In 2008, Lisa D. Grant, a professor of Jewish education, put the issue differently: "The root cause of our inability to develop a compelling vision for Israel education lies in a paradoxical comfort with our ambiguous stance towards Israel. Inasmuch as Israel education can be used as a way to reinforce *American* Jewish identity, it is viewed as a positive." But to remain positive, educators "avoid problematizing or over-complicating in order to ensure a love of Israel." Such an approach results in an American Jewish education that provides, "at best, a superficial understanding of why Israel is or should be significant in American Jewish life."[72]

This "superficial understanding" is at the center of new criticisms of Israel education among American Jewish young people today. Issues surrounding what kinds of Zionist education and advocacy Jewish youth should receive and be prepared to take on themselves have simmered since the early 2000s, but a major turning point for camping took place only in 2017, when If-

NotNow, an activist movement of Jewish youth fighting against US support of the Israeli occupation of Palestinians, launched a social media campaign called "#YouNeverToldMe." Through the campaign, recent alumni of Jewish summer camps, and in some cases current counselors, called out what they saw as a misleading Zionist education they had received at their summer camps. Participants passionately reject how their camps placed Israel at the center of their identity-building projects and accuse them of lying by omission about the Israeli occupation and Israel's treatment of Palestinians.[73]

In the summers since the launch of the campaign, tensions have bubbled up beyond social media at Ramah, Reform, and Zionist camps over what kind of Israel education is appropriate, necessary, and just.[74] In 2018, furthermore, IfNotNow began sponsoring training specifically for camp counselors, teaching them how and why camps have come to teach Israel the way they do and gearing them up for changing the status quo on the ground.[75] Even as the summer of 2020 was a relatively quiet one regarding Israel education at camp, given the closure of most camps due to the coronavirus, the issue continued to appear on social media and in the Jewish press. A high-profile controversy over the actor Seth Rogen, who grew up attending Jewish schools and Jewish camp in Vancouver, mirrored the state of affairs. After stating on a popular comedy podcast that he was "fed a huge amount of lies about Israel" in both school and camp, a Jewish media frenzy indicated that we are only at the beginning of this particular moment of reckoning in the history of camping and Jewish education writ large.[76] While individual campers may have questioned certain aspects of Israeli and Zionist culture and narratives at camp in earlier decades, these organized and public protests mark a significant turn in the history of Jewish summer camping, pointing to yet another way in which campers and counselors may end up altering the agendas of camps in the years to come.

As some former campers reject the kinds of Zionism they learned at camp in young adulthood, many also seek alternative ways of identifying with their Jewishness that decenters Israel entirely. A renewed interest in alternative forms of Jewish practice, represented by growing independent prayer groups and Beit Midrash programs in large cities, provides a contemporary version of sixties' Ramah alumni, who achieved their educators' goals of caring about Judaism (wearing a kippah proudly and being enthusiastic about prayer and learning) while decrying the inauthenticity of the movement's synagogues and breaking away by way of the Havurah movement.[77] Millennial Jews also gather and organize in specifically Jewish political movements such as IfNotNow, Jews for Racial and Economic Justice, and Jewish Voice for Peace, among others. The number of Jewish magazines, podcasts, and other online resources by and for young Jews have also grown tremendously, some independent and others sponsored by larger Jewish institutions and foundations.[78] Some young Jews are choosing to embrace a new sense of "diasporism," or, as Bundists called it, *dokayt* or "hereness," "a critical awareness of Israel coupled with a commitment to struggling primarily in the communities in which we live," inviting Jews "to dig in and build a political, spiritual and material fullness."[79] Diasporism relates to the renewed Jewish leftist activism of the Trump era, as well as to a wider understanding of Mizrahi and Sephardic culture, of Jews of Color, and of the Ashkenazi-centrism or Ashkenormativity of American Jewish culture.[80] As part of this interest in diaspora, moreover, young Jews are also embracing Yiddish and Yiddishism in larger numbers than ever before, demonstrating how the American Yiddishism that Boiberik and Hemshekh cultivated has had a longer life than the camps themselves.[81]

None of these movements and trends are new. Yiddish revival began in the 1960s, Klezmer revival grew in the 1980s, and an idea of "Queer Yiddishkayt" proliferated mainly in the 1990s. Breira, which could be seen as a precursor to IfNotNow, was founded in the 1970s; the sardonic Jewish magazine *Heeb*, a quarterly magazine that ran from 2001 to 2010, is just one example of the many precursors of newer youthful Jewish media emerging from social media. None of these developments or movements are numerically massive when considered on their own. Taken together, however, these trends point to how former campers of the 1990s and 2000s are simultaneously embracing the Jewish identities they gained in camps and youth movements while questioning, pushing, and reimagining their boundaries. Slowly but surely, these trends are also gaining steam within summer camps themselves, challenging educators but pushing camps to better reflect the Jewish present.

As camps move forward into the future, the voices of young Jews will no doubt continue to alter their goals and practices. So too will financial and market factors. As teenagers face more pressure than ever before to use their summers to make their college applications shine, today's camps face new problems regarding recruitment and the durability of their month or two-month long programs. And yet the Jewish summer camp's extraordinary ability to evolve according to such changing circumstances has allowed it to maintain its place as a beloved and highly invested part of Jewish life in the first place. With continued communal investments, camps are facing these issues head on, developing specialty programs and altering their content to match the market forces and the political, cultural, and social issues of the American and Jewish present.

———

When the coronavirus sent the world into lockdown in March 2020, a desperate dialogue ensued in the Jewish press among parents, doctors, and camp leaders who argued that camps could open safely and those who argued that camps had to close for the summer for reasons of safety and *pikuach nefesh*, the Jewish value of putting the preservation of human life above all else. *Forward* editor and camp parent Judi Ruderon wrote in one article, "I know that people are dying, and the economy is flailing, and that it is only from a position of privilege that I could possibly be making this plea, but we need camp." Campers would no doubt be devastated over their camp's closure and would lose out on the personal growth that a year of camp provides. But as Ruderon explained, the impetus was bigger than these personal reasons: "The Jewish world needs camp, the way it creates a feeling of home rarely replicated in synagogue or school. That intensity, that closeness, that warmth and pure fun—all essentially, intrinsically, tied up in Jewish identity and sealed with a singalong."[82]

While many state health departments made the decision to close camps before camp directors had to, this public dialogue offered a window into how American Jews continue to see the significance and transformational power of camp. Concerned over changes in socioeconomic status and mournful in the wake of the Holocaust, postwar Jews turned to summer camps as solutions to their perceived communal ills. In the decades that followed, camps changed their messaging, responding to both the culture outside their gates and the wills of those within them, functioning once again as mirrors and mediators of American and Jewish life. Many structural elements of camping have remained unchanged, reflecting the remarkable durability of camp rituals and routines; indeed, camps' persistent sense of nostalgia and "camp tradition" lies at the center of what keeps them in the hearts and minds of its promoters, leaders, attendees, and supporters. And yet camps' abilities to face cultural change is what has pushed them into new directions and allowed them to incubate new forms of Jewish culture. In the face of market forces, some Jewish camps will inevitably close over the next few decades; their romantic and sexual cultures will continue to adjust to new norms around youth sexuality, consent, and LGBTQ+ experiences; their political messaging surrounding Israel will likely face greater pushback from teenage campers and young adult counselors, forcing camp leaders to reevaluate Israel's role as an educational and transformational tool. As camp leaders and participants face this dynamic economic, cultural, and political future, however, it is this dialectic—the stable and the unstable, the routine and the innovative, the influences of both the present and the past—that will allow camps to continue as mirrors and generators of Jewish life.

# CONCLUSION

IN THE EARLY 1970S, Rabbi Simon Greenberg, then vice chancellor of the Jewish Theological Seminary, flew to Israel to address a group of young Israelis set to work at various American Jewish camps that upcoming summer. In his remarks, Greenberg aimed to prepare the shlichim, or emissaries, for their mission, focusing on what he saw as the central challenge facing American Jewry: assimilation. To Greenberg, the problem of assimilation did not begin in suburbia, where Jews had experienced unprecedented social and economic mobility but rather with "the end of the shtetl" in Europe, when "the old Jewish ways . . . [were] replaced by the 'modern' ways of other nations." Nearly a century since the end of the Haskalah, the Jewish enlightenment, the troubles posed by modernity continued to plague Jews outside of Israel, creating a "pressing need to develop a Jewish way of life in the new culture of the *golah* [diaspora or exile])." The campers that the Israelis would encounter that summer, he continued, were born and raised within this weakened culture, a place and a time that "could not nourish an adequate Jewish identity."[1] Without intervention, the American suburb, with its lavish synagogues and uninspired Hebrew schools, would encompass all they knew of Jewish life.

Greenberg had his reasons for measured optimism. Inspired by the wider embrace of ethnicity and multiculturalism, American Jewish young people of the late sixties and early seventies were "looking for ways of 'being' Jewish," trading in the assimilationist tendencies their parents' and grandparents' generations felt pressure to take on in exchange for greater engagement with Jewish heritage and culture. College-aged and postcollege Jews generated all sorts of new modes of Jewish practice, activism, and identity in this time of ethnic revival, including the independent prayer groups of the Havurah movement, the Soviet Jewry movement, Zionism, and, for a smaller subset of young Jews, an embrace of Yiddish. But for Greenberg, camps offered the crucial opportunity to provide direction for younger children and teens, filling an educational void through 24/7 Jewish living.

The mere presence of the shlichim—their Hebrew fluency, cultural differences, and stories of Israeli childhood and army life —served to inflect camp life with a sense of Jewish authenticity many educators saw as invigorating and transformative. But while all Jewish camps embraced some notion or another of authenticity, not all believed that Israeliness represented its peak form. In many ways, camps diverged when it came to "which attitudes are to be indoctrinated." Yiddishists offered a distinctive contrast to the Zionist vision of authentic Jewishness, looking toward the Eastern European past for inspiration; while embracing and using some Zionist ideas, Reform and Conservative camps presented a wider vision of Jewishness, imbued by their movement's values and approaches to Jewish practice.[2] These differences came through in every element of daily life, from the symbols they drew on to the languages they spoke to the Jews from other times and places they role-played and revered. At the same time, Zionists, Yiddishists, Reform, and Conservative Jews ultimately shared strikingly similar fantasies of repairing postwar Jewish culture and similarly used the immersivity and intensiveness of the summer camp toward their ends. If the American sleepaway camp was what psychologist Fritz Reall once called a "powerful drug," with the potential to alter the behaviors and identities of young people, Jewish educators across the spectrum prescribed it liberally, believing in it as a cure-all for their perceived communal ills caused by social mobility, modernity, and affluence.[3]

Affluence played a particularly important and paradoxical role in the history of camping. Rising middle-classness sat at the core of the anxieties of those who funded, founded, and led Jewish camps. Many communal leaders wondered who Jews would become under conditions of comfort and how the Jewish summer camp could serve to counter the perilous effects that affluence had on the identity development of the young. At the same time, affluence also played an essential role in the postwar Jewish camping sector's ability to expand and thrive. While philanthropic and small, private Jewish camps existed prior to the prosperity of the postwar decades, postwar Jews had more means to put toward their children's education and recreation, and Jewish movements and institutions had more ability to purchase acres of land and build modern and permanent campsites. The educational Jewish summer camping sector that the postwar period spawned—varied, interconnected, modernized, subsidized for those in need, and professionalized—could not have happened without Jews entering the middle class. Rather than sitting in contradiction, *The Jews of Summer* shows how tensions between economic success and anxiety over cultural decline pushed Jewish life in new directions. Affluence made the middle-class marker of the sleepaway camp both a Jewish rite of passage and a communal cause.

Despite their geographic removal and unique traditions and routines, camps are incubators of culture, religious practice, and political attitudes. As such, they necessarily respond to the goings-on outside their boundaries, serving as mirrors of their historical moments. Everyday life in the postwar Jewish summer camp not only reflected the changing concerns of the organized American Jewish community, but transformations in American education, childhood, youth culture, and global Jewish affairs. The responsiveness of Jewish camps to the historical developments of the mid-1940s through the early 1970s led to substantial changes. Most camps increased their focus on Israel in response to growing Zionist sentiment, abandoned goals of spoken Hebrew or Yiddish in favor of a more symbolic use of the languages, centered their programs on teenagers as the youth culture emerged a broader phenomenon of concern, and harnessed laxity and freedom as a means of controlling an increasingly defiant teen culture. A separate and more defined Orthodox camping sector, furthermore, developed in step with the growth of Modern

Orthodoxy. Several social, cultural, and economic factors challenged camps like Boiberik, Hemshekh, and Massad at the end of the 1970s, but their inabilities to evolve enough to face these challenges ultimately spelled their ends. Campers, staff members, and alumni glorify camp tradition, holding near and dear to their hearts the ideologies, routines, and rituals that they see as essential and unshakeable parts of camp life. Camps only moved forward, however, when they were willing and capable of substantial change.

Researchers, camp advocates, and communal leaders alike have placed tremendous energy on demonstrating the Jewish summer camp's status as an educational and transformational success. While Greenberg's use of the term *indoctrination* as a positive educational approach is generally frowned on today, the notion of Jewish camps' unparalleled power to transmit identity and ideology became widespread in the postwar decades and led a wider array of Jewish communal camps to adopt more intensive educational styles and goals in the 1970s. Watching many of the alumni of postwar camps go on to lead the American Jewish community, move to Israel, or become Yiddish cultural activists, camp leaders and proponents saw their proof in the pudding. The notion of the summer camp's power remains prevalent in Jewish communal discourse, and Jewish camps today still answer to and serve communal anxieties, ideals, and missions. After decades of promoting, supporting, and declaring their success, Jewish organizations have even come to harness camp-like forms of socialization and education for Jews in their twenties and early thirties, as notions of youth expand to include the postcollege, premarriage "emerging adult."

Schools, camps, and youth groups of all kinds are shaped by adult desires, goals, and expectations; it is both sensible and predictable that education scholars, demographers, and sociologists would seek to evaluate whether the goals of the institutions at the heart of their research have been met. Such research has had tangible material effects on the Jewish camping sector, leading to larger investments in infrastructure, scholarships, and professionalization. The success narrative also plays a leading role in a widespread belief among American Jews that summer camp is somehow inherently a "Jewish thing," although this is not technically the case.[4] Out of nearly twenty-three hundred overnight camps available in the search engine of the American Camping Association today, only sixty-eight, or about 3 percent, identify specifically as Jewish summer camps.[5] According to the 2006 National Study of Youth and Religion, moreover, nearly 80 percent of Mormon teens have attended an overnight camp, 53 percent of conservative Protestants, and 48 percent of mainline Protestants. Jewish teens come in fourth, at 43 percent.[6] That said, no other organized community in America has seemed to believe quite as unanimously and passionately in the power of camp to transform cultural identities, invested as much in its expansion and professionalization, and sent their kids to camp for month-long sessions in such large proportions. Other religious groups tend to hold shorter sessions and generally have different aims. As Jacob Sorensen explains, one-week Christian camps tend to have "five fundamental characteristics: relational, safe space, participatory, unplugged from home, and faith-centered." Sorensen also notes that research on the effectiveness of Christian camps is new, despite their prevalence and long history.[7] Research on Jewish camping, in contrast, began in the 1960s and has flourished since then. What may make Jewish educational camps unique, then, is not the number of them but the persistent belief Jews have held in their unparalleled power to produce strong cultural identities.

A focus on success, however, can sideline other important issues. By centering my analysis on the lived experiences of campers and staff members, my goals have been threefold. First, this book demonstrates that the shape of camp life never rested in the hands of adult leaders alone, and that asserts that all kinds of educational phenomena can be better understood by paying attention to age and stage in life. Campers challenged the plans of their counselors, educators, rabbis, and head staff members. And yet tensions between the generations also produced new interpretations of and paths for the ideologies camps promoted. Camper resistance to the idea of Hebrew and Yiddish immersion, for instance, not only reshaped the roles those languages would play in camp life but reconstituted the linguistic movements to better match their American historical moments in ways that have had lasting impacts. As campers sought to foster their own youth cultures within camps, moreover, their interests in dating and sex and their resistance to adult plans altered camp leaders' priorities, changed their approaches to pedagogy, and brought adults to use campers' interest in romance and sexuality to their own ends. Fostering a balance between control and freedom was an economic imperative, as campers needed to be happy enough during the summer to return the next year. But adult leaders also understood the importance of intergenerational negotiation to their educational goals. Answering to the desires of youth produced the educational buy-in required to transform youth according to the camp's visions and goals. The Jewish summer camp took its shape not from the top down but in the space between the plans and hopes of adults and the desires and interests of children and teenagers.

Second, *The Jews of Summer* places attention on a group that has been bypassed in camping studies and histories centered on success: Yiddish camps. Yiddishists did not fit neatly into the mainstream Jewish communal agenda in the postwar period, nor do they today. They were not, as a rule, particularly Zionistic; they generally identified as adamantly secular and leaned further left than other Jews in the immediate postwar decades. Their goals as a group deviated from those of the organized Jewish community, putting aside Israel and concerns over "Jewish continuity" in favor of a focus on the continuation of Yiddish culture. Although they sat at the margins of the postwar sector, Yiddish camps underscore the overwhelming similarities among postwar Jewish leaders. They all ascribed camp life with unparalleled power and harnessed the summer camp's intensity to serve their ends. Postwar Jewish camping ran on a shared understanding of cultural decline, an anxious line of thinking that linked Jews who agreed on little else. Placing Yiddish camps in the history of postwar Jewry, moreover, complicates the idea that the Yiddishist movement simply disappeared after the war. Far from presenting a sudden revival, the vibrancy of Yiddish education, activism, and cultural production in the twenty-first century has relied directly on the alumni of Yiddish summer camps, who still serve as teachers and caretakers of Yiddish culture today. While Hemshekh and Boiberik did not survive the turmoil of the 1970s, they undoubtedly succeeded by a very different, overlooked metric: perpetuating Yiddish cultural and linguistic activism and carrying the torch of a kind of "diasporism" that is slowly gaining traction among American Jewish young people today.[8]

Most important, the history of Yiddish camping may be helpful as American Jews face a complex contemporary moment. Over the years I worked on this project, Jewish teens and young people began to increasingly and publicly probe the ideologies they learned in their camps and youth movements, particularly with regard to Israel and Zionism. A linking of the #MeToo movement with the trajectory of the continuity crisis, moreover, has complicated young Jews' understandings of their camps and youth movements as positive places of sexual freedom and brought to light the ideological underpinnings that make Jewish camps and youth groups associated with hook-up culture. Rather than continuing to focus primarily or intensely on Zionism as a source of identity or the encouragement of in-marriage—issues that remain important to many in the Jewish establishment but are apparently losing favor among Jewish youth from non-Orthodox backgrounds[9]—the history of Yiddish camping reveals other options, some of which are already gaining ground: Jewish educational programs that pointedly celebrate, and aim to continue, diaspora Jewish cultures, not only Ashkenazi, but Sephardic and Mizrahi; that center the oft-cited Jewish value of *tikkun olam*, or "repairing the world," placing particular value on issues closer to home; and that encourage and support youth as they critique and question all kinds of Jewish ideas and ideologies, without a list of issues that remain off-limits.[10] It would be easy to let this book sink us into a comfortable nostalgia for simpler summers past—a time when Jews seemed to align, at the very least, on the problems that plagued them most. In this moment of reckoning, however, my greatest hope is that its chapters encourage the very opposite, emboldening readers to contemplate the ideological weights adults place on children, the roles youth play in the making of culture, and how conceptions of authenticity can be creatively and productively expanded for the sake of the Jewish future.

# Notes

**Introduction**

1. Jo Backer, "Thoughts on What Fiddler Made Me Think about Mame Loshn/Yiddish Loshn," *Di Hemshekh Vokh*, n.d., 015009254, YIVO Archives, YIVO Institute for Jewish Research, New York.

2. See Jonathan Sarna, *American Judaism* (New Haven: Yale University Press, 2004), 281–282.

3. Regarding Jewish acclimation to middle-classness, see Deborah Dash Moore, *To the Golden Cities: Pursuing the American Dream in Miami and L.A.* (New York: Simon & Schuster, 1994); Jenna Weissman Joselit, *The Wonders of America: Reinventing Jewish Culture, 1880–1950* (New York: Hill and Wang, 1994); Andrew Heinze, *Adapting to Abundance: Mass Consumption, and the Search for American Identity* (New York: Columbia University Press, 1990); Etan Diamond, *And I Will Dwell in Their Midst: Orthodox Jews in Suburbia* (Chapel Hill: University of North Carolina Press, 2000).

4. See Herbert J. Gans, "The Origins and Growth of a Jewish Community in the Suburbs: A Study of the Jews in Park Forest," in *The Jews: Social Patterns of an American Group*, ed. Marshall Sklare (New York: Free Press, 1958), 205–248.

5. See Rachel Kranson, *Ambivalent Embrace: Jewish Upward Mobility in Postwar America* (Chapel Hill: University of North Carolina Press, 2017); Riv-Ellen Prell, "Community and the Discourse of Elegy: The Post War Suburban Debate," in *Imagining the American Jewish Community*, ed. Jack Wertheimer (Hanover, NH: University Press of New England,

2007); Lila Corwin Berman "American Jews and the Ambivalence of Middle-Classness," *American Jewish History* 93, no. 4 (2007): 409–436; Eli Lederhandler, *New York Jews and the Decline of Urban Ethnicity, 1950–1970* (Syracuse, NY: Syracuse University Press, 2001); Edward S. Shapiro, *A Time for Healing: American Jewry since World War II: "The Jewish People in America,"* vol. 5 (Baltimore: Johns Hopkins University Press, 1992).

6. Riv-Ellen Prell's work on camp also addresses anxieties over the state of postwar Judaism. See Riv-Ellen Prell, "Summer Camp, Post-War American Jewish Youth and the Redemption of Judaism," in *The Jewish Role in American Life: An Annual Review*, vol. 5, ed. Bruce Zuckerman and Jeremy Schoenberg (West Lafayette, IN: Purdue University Press, 2007), 77–106.

7. For more on the history of prewar Jewish summer camps, see Jonathan B. Krasner, *The Benderly Boys and American Jewish Education* (Waltham, MA: Brandeis University Press, 2012); on camps at the transition into and beginning of the postwar period, see Jonathan Sarna, "The Crucial Decade in Jewish Camping" in *A Place of Our Own: The Rise of Reform Jewish Camping: Essays Honoring the Fiftieth Anniversary of Olin-Sang-Ruby Union Institute*, ed. Gary Phillip Zola (Tuscaloosa: University of Alabama Press, 2006); Daniel Isaacman, "Jewish Education in Camping," in *American Jewish Year Book* (American Jewish Committee and Springer, 1967), 245–252; Jenna Weissman Joselit, Karen S. Mittelman, and National Museum of American Jewish History, "A Worthy Use of Summer: Jewish Summer Camping in America" (Philadelphia: National Museum of American Jewish History, 1993). On general American camping, see Leslie Paris, *Children's Nature: The Rise of the American Summer Camp* (New York: New York University Press, 2008).

8. See Sarna, "Crucial Decade in Jewish Camping"; Shuly Rubin Schwartz, "Camp Ramah: The Early Years, 1947–1952," *Conservative Judaism* 40 (Fall 1987): 17, 22; Prell, "Summer Camp"; Joselit et al., "A Worthy Use of Summer"; Celia E. Rothenberg, *Serious Fun at a Jewish Community Summer Camp: Family, Judaism, and Israel* (Lanham, MD: Lexington Books, 2016). For alumni literature and memoir, see Ariel Hurwitz, *Against the Stream: Seven Decades of Hashomer Hatzair in North America* (Tel Aviv: Yad Yaari, 1994); World Hashomer Hatzair, *With Strength and Courage: 50 Years Hashomer Hatzair, 1913–1963* (New York: Education Department of Hashomer Hatzair, 1963); David Breslau, *Story of 25 Years of Habonim Camping* (New York: Chai Commission of LZOA Movement, 1957); David Breslau, *Arise and Build: The Story of American Habonim* (New York: Ichud Habonim Labor Zionist Youth, 1961); *Massad Reminiscences*, Massad Hebrew Summer Camps Alumni Organization and the Oral History Division of the Abraham Harman Institute of Contemporary Jewry, Hebrew University, Jerusalem, 1996.

9. Sarah Bunin Benor, Jonathan Krasner, and Sharon Avni, *Hebrew Infusion: Language and Community at American Jewish Summer Camps* (New Brunswick, NJ: Rutgers University Press, 2020), 1.

10. Jacob Sorensen, "A Theological Playground: Christian Summer Camp in Theological Perspective" (PhD diss., Luther Seminary, 2016), 77. Since the bulk of the writing of this

book, Sorensen has published a book based on his dissertation: *Sacred Playgrounds: Christian Summer Camp in Theological Perspective* (Eugene, OR: Cascade Books, 2021).

11. For more on Yiddish secular education, see Fradle Freidenreich, *Passionate Pioneers: The Story of Yiddish Secular Education in North America, 1910–1960* (Teaneck, NJ: Holmes & Meier, 2010); Naomi Prawer Kadar, *Raising Secular Jews: Yiddish Schools and Their Periodicals for American Children, 1917–1950*, (Waltham, MA: Brandeis University Press, 2016).

12. Jeffrey Shandler, *Adventures in Yiddishland: Postvernacular Language and Culture* (Berkeley: University of California Press, 2005), 1.

13. Some examples of Yiddish revival coverage in the press include Lidar Grade-Lazi, "It's Cool and Fringe, It's Yiddish," *Jerusalem Post*, July 23, 2016, https://www.jpost.com/Israel-News/Culture/Its-cool-and-fringe-its-Yiddish-462184; D. B., "Yiddish on the Rise," *Economist*, July 21, 2015, https://www.economist.com/prospero/2015/07/21/yiddish-on-the-rise. For more on Yiddish activism among American Jewish youth, see Sandra Fox, "'The Passionate Few': Youth and Yiddishism in American Jewish Culture, 1964 to Present," *Jewish Social Studies* 26, no. 3 (2021): 1–34; Joshua Friedman, "Serious Jews: Cultural Intimacy and the Politics of Yiddish," *Cultural Dynamics* 32, no. 2 (August 2020).

14. Paris, *Children's Nature*, 150.

15. "Standards Report for the Accreditation of Organized Camps" (Martinsville, IN: American Camping Association, 1966). Tom Rosenberg, CEO of the ACA, sent this PDF to me in October 2017.

16. As Paris writes in *Children's Nature*, "Although the counselors were young, often college students, they represented an intermediate generation in some ways like parents and in other ways like older peers" (134).

17. See Elliott West and Paula Petrik, eds., *Small Worlds: Children and Adolescents in America, 1850–1950* (Lawrence: University Press of Kansas, 1992), 1; Mona Gleason, "Avoiding the Agency Trap: Caveats for Historians of Children, Youth, and Education," *History of Education* 45, no. 4 (2016): 447.

18. Gleason, "Avoiding the Agency Trap," 457. For more on the field of history of childhood and youth grappling with agency, see Joseph M. Hawes and N. Ray Hiner, "Reflection on the History of Children and Childhood in the Postmodern Era," in *Major Problems in the History of American Families and Children*, ed. Anya Jabour (Boston: Houghton Mifflin, 2005); Leslie Paris, "Through the Looking Glass: Age, Stages, and Historical Analysis," *Journal of the History of Childhood and Youth* 1, no. 1 (2008); Steven Mintz, "Children's History Matters," *American Historical Review* 125, no. 4 (October 2020); Sarah Maza, "The Kids Aren't All Right: Historians and the Problem of Childhood," *American Historical Review* 125, no. 4 (October 21, 2020): 1261–1285.

19. Jacob Sorensen, "Sacred Playgrounds: Chapter 2 Draft," unpublished manuscript, sent to me via email, May 17, 2020, 23.

20. Sarna, "Crucial Decade in Jewish Camping."

21. Jacob Sorensen, conversation with the author, May 21, 2020.

22. Nadine Karachi, conversation with the author, May 21, 2020. Karachi is the director of Camp Deen, a Muslim camp established in the 1970s in Ontario, Canada,

23. Sarna, "Crucial Decade in Jewish Camping," 35.

24. For more on Nathan Birnbaum, see Jess Olson, *Nathan Birnbaum and Jewish Modernity: Architect of Zionism, Yiddishism, and Orthodoxy* (Stanford: Stanford University Press, 2013).

25. See Avraham Schenker, "Zionist Camping in America," *Jewish Education* 36, no. 2 (January 1, 1966).

26. See Yitzhak Conforti, "'The New Jew' in the Zionist Movement: Ideology and Historiography," *Australian Journal of Jewish Studies* 25 (2011).

27. See Shlomo Shulsinger, "Introduction: Hebrew Camps—Their Role and Place," translated from Hebrew, Camp Massad records, 1944–2003 (bulk 1949–1990), n.d., box 2, folder 7, American Jewish Historical Society, New York.

28. Due to source availability, this project puts more emphasis on Camps Hemshekh and Boiberik than on Kinder Ring and Kinderland. For more about Yiddish camps within the context of communist camping, see Paul Mishler, *Raising Reds: The Young Pioneers, Radical Summer Camps, and Communist Political Culture in the United States* (New York: Columbia University Press, 1999).

29. See "Imagining Yiddishland," in Jeffrey Shandler, *Adventures in Yiddishland: Postvernacular Language and Culture* (Berkeley: University of California Press, 2005), 38.

30. My understanding of the trajectory of Reform camping came from research in the American Jewish Archive and from Zola, ed., *A Place of Our Own*. My reading of the Ramah summer camps evolved out of extensive research of the National Ramah Commission's collection at the Jewish Theological Seminary Archives (For more on the foundational years of Conservative camping, see the special issue of *Conservative Judaism on Ramah* (Fall 1987).

31. For more on the history of the Ramah summer camps, see Sylvia C. Ettenberg and Geraldine Rosenfield, eds., *The Ramah Experience: Community and Commitment* (New York: Jewish Theological Seminary of America, 1989).

32. Sarna, "Crucial Decade in Jewish Camping," 32–35.

33. See Norman Schanin, "Young Judaea: A Survey of a National Jewish Youth Movement in 1951–1952" (PhD diss., New York University, 1959), 86.

34. Schenker, "Zionist Camping in America," 104.

35. Sandra Fox, "'Laboratories of Yiddishkayt': Postwar American Jewish Summer Camps and the Transformation of Yiddishism," *American Jewish History* 103, no. 3 (2019).

36. Daniel Isaacman, "Jewish Education in Camping," *American Jewish Yearbook* 67 (1966), 247. My understanding of Reform camping comes from visits to the American Jewish Archive and from the crucial work on the subject, *A Place of Our Own*.

37. Shuly Rubin Schwartz, "Camp Ramah: The Early Years, 1947–1952," *Conservative Judaism* 40 (1987): 17, 22.

38. "Camp Ramah History," *Ramah Outdoors* (blog), November 27, 2017, http://old

.ramahoutdoors.org/ramahhistory/. Additional Ramah camps have opened in recent decades, including Ramah Darom in 1996, Ramah Rockies in 2010, and Ramah NorCal in
2016.

39. Sarna, "Crucial Decade in Jewish Camping," 43.

40. "A Finding Aid to the Swig Camp Institute Records. 1964–1967," American Jewish
Archives, processed by Melinda McMartin, November 2001, http://collections.american
jewisharchives.org/ms/ms0671/ms0671.html.

41. Sarna, "Crucial Decade in Jewish Camping," 44.

42. See Zola, *A Place of Our Own*, 28.

43. My understanding of Orthodoxy's time line regarding camping and youth culture
came in large part from Diamond, *And I Will Dwell in Their Midst*; Zev Eleff, *Living from
Convention to Convention: A History of the NCSY, 1954–1980* (Brooklyn: Ktav Publishing
House, 2009), and Zev Eleff, *Authentically Orthodox: A Tradition-Bound Faith in American
Life* (Detroit: Wayne State University Press, 2020).

44. For more on Jewish movement toward the sunbelt, see Moore, *To the Golden Cities*.

45. This general model matched the suggested standard for camp staff hierarchies in the
American Camping Association's "Standards Report for the Accreditation of Organized
Camps" (Martinsdale, MI: American Camping Association, 1966), 13.

46. See the special issue, "Chronological Age: A Useful Category of Analysis," *American
Historical Review* 125, no. 2 (April 2020).

47. Oral history with Judith Lerner by the author, November 11, 2020.

48. Nancy Mykoff, "Summer Camping in the United States," Jewish Women's Archive,
accessed February 10, 2022, https://jwa.org/encyclopedia/article/summer-camping-in-uni
ted-states. For more on the idea of the camp family, see "Tensions in the Camp Family" in
Paris, *Children's Nature*.

49. One line in Norman Schanin's 1959 dissertation on Young Judaea reflects the sexism
of the period, as the writer noted that "the lack of effective leadership had limited the
growth of Young Judaea" and blamed the movement's problems on the "preponderance of
female leaders, in a movement that was, in the school-year of 1951–1952, 82% female." See
Schanin, "Young Judaea," 2.

50. For studies on camps' impacts since the 1970s, see Gerald B. Bubis and Lawrence E.
Marks "Changes in Jewish Identification: A Comparative Study of a Teen Age Israel Camp-
ing Trip, a Counselor-in-Training Program, and a Teen Age Service Camp" (New York:
JCC Association, 1975); Steven M. Cohen, "Impact of Varieties of Jewish Education upon
Jewish Identity: An Inter-Generational Perspective," *Contemporary Jewry* 16 (1995): 68–96;
Steven M. Cohen, "Camp Ramah and Adult Jewish Identity," in *RAMAH: Reflections at
50: Visions for a New Century, National Ramah Commission*, ed., Sheldon A. Dorph (Na-
tional Ramah Commission, 2000), 95–129; Steven M. Cohen, "Jewish Overnight Summer
Camps in Southern California: A Marketing Study" (New York: Foundation for Jewish
Camp, 2007); Steven M. Cohen and Judith Veinstein, "Jewish Overnight Camps: A Study

of the Greater Toronto Area Market" (New York: Foundation for Jewish Camp, 2009); Uri Farago, "The Influence of a Jewish Summer Camp's Social Climate on the Camper's Identity" (PhD diss., Brandeis University, 1971); Seymour Fox with William Novak, "Vision at the Heart: Lessons from Camp Ramah. On the Power of Ideas in Shaping Educational Institutions" (Jerusalem and New York: Mandel Institute and the Council for Initiatives in Jewish Education, 1997); Steven M. Cohen and Laurence Kotler-Berkowitz, "The Impact of Childhood Jewish Education upon Adults' Jewish Identity: Schooling, Israel Travel, Camping and Youth Groups," United Jewish Communities Report Series on the National Jewish Population Survey 2000–2001, report 3, 2004, www.ujc.org/njps. See also Steven M. Cohen, Ron Miller, Ira M. Scheskin, and Berna Torr, "Camp Works: The Long-Term Impact of Jewish Overnight Camp," spring 2011, https://jewishcamp.org/campopedia/camp-works-the-long-term-impact-of-jewish-overnight-camp/.

51. Many researchers interested in interfaith families do not operate under the assumption that interfaith marriages present a threat to American Jewish life. See Jennifer Thompson, *Jewish on Their Own Terms: How Intermarried Couples Are Changing American Judaism* (New Brunswick, NJ: Rutgers University Press, 2014); Keren R. McGinity, *Marrying Out: Jewish Men, Intermarriage, and Fatherhood* (Bloomington: Indiana University Press, 2014); Keren McGinity, *Still Jewish: A History of Women and Intermarriage in America* (New York: NYU Press, 2009); and Samira K. Mehta, *Beyond Chrismukkah: Christian-Jewish Interfaith Families in the United States* (Chapel Hill: University of North Carolina Press, 2018). However, scholarship on the impacts of camps have overwhelmingly pursued this assumption, particularly in the work of Steven M. Cohen, who was prolific on the subject regarding camp and American Jewry more broadly, including in "Seeking a Third Way to Respond to the Challenge of Intermarriage" (New York: Central Conference of American Rabbis, March 2008) and "A Tale of Two Jewries: The 'Inconvenient Truth' for American Jews" (New York: Steinhardt Foundation for Jewish Life, November 2006). It must be noted that Cohen was accused of sexual harassment and assault in 2018 by female colleagues in both scholarly and Jewish communal settings. Cohen apologized for the behavior and did not dispute the allegations. This issue is addressed further in chapter 8.

52. Jodi Ruderon, "Let There Be Camp—Please!" *Forward*, April 19, 2020, https://forward.com/opinion/444100/jewish-summer-camp-coronavirus/.

53. Shraga Arian, Superintendent Board of Jewish Education Chicago, "Camping and Creative Jewish Education" in "The Future of Jewish Camping—Directions and Emphases: Proceedings of the National Conference on Jewish Camping," January 10–13, 1973, BM 135. N2.85, Hebrew Union College Library, Cincinnati.

54. See Ari Y. Kelman, "Counting Jews of Color: Are We Asking the Right Questions?," *J Weekly: The Jewish News of Northern California* May 21, 2020, https://www.jweekly.com/2020/05/21/counting-jews-of-color-are-we-asking-the-right-questions/. Kelman's article was in response to Ira M. Sheskin and Arnold Dashefsky "How Many Jews of Color Are There?," *eJewish Philanthropy* (blog), May 17, 2020, https://ejewishphilanthropy.com/how-many-jews-of-color-are-there/, which countered the findings of Ari Y. Kelman, Aaron Hahn

Tapper, Izabel Fonseca, and Aliyah Saperstein's 2019 study, "Counting Inconsistencies: An Analysis of American Jewish Population Studies, with a Focus on Jews of Color," https://jewsofcolorfieldbuilding.org/wp-content/uploads/2019/05/Counting-Inconsistencies-052119.pdf

55. While researchers and the public use various terms to describe marriages between Jews and non-Jews, including both *mixed marriage* and *interfaith marriage*, I use the term *intermarriage* as used by my historical subjects and by those who studied camps' influences on the marriage choices of alumni.

## Chapter One

1. David Mogilner, "The Role of Israel in Camp," in *Strengthening the Jewish Experiences of Children at Camp: Proceedings of the National Conference on Jewish Camping*, January 5–8, 1969, BM 135.N2.85, Hebrew Union College Library, Cincinnati.

2. See Hasia R. Diner, *The Jews of the United States, 1654 to 2000* (Berkeley: University of California Press, 2006), 88–89.

3. See Sol Steinmetz, *Yiddish and English: A Century of Yiddish in America* (Tuscaloosa: University of Alabama Press, 1986).

4. For more on "Yiddish socialism" and the labor movements of the turn of the century, see Tony Michaels, *A Fire in Their Hearts: Yiddish Socialists in New York* (Cambridge, MA: Harvard University Press, 2005).

5. On Jews and McCarthyism, see Deborah Dash Moore, "Reconsidering the Rosenbergs: Symbol and Substance in Second-Generation American Jewish Consciousness," *Journal of American Ethnic History* 8 (1988): 21–37.

6. Rachel Kranson, "Grappling with the Good Life: Jewish Anxieties over Affluence in Postwar America, 1945–1976" (PhD diss., New York University, 2012), 31–32.

7. "Two Thirds of America's Jews Now Live in Suburbs, Expert Estimates," Jewish Telegraphic Agency, October 16, 1959, accessed November 17, 2020, http://archive.jta.org.

8. See Rachel Kranson, *Ambivalent Embrace: Jewish Upward Mobility in Postwar America* (Chapel Hill: University of North Carolina Press, 2017), 3; see also Diner, *Jews of the United States*, 205–258.

9. For more on the synagogue in this period, see Paula Hyman, "From City to Suburb: Temple Mishkan Tefila of Boston," in *The American Synagogue*, ed. Jack Wertheimer (Cambridge: Cambridge University Press, 1987); and Deborah Moore, *At Home in America* (New York: Columbia University Press, 1981), 123–147.

10. Kranson, *Ambivalent Embrace*, 3–4.

11. Ibid., 13.

12. See Hasia R. Diner, *We Remember with Reverence and Love: American Jews and the Myth of Silence after the Holocaust, 1945–1962* (New York: NYU Press, 2010).

13. For more on Black-Jewish relations in the earlier twentieth century, see Hasia R. Diner, *In the Almost Promised Land: American Jews and Blacks, 1915–1935* (Westport, CT: Greenwood Press, 1977).

14. On Jews and the issue of whiteness, see Eric Goldstein, *The Price of Whiteness: Jews, Race, and American Identity* (Princeton: Princeton University Press, 2006). On Jews, white ethnic revival, and identity politics, see Matthew Frye Jacobson, *Roots Too: White Ethnic Revival in Post–Civil Rights America* (Cambridge, MA: Harvard University Press, 2006).

15. Kranson, "Grappling with the Good Life," 166. For more about the notion of the shtetl, see Jeffrey Shandler, *Shtetl: A Vernacular Intellectual History* (New Brunswick, NJ: Rutgers University Press, 2014).

16. For more on this, see Sandra F. Fox, ""Laboratories of Yiddishkayt": Postwar American Jewish Summer Camps and the Transformation of Yiddishism," *American Jewish History* 103, no. 3 (2019): 279–301, and Fox, "'The Passionate Few': Youth and Yiddishism in American Jewish Culture, 1964 to Present," *Jewish Social Studies* 26, no. 3 (2021): 1–34.

17. Shaul Magid, *American Post-Judaism: Identity and Renewal in a Postethnic Society*, rev. ed. (Bloomington: Indiana University Press, 2013), 16; Emily Alice Katz, *Bringing Zion Home: Israel in American Jewish Culture, 1948–1967*, reprint ed. (Albany: State University of New York Press, 2016), 2–3; Kranson, "Grappling with the Good Life," 71.

18. See Riv-Ellen Prell, "Summer Camp, Post-War American Jewish Youth and the Redemption of Judaism," in *The Jewish Role in American Life: An Annual Review*, vol. 5, ed. Bruce Zuckerman and Jeremy Schoenberg (West Lafayette, IN: Purdue University Press, 2007), 77-106; Joshua Furman, "'Jewish Education Begins at Home': Training Parents to Raise American Jewish Children after World War II," in *Mishpachah: The Jewish Family in Tradition and in Transition*, ed. Leonard J. Greenspoon (West Lafayette, IN: Purdue University Press, 2016).

19. Leslie Paris, *Children's Nature: The Rise of the American Summer Camp* (New York: New York University Press, 2008), 4.

20. On changing conceptions of youth and age, see Howard P. Chudacoff, *How Old Are You? Age Consciousness in American Culture* (Princeton, NJ: Princeton University Press, 1989); G. Stanley Hall, *Adolescence: Its Psychology and Its Relations to Physiology, Anthropology, Sociology, Sex, Crime, Religion and Education* (New York: Appleton, 1907); Julia Guarneri, "Changing Strategies for Child Welfare, Enduring Beliefs about Childhood: The Fresh Air Fund, 1877–1926," *Journal of the Gilded Age and Progressive Era* 11, no. 1 (2012): 27–70. On mandatory schooling and other shifts in American public education, see John L. Rury, *Education and Social Change: Contours in the History of American Schooling* (New York: Routledge, 2009); David Tyack, *The One Best System: A History of American Urban Education* (Cambridge, MA: Harvard University Press, 1974); Patricia Albjerg Graham, *Schooling America: How the Public Schools Meet the Nation's Changing Needs* (New York: Oxford University Press, 2005); William J. Reese, *America's Public Schools: From the Common School to "No Child Left Behind"* (Baltimore: Johns Hopkins University Press, 2005).

21. On the postwar family, see Elaine Tyler May, *Homeward Bound: American Families in the Cold War Era* (New York: Basic Books, 2008), and Rima D. Apple, *Perfect Motherhood: Science and Childrearing in America* (Piscataway, NJ: Rutgers University Press, 2006).

22. See Cheryl Russell, *The Baby Boom: Americans Born 1946 to 1964*, 7th ed. (Ithaca, NY: New Strategist Publications, 2012), 1, and May, *Homeward Bound*, 3.

23. Rury, *Education and Social Change*, 165.

24. On postwar youth culture, activism, and dating habits, see William Graebner, *Coming of Age in Buffalo: Youth and Authority in the Postwar Era;* Gael Graham, *Young Activists: American High School Students in the Age of Protest* (DeKalb: Northern Illinois University Press, 2006); Beth L. Bailey, *From Front Porch to Back Seat: Courtship in Twentieth-Century America* (Baltimore: Johns Hopkins University Press, 1988).

25. On the topic of juvenile delinquency, see James Gilbert, *A Cycle of Outrage: America's Reaction to the Juvenile Delinquent in the 1950s* (New York: Oxford University Press, 1986).

26. Graebner, *Coming of Age in Buffalo*, 7.

27. Beth Bailey, "From Panty Raids to Revolution: Youth and Authority, 1950–1970," in *Generations of Youth: Youth Cultures and History in Twentieth-Century America*, ed. Joe Austin and Michael Nevin Willard (New York: New York University Press, 1998).

28. I gathered this from searching for articles within the Historical Jewish Press database of the National Library of Israel. More research on Jews and the issue of delinquency is needed, but trends in the press show that the issue was of interest to American Jewry. See as an example, "Juvenile Delinquency May Be Avoided Says Youth Director," *B'nai B'rith Messenger*, May 27, 1955.

29. Rury, *Education and Social Change*, 185.

30. Ibid. See also Stephen Lassonde, "Age and Authority: Adult-Child Relations during the Twentieth Century in the United States," *Journal of the History of Childhood and Youth*, no. 1 (2008), 95; Reese, *America's Public Schools*, 7.

31. Joseph F. Kett, *Rites of Passage: Adolescence in America, 1790 to the Present* (New York: Basic Books, 1977), 267. For more on youth in the civil rights movement, see Rebecca de Schweinitz, *If We Could Change the World: Young People and America's Long Struggle for Racial Equality* (Chapel Hill: University of North Carolina Press, 2011); Philip Davies, *From Sit-Ins to SNCC: The Student Civil Rights Movement in the 1960s* (Gainesville: University Press of Florida, 2012); Andrew B. Lewis, *The Shadows of Youth: The Remarkable Journey of the Civil Rights Generation* (New York: Hill and Wang, 2009). On high school feminism, see Matthew Ides, "'Dare to Free Yourself': The Red Tide, Feminism, and High School Activism in the Early 1970s," *Journal of the History of Childhood and Youth* 7, no. 2 (2014): 295–319. For youth involvement in gay rights, see Stephan Cohen, *The Gay Liberation Youth Movement in New York: "An Army of Lovers Cannot Fail"* (Hoboken: Taylor & Francis, 2008).

32. Regarding the Jews in Students for a Democratic Society (SDS) and the Weatherman, see Mark Rudd, "Why Were There so Many Jews in SDS? (Or, The Ordeal of Civility)," November 2005, https://www.markrudd.com/indexcd39.html?about-mark-rudd/why-were-there-so-many-jews-in-sds-or-the-ordeal-of-civility.html, Jeremy Varon, *Bringing the War Home: The Weather Underground, the Red Army Faction, and Revolutionary Violence in the Sixties and Seventies* (Berkeley: University of California Press, 2004), 28. On Jews and the

Freedom Summer, see "Mississippi Freedom Summer—Fifty Years Later, Part One," *Jewish Currents*, June 15, 2014, https://jewishcurrents.org/mississippi-freedom-summer-fifty-years -later-part-one/, and Diner, *Jews of the United States*, 268–269.

33. See Riv-Ellen Prell, *Prayer and Community: The Havurah in American Judaism* (Detroit: Wayne State University Press, 1989).

34. Kranson, "Grappling with the Good Life," 59–60.

35. Kranson, *Ambivalent Embrace*, 152. See also David Glanz, "An Interpretation of the Jewish Counterculture," *Jewish Social Studies* 39 (1977): 117–128

36. Ibid., 167; see also Rachel Kranson, "'To Be a Jew on America's Terms Is Not to Be a Jew at All': The Jewish Counterculture's Critique of Middle-Class Affluence," *Journal of Jewish Identities* 8, no. 2 (July 2015), and Lila Corwin Berman, "American Jews and the Ambivalence of Middle-Classness," *American Jewish History* 93, no. 4 (2007): 409–434.

37. Kranson, *Ambivalent Embrace*, 167.

38. For general background regarding the American Progressive Era, see Michael McGerr, *A Fierce Discontent: The Rise and Fall of the Progressive Movement in America, 1870–1920* (New York: Oxford University Press, 2005).

39. Paris, *Children's Nature*, 55.

40. Ibid., 18. See also Julia Guarneri, "Changing Strategies for Child Welfare, Enduring Beliefs about Childhood: The Fresh Air Fund, 1877–1926," *Journal of the Gilded Age and Progressive Era* 11, no. 1 (2012): 27–70.

41. On the crisis of masculinity in the Progressive Era, see E. Anthony Rotundo, *American Manhood: Transformations in Masculinity from the Revolution to the Modern Era* (New York: Basic Books, 1993); T. J. Jackson Lears, *No Place of Grace: Antimodernism and the Transformation of American Culture, 1880–1920* (New York: Pantheon, 1981); and Mark C. Carnes and Clyde Griffen, eds., *Meanings for Manhood: Constructions of Masculinity in Victorian America* (Chicago: University of Chicago Press, 1990).

42. Paris, *Children's Nature*, 19, 56.

43. Ibid., 61.

44. Jacob Sorenson, *Sacred Playgrounds: Christian Summer Camp in Theological Perspective* (Eugene, OR: Cascade Books, 2021), 23.

45. Paris, *Children's Nature,* 167.

46. American Camping Association, "Standards Report for the Accreditation of Organized Camps" (1966).

47. American Camping Association, for the Accreditation of Organized Camps "Camp Standards with Interpretations, " 1976. Tom Rosenberg, CEO of the ACA, sent this PDF to me in October 2017.

48. Paris, *Children's Nature,* 93.

49. Sorensen, *Sacred Playgrounds*, 3.

50. Horace Bushnell, *Christian Nurture* (New Haven: Yale University Press, 1953), 15.

51. Sorenson, *Sacred Playground*.

52. Regarding Muslim camping, for which there is scant scholarship, I refer to my conversation with Nadine Karachi, May 21, 2020.

53. On Jews and public schooling, see Diner, *Jews of the United States*, 294.

54. As Jenna Weissman Joselit explained, "Preferring to spend vacations in the company of their own kind rather than run a gauntlet of disapproving gentiles, Eastern European Jewish immigrants created a summer world" in the Catskill Mountains, "of boardinghouses, bungalows, inns, and 'exclusive' hotels populated entirely by Jews." Jenna Weissman Joselit, "Leisure and Recreation in the United States," accessed November 27, 2017, Jewish Women's Archive, Brookline, MA.

55. See Jonathan Sarna, "The Crucial Decade in Jewish Camping," in *A Place of Our Own: The Rise of Reform Jewish Camping: Essays Honoring the Fiftieth Anniversary of Olin-Sang-Ruby Union Institute*, ed. Gary Phillip Zola (Tuscaloosa: University of Alabama Press, 2006). See also the records of the National Jewish Welfare Board, 1889–1995 (bulk 1917–1990), Finding Aid, I-377, n.d., American Jewish Historical Society (AJHS).

56. Itzik Gottesman, "A Short History of Camp Boiberik," Camp Boiberik home page, https://boiberik.media.mit.edu/history.html.

57. See Sarna, "Crucial Decade in Jewish Camping," 48, and Fradle Freidenreich, *Passionate Pioneers: The Story of Yiddish Secular Education in North America, 1910–1960* (Teaneck, NJ: Holmes & Meier, 2010), 363–364. See also Barnett Zumoff, "The Secular Yiddish School and Summer Camp: A Hundred-Year History," *Jewish Currents*, August 9, 2013, http://jewishcurrents.org/the-secular-yiddish-school-and-summer-camp-a-hundred-year-history/.

58. See David Breslau, *Story of 25 Years of Habonim Camping* (New York: Chai Commission of LZOA Movement, 1957); "About Habonim Dror North America," accessed June 30, 2020, https://www.habonimdror.org/about-us/.

59. Alan L. Mintz, *Hebrew in America: Perspectives and Prospects* (Detroit: Wayne State University Press, 1993), 115. For more on Camp Achvah, see Jonathan Krasner, *The Benderly Boys and American Jewish Education* (Waltham, MA: Brandeis University Press, 2011), 268–322.

60. Sarna, "Crucial Decade in Jewish Camping," 37.

61. "American Jewish University Website—History of the Brandeis-Bardin Campus," accessed November 2017, https://www.aju.edu/about-aju/history

62. Sarna, "Crucial Decade in Jewish Camping," 35. Sarna and Isaacman both gave Yiddish camps short shrift in their research. Portraying the Hebrew infusion methods of many Jewish educational camps as productive and positive, Isaacman dismissed the similar use of "Yiddishisms and . . . Yiddish camp expressions" established in "earlier years" of Yiddishist camping, "when Yiddish was indeed in use." To Isaacman, there was no need to elaborate "on the lack of Yiddish in the so-called Yiddish camps." While a footnote in Sarna's essay acknowledged that Fradle Freidenreich had "persuasively argued" that Yiddish camps "promoted an educational agenda as early as the 1920s and were therefore forerunners of Jewish educational camping," and that "Zionist camps such as Moshava, sponsored

by the Habonim movement, likewise promoted an educational agenda," Sarna writes that these camps' "distinctly ideological" forms of education place them in a different category, making their divergent historical timelines irrelevant to the 1941–1952 decade. Daniel Isaacman, "Jewish Education in Camping," *American Jewish Yearbook* 67 (1966), 245–252.

63. Shulamith Z. Berger, "Summers at Camp Machanaim, 1929–1938" (blog), Yeshiva University Library, August 9, 2018, https://blogs.yu.edu/library/2018/08/09/summers-at-camp-machanaim-1929-1938/.

64. See Camp Shari, Jacob Hartstein Collection, box 43, 4/19–20, Yeshiva University Archives; Camp Machanaim, Jacob Hartstein Collection, box 43, 4/10–11, Yeshiva University Archives. See also Ilana Abramovitch and Seán Galvin, eds., *Jews of Brooklyn* (Waltham, MA: Brandeis University Press, 2002), 244.

65. Berger, "Summers at Camp Machanaim, 1929–1938."

66. "Camp Agudah—At Last!" *Orthodox Tribune* 2, no. 4 (Adar 5702/March 1942).

67. For more on this period in the history of Orthodoxy, see Zev Eleff, *Authentically Orthodox: A Tradition-Bound Faith in American Life* (Detroit, MI: Wayne State University Press, 2020).

68. "Data on Jewish Sponsored Camps in Greater New York Area: Habonim Naaleh," n.d., box 900, Folder "Habonim Camp Naaleh, 1963–1970," United Jewish Appeal, Federation of New York Collection 1909–2004, I-433, AJHS.

69. Issacman, "Jewish Education in Camping," 248.

70. Ibid., 250.

71. Mogilner, "Role of Israel in Camp," 71.

72. Leibush Lehrer, Leibush Lehrer, "Camp Boiberik: The Growth of an Idea" (1959), 26, YIVO Library, YIVO Institute for Jewish Research, New York. "Summer Report," 1956, Camp Boiberik, box 6, folder 220, Sholem Aleichem Folk Institute, Camp Boiberik Collection 1923–1978, YIVO Archives. See also Judah Pilch, *A History of Jewish Education in the United States* (New York: National Curriculum Research Institute of the American Association for Jewish Education, 1969), 130.

73. As Daniel Isaacman stated in the 1966 *American Jewish Yearbook*, "The Yiddishist camps, organized to provide an environment in keeping with the philosophy of the parent body—Yiddish culturist or Zionist with Yiddish cultural concerns—have deviated considerably from their original purposes.... There was no mention of Yiddish" (Isaacman, "Jewish Education in Camping," 247). Isaacman, my research shows, overstated these changes: all of the camps studied in this work still used Yiddish at camp in myriad ways symbolically and educationally, even as spoken Yiddish had significantly declined.

## Chapter Two

1. Morris Freedman, "Camp Ramah: Where Hebrew Is the Key: A Full Jewish Education for a Full Jewish Life," *Commentary* (May 1955), https://www.commentarymagazine.com/articles/camp-ramah-where-hebrew-is-the-key-a-full-jewish-education-for-a-full-jewish-life/.

2. Daniel Isaacman, "Jewish Education in Camping," *American Jewish Yearbook* 67 (1966): 246.

3. Leibush Lehrer, "The Objectives of Camp Boiberik," 1962 pamphlet, 61, YIVO Library, YIVO Institute for Jewish Research, New York.

4. Asher Meltzer, "A Program Guide for the Jewish Camp" (American Zionist Youth Foundation, 1972).

5. Jonathan B. Krasner, *The Benderly Boys and American Jewish Education* (Waltham, MA: Brandeis University Press, 2012), 284.

6. Abigail A. Van Slyck, *A Manufactured Wilderness: Summer Camps and the Shaping of American Youth, 1890–1960* (Minneapolis: University of Minnesota Press, 2006), 43.

7. "Camp Ramah in Wisconsin: Introduction to the Junior Counselor Program," 1970, box 8, folder 1, Records of the National Ramah Commission, Jewish Theological Seminary Archives (JTSA), New York, 1951–1989.

8. Eviatar Zerubavel, *Hidden Rhythms: Schedules and Calendars in Social Life* (Berkeley: University of California Press, 1985), 67. For more on total institutions, see Erving Goffman, *Asylums: Essays on the Social Situation of Mental Patients and Other Inmates* (New York: Anchor Books/Doubleday, 1961).

9. Meryl Nadel and Susan Scher, "From Fresh Air to Summer Camp: Social Work Enters the Picture, " in *Not Just Play: Summer Camp and the Profession of Social Work* (New York: Oxford University Press, 2019), 63.

10. Jonathan B. Krasner, *The Benderly Boys and American Jewish Education* (Waltham, MA: Brandeis University Press, 2012), 285.

11. "15 Ways You Know You Went to Jewish Summer Camp," *Foundation for Jewish Camp* (blog), January 27, 2017, https://jewishcamp.org/15-ways-you-know-you-went-to-jewish-summer-camp/.

12. Rachel Mann, "Running on Camp Time," *Forward*, July 26, 2016, https://forward.com/scribe/345964/running-on-camp time/.

13. A similar vision of camp time was described by Celia Rothenberg in her study of a Jewish summer camp in St Louis. See Celia E. Rothenberg, *Serious Fun at a Jewish Community Summer Camp: Family, Judaism, and Israel* (Lanham, MD: Lexington Books, 2016), 13.

14. "Counselors Checklist," box 8, folder 1, Louis Newman Papers, 1936–2006, MS-839, American Jewish Archive (AJA), Cincinnati.

15. In 1963, the Association of American Jewish Education's study of sixty-one Jewish summer camps found that 32 percent of camps held daily prayer services. Daniel Isaacman, "Jewish Education in Camping," *American Jewish Year Book* 67 (1966): 250.

16. "Cejwin Prayer Book," 1969, box 23, folder 4, Schoolman Family Collection, undated, 1889–1994, AJHS.

17. "Director's Report," Tel Yehudah, 1948, and advertising pamphlet, 1956, Camp Tel Yehudah DD1–52321, Central Zionist Archive, Jerusalem.

18. "OSRUI Promotional Pamphlet," 1965, box 1, folder 9, Olin-Sang-Ruby Union Institute (Oconomowoc, WI) Records, 1941–2001, AJA.

19. Ismar Schorsch, "Ramah: Adventure in Jewish Education," in "Camp Ramah: The Early Years, 1947–1952," *Conservative Judaism* 40, no. 1 (1987): 7.

20. "Prayer Materials," box 8, folder 11, Records of the National Ramah Commission, 1951–1989, RG-28, JTSA.

21. See Riv-Ellen Prell, "'How Do You Know That I Am a Jew?': Authority, Cultural Identity, and the Shaping of Postwar American Judaism," in *Jewish Studies at the Crossroads of Anthropology and History: Authority, Diaspora, Tradition*, ed. Ra'anan Boustan, Oren Kosansky, and Marina Rustow (Philadelphia: University of Pennsylvania Press, 2011), 37.

22. See Shuly Rubin Schwartz "Camp Ramah: The Early Years, 1947–1952," *Conservative Judaism* 40, no. 1 (1987).

23. Daniel J. Elazer and Rela Mintz Geffen, *Conservative Movement in Judaism: Dilemmas and Opportunities* (Albany: State University of New York Press, 2000), 56–7.

24. Schorsch, "Ramah: Adventure in Jewish Education," 7.

25. Donald Splansky's "Creating a Prayer Experience in Reform Movement Camps and Beyond," in *A Place of Our Own: The Rise of Reform Jewish Camping: Essays Honoring the Fiftieth Anniversary of Olin-Sang-Ruby Union Institute*, ed. Gary Phillip Zola (Tuscaloosa: University of Alabama Press, 2006), 158.

26. Ibid.

27. Schwartz, "Camp Ramah," 32.

28. Sarah Bunin Benor, Jonathan Krasner, and Sharon Avni, *Hebrew Infusion: Language and Community at American Jewish Summer Camps* (New Brunswick, NJ: Rutgers University Press, 2020), 82.

29. "WE SPEAK OUT," 1967, box 1, folder 13, Swig Camp Institute Records, 1964, 1967, AJA.

30. See "Habonim Spies," n.d., box 8, folder 1 "Plays and Musicals," Camp Hemshekh Collection, YIVO Archives. For more on SKIF, see David Slucki, "The Goldene Medineh? Bund and Jewish Left in the Post-War United States," in *Bundist Legacy after the Second World War*, ed. Vincenzo Pinto (Leiden: Brill, 2018), 70–89.

31. For more on Jews and physical culture, see Moshe Zimmermann, "Muscle Jews versus Nervous Jews" in *Emancipation Through Muscles: Jews and Sports in Europe*, ed. Michael Brenner and Gideon Reuveni (Lincoln: University of Nebraska Press, 2006); see also Filip Marcinowski and Tadeusz Nasierowski, "Rafael Becker: Psychiatrist, Eugenist, Zionist," *Psychiatria Polska* 50, no. 1 (2016): 261–268; and Susan Grant, *Physical Culture and Sport in Soviet Society* (New York: Routledge, 2012), 10.

32. "Shomria Advertisement," folder, 60–1, 2942, Hashomer Hatzair Collection, Givat Haviva Archives.

33. "Farm Life to Be Demonstrated at Camp Shomria" *Bnai Brith Messenger*, May 31 1957, 9.

34. Prell, "'How Do You Know That I Am a Jew?'" 91.

35. "Tel Yehudah," *Senior*, March 1962, Page 70, box 51, Jewish Student Organizations Collection, AJHS.

36. Iton Moshava, "Sixteen Kids," 1970–1971, p. 3, 60–61, 2968, Hashomer Hatzair Collection.

37. "An Outline of Projections for the Compilation of a Course of Study for Ramah Camps," Alvin Mars, box 2, folder 8, Records of the National Ramah Commission, New York.

38. "Tel Yehudah," 70, Young Judaea, North American Jewish Students Appeal Records, American Jewish Historical Society (AJHS), New York.

39. "Advertising Pamphlet," 1956, Camp Tel Yehudah DD1–52321, Central Zionist Archive, Jerusalem.

40. "Letter to Parents from director of Shomria, Jaacov Lior," 1972, 60–1, 2942, Hashomer Hatzair Collection, Yad Yaari Archives, Haifa.

41. "Advertising Pamphlets, n.d." 60–1, 2942. Hashomer Hatzair Collection.

42. David Breslau, *Story of 25 Years of Habonim Camping* (New York: Chai Commission of LZOA Movement, 1957), 43.

43. "Tentative Program of the Counselor Committee," 1963, box 1, folder 1, Camp Hemshekh Collection, YIVO.

44. "Machaneh Avodah in Ramah," n.d., box 9, folder 16, Records of the National Ramah Commission, 1951–1989, RG-28, JTSA.

45. Ibid.

46. "Chugim," folder, 60–1, 2972, Hashomer Hatzair Collection.

47. "Camp Tel Yehudah Advertising Pamphlet," 1956, file DD1–5232, Central Zionist Archive, Jerusalem. In Young Judaea's camps, the counselors who taught scouting came as representatives of the Israeli Scouts youth movement. See "Israel Scout to Join Camp Staff," *Bnai Brith Messenger*, May 31, 1968, 18. "Israeli Boy Scout to Spend Summer with Young Judaea," *Bnai Brith Messenger*, April 22, 1966, 16.

48. See Breslau, *25 Years of Habonim Camping*; Yavneh Yearbook "Eshkol," 1962, Camp Yavneh website, https://www.campyavneh.org/yavneh-alumni/.

49. "Machaneh Avodah in Ramah," n.d., box 9, folder 16, Ramah.

50. A *Tablet* magazine article in 2016 attempted to untangle the mythology surrounding the game of Gaga, but came up with no conclusive evidence of its origins. See Stephen Silver, "The Ga-Ga Saga," August 17, 2016, http://www.tabletmag.com/jewish-life-and-religion/210407/the-ga-ga-saga, and Karen Alexander, "Jewish Camps Spawn a U.S. Playground Hit," *New York Times*, July 19, 2012, https://www.nytimes.com/2012/07/19/us/gaga-play ground-game-is-popular-at-camps.html.

51. Philip Goodman. "The Jewish Home Camp, " *Jewish Education* 17 (June 1946): 30–35.

52. I. Sheldon Posen, "Lomir Zingn, Hava Nashira (Let Us Sing): An Introduction to Jewish Summer Camp Song," in *A Worthy Use of Summer: Jewish Summer Camping in*

*America*, ed. Jenna Weissman Joselit and Karen S. Mittelman (Washington, DC: National Museum of American Jewish History, 1995), 30.

53. "The Educational Principles of Camp Hemshekh," 1962, box 5 "Miscellaneous," Hemshekh Collection.

54. "Mir Zingen," 1960, Camp Kinderring, 000082359, YIVO Library.

55. "Kol Ba'Ramah," Louis Newman Papers, 1936–2006, box 8, folder 1, AJA.

56. Asher Meltzer, "A Program Guide for the Jewish Camp," 1972, American Zionist Youth Foundation, HUC BM.135.M4, HUC, 21.

57. Ibid.

58. "Folk Dancing Chug," 1971, box 4, folder 10, Myron S, Goldman Camp Institute Collection, AJA; "Dance: Israeli, Folk, Modern—Second Year," 1962, box 8, folder 4, Louis Newman Papers, 1936–2006, AJA.

59. "We Learn," Haboneh 1959, Lisa Kurtzman, box 7, folder 3, Jewish Student Organizations Collection, I-61, AJHS.

60. "Dramatics," n.d., Massad Collection, F51/66, Central Zionist Archives.

61. "Alizah in Wonderland," n.d. 1950s, box 23, folder 19—Plays and Program Kits, Schoolman Family Collection, AJHS; "My Fair Sabra" and "Portrait of the Shtetl," 1960, box 12, "Dramatizations and Plays" folder, Young Judaea Collection, North American Jewish Students Appeal Records, AJHS.

62. Walter Ackerman, "A World Apart: Hebrew Teachers Colleges and Hebrew-Speaking Camps," ed. Alan L. Mintz (Detroit: Wayne State University Press, 1993), 118; see also "Index of Dramatic Material," in Series B. Alphabetical, 1954–1988, n.d., Records of the National Ramah Commission, 1951–1989, RG-28, JTSA.

63. "Season Directors Report and Evaluation," 1966, DCS Camp Morasha, 1963–1966, Mendel Gottesman Library, Yeshiva University.

64. "The Educational Principles of Camp Hemshekh," 1962, box 5, "Miscellaneous," Hemshekh Collection.

65. "Counselor's Play: Amkho sher un ayzn," *Di Hemshekh Vokh* 10, no. 6 (1968), 015009254, YIVO.

66. All of these plays can be found in "Plays/Scripts," 1968, box 4, folder 20, Myron S. Goldman Union Camp Institute, AJA.

67. "The Jewish American Princess" 1972, box 3, folder 4, Myron S. Goldman Union Camp Institute.

68. "Plays," 1963, box 5, Myron S. Goldman Union Camp Institute.

69. "Shabbat Schedule," 1965, box 9, folder 35, Records of the National Ramah Commission.

70. "Shabbat Rest," Camp Yavneh Yearbook, 1966, Camp Yavneh website, https://www.campyavneh.org/yavneh-alumni/.

71. "Tel Yehudah," *Senior*, March 1962, p. 70, box 51, Jewish Student Organizations Collection, AJHS.

72. Zevi Scharfstein, *Massad: The Story of Hebrew Camping in the United States* (New York: Massad Camps, 1959), BM135.S4.613, HUC, 17.

73. "Schedules," folder, 60–1, 2972, Hashomer Hatzair Collection.

74. Rukhl Schaechter and Gitl Schaechter-Viswanath, episode 37 of *Vaybertaytsh: A Feminist Podcast in Yiddish*, recorded at the Yiddish Week in Copake, New York, August 20, 2018; Miriam Oxenhandler, conversation in Hemshekh Alumni Facebook Group, October 2018.

75. Author interview with Miriam Forman, November 10, 2020.

76. Leibush Lehrer, "Camp Boiberik: The Growth of an Idea," 9, 1959, YIVO Library.

77. Mara Sokolsky, "Article from The Forward," May 29, 1998, "The Return to Shabbes Rock (Reunion 1998)," Boiberik Alumni website, boiberik.media.mit.edu.

78. Naomi Prawer Kadar attributed this change in Lehrer and others like him, which she saw as beginning around 1936, to the rise of Hitler. See Naomi Prawer Kadar, *Raising Secular Jews: Yiddish Schools and Their Periodicals for American Children, 1917–1950*, (Waltham, MA: Brandeis University Press, 2016), 9.

79. "Summer Camps Guide" from the Jewish National Fund: 1953, 1957, HUC- BM.135. S9/1953.

80. Mann, "Running on Camp Time."

### Chapter Three

1. "Special Days," *Kol Machane*, Midwest Camp Habonim, 1964, in Near-Print: Special Topics: Jewish Camp, box 2, American Jewish Archives (AJA), Cincinnati.

2. Roger Caillois, *Man, Play, and Games* (New York: Free Press, 1961), 83.

3. For more on children's play through history and theories about play, see Howard Chudacoff, *Children at Play: An American History* (New York: New York University Press, 2007), xii.

4. "Translator's Introduction," in Roger Caillois, *Man, Play, and Games*, 2nd ed. (Champaign: University of Illinois Press, 2001), ix. The original book, *Les jeux et les hommes*, was published in 1958 by Librarie Gallimard, Paris.

5. Leslie Paris, *Children's Nature: The Rise of the American Summer Camp* (New York: New York University Press, 2008), 5.

6. John Dewey, *Democracy and Education: An Introduction to the Philosophy of Education* (1916; Waiheke Island: Floating Press, 2009), 335. For more on Dewey's influence on American Jewish education, see also Jonathan B. Krasner, *The Benderly Boys and American Jewish Education* (Waltham, MA: Brandeis University Press, 2012), and Ronald Kronish, "The Influence of John Dewey on Jewish Education in America" (PhD diss., Harvard Graduate School of Education, 1979).

7. For more on group work, see Meryl Nadel and Susan Scher, *Not Just Play: Summer Camp and the Profession of Social Work* (New York: Oxford University Press, 2019), 18–30.

8. Paris, *Children's Nature*, 120–121.

9. Louis H. Blumenthal, *Group Work in Camping* (New York: Association Press, 1937), 77.

10. Ibid., 77–78.

11. Lila Corwin Berman, *Speaking of Jews: Rabbis, Intellectuals, and the Creation of an American Public Identity* (Berkeley: University of California Press, 2009), 3, 35, 2.

12. See Nadel and Sher, 76-86. See also "The Future of Jewish Camping—Directions and Emphases," in *Proceedings of the National Conference on Jewish Camping*, January 10–13, 1973, BM 135.N2.85, HUC Library, Cincinnati, and *Proceedings of the National Conference on Jewish Camping*, January 5–8, 1969, BM 135.N2.85, Hebrew Union College Library (HUC), Cincinnati.

13. David Mogilner, "The Role of Israel in Camp," in *Strengthening the Jewish Experiences of Children at Camp: Proceedings of the National Conference on Jewish Camping*, January 5–8, 1969, BM 135.N2.85, HUC Library.

14. Samuel Green, "Serving the Jewish Teenager in the Camp," in *Strengthening the Jewish Experiences of Children at Camp: Proceedings of the National Conference on Jewish Camping*, January 5–8, 1969, HUC Library.

15. Samuel J. Citron, "Dr. Benderly's Love of Drama," *Journal of Jewish Education*, June 1, 1949, 74.

16. Ibid., 71.

17. Samuel J. Citron, "They Live Together through Dramatics," *Journal of Jewish Education*, September 1, 1952, 51.

18. Fannie R. Shaftel and George Armin Shaftel, *Role Playing in the Curriculum*, 2nd ed. (Englewood Cliffs, NJ: Prentice Hall, 1982).

19. Borge Kristoffersen, "Jacob Levy Moreno's Encounter Term: A Part of a Social Drama," *Zeitschrift Für Psychodrama Und Soziometrie* 13, no. 1 (2014): 69.

20. Jonathan D. Moreno, *Impromptu Man: J. L. Moreno and the Origins of Psychodrama, Encounter Culture, and the Social Network*, illustrated ed. (New York: Bellevue Literary Press, 2014), 50.

21. Jonathan L. Moreno. "The Concept of Sociodrama: A New Approach to the Problem of Inter-Cultural Relations," *Sociometry* 6, no. 4 (1943): 437.

22. For more on the relationship between Dewey and Kallen, see Ronald Kronish, "John Dewey and Horace M. Kallen on Cultural Pluralism: Their Impact on Jewish Education," *Jewish Social Studies* 44, no. 2 (1982): 137.

23. Fannie R. Shaftel and George Armin Shaftel, *Role-Playing for Social Values: Decision-Making in the Social Studies* (Englewood Cliffs, NJ: Prentice Hall, 1967), 147–149.

24. Michael Zeldin, "Making the Magic in Reform Jewish Camps," in *A Place of Our Own: The Rise of Reform Jewish Camping: Essays Honoring the Fiftieth Anniversary of Olin-Sang-Ruby Union Institute*, ed. Gary Phillip Zola (Tuscaloosa: University of Alabama Press, 2006), 109.

25. "Summer Camps Guide," Jewish National Fund, 1953, BM135.S9/1953, and 1957, BM.135.J4.7, HUC Library.

26. Eli Weber, "Games for Summer Camps," early 1970s, American Zionist Youth Foundation Education Department, box 3, Special Topics: Nearprint, AJA.

27. Ibid.

28. Ibid.

29. Ibid.

30. "Special Days," *Kol Machane*, Midwest Camp Habonim, 1964, in Near-Print: Special Topics: Jewish Camp, box 2, AJA.

31. Weber, "Games for Summer Camps."

32. Author oral history interview with Mike (pseudonym), November 11, 2020.

33. Author oral history interview with Judith Lerner, November 11, 2020.

34. Asher Meltzer, "A Program Guide for the Jewish Camp," 1972, American Zionist Youth Foundation, HUC BM.135.M4, HUC Library.

35. "Yoman Solel—Mifal HaYom," box 1, folder 16, Swig Camp Institute Collection, AJA.

36. "Zionist Congress," box 10, folder 11, Swig Camp Institute Collection.

37. Zeldin, "Making the Magic," 86.

38. For more on the significance of the shtetl to American Jewry, see Jeffrey Shandler, *Shtetl: A Vernacular Intellectual History* (New Brunswick, NJ: Rutgers University Press, 2014).

39. "Cossacks Raid Campers," June 22, 1969, *GUCI Camp Newspaper*, vol. 1, no. 1, box 5: Publications 1968, Myron S. Goldman Camp Institute Collection, AJA.

40. Author oral history interview with Judith Lerner, November 11, 2020.

41. "Our Jewish World," 1964, box 10, folder 10, Swig Camp Institute Collection, AJA.

42. "Program Based on the Prayer Book," 1960s, box 8, folder 11, Records of the National Ramah Commission, Jewish Theological Seminary Archives (JTSA).

43. "The Zionsville Platforms," n.d., box 5, folder 5, Myron S. Goldman Camp Institute Collection.

44. Meltzer, "Program Guide."

45. "Yada and Culture Nights," n.d., Camp Hemshekh, box 4, folder 2, YIVO Institute for Jewish Research, New York.

46. Paris, *Children's Nature*, 120.

47. Blumenthal, *Group Work*, 78.

48. Paris, *Children's Nature*, 120–121.

49. For more on the history of the international Maccabiah Games, see Yair Galily and Amir Ben Porat, *Sport, Politics and Society in the Land of Israel: Past and Present* (New York: Routledge, 2013).

50. "Maccabia in Massad," 1953, I 550, box 3, folder 6, Camp Massad Collection, American Jewish Historical Society (AJHS).

51. "Maccabiah: Katarnim and Kfarim," 1956, box 3, folder 9, Camp Massad Collection.

52. "Maccabiah: Galim and Tslilim," 1973, box 3, folder 9, Camp Massad Collection.

53. Ibid.

54. "Maccabia" 1964, Olin-Sang-Ruby Union Institute Records, 1941–2001, box 6, folder 4, AJA.

55. "Yada and Culture Nights," n.d., Camp Hemshekh Collection , box 4, folder 2.

56. "YADA," 1971, box 4, folder 2, Camp Hemshekh Collection.

57. See "Yada" and "Hemshekh Yada," box 4, folders 2 and 4, Camp Hemshekh Collection.

58. Ibid.

59. "Mazel Tov Day," n.d., box 7, folder 290, SAFI Camp Boiberik, YIVO.

60. "Di Yontefdike Teg," 1964, Camp Hemshekh, box 4, folder 3.

61. Ibid.

62. "1968: Chanukah Play Pamphlet," n.d., box 4, folder 2, Camp Hemshekh Collection.

63. "Shavuos," 1967, box 4, folder 2, Camp Hemshekh Collection.

64. "Olympics 1964," 1964, box 4, folder 3 "Olympics," Camp Hemshekh Collection.

65. "Maccabiah," July 1964, box 6, folder 33, Swig Camp Institute Collection.

66. "Chana Schachner's Oral History," interview by Pauline Katz, Yiddish Book Center, April 7, 2011, http://www.yiddishbookcenter.org/collections/oral-histories/interviews/woh -fi-0000116/chana-schachner-2011/woh-fi-0000116.

67. "Director's Report," Tel Yehudah, 1948, gifted to me by Jamie Maxner, assistant director of Camp Tel Yehudah in October 2015.

### Chapter Four

1. "Tisha B'Av," Reuben Cohen, Camp Yavneh Yearbook, Eshkol 1961, Camp Yavneh website, https://www.campyavneh.org/yavneh-alumni/.

2. See Larry Domnitch, *The Jewish Holidays: A Journey through History* (Lanham, MD: Jason Aronson, 2000), and Rabbi Paul Steinberg, *Celebrating the Jewish Year: The Spring and Summer Holidays: Passover, Shavuot, the Omer, Tisha B'Av* (Philadelphia: Jewish Publication Society, 2009).

3. See Tova Birnbaum, "Most Jews Don't Know Much about Tisha B'Av. That Gives Us Educators a Huge Opportunity," *Jewish Telegraphic Agency* (blog), July 28, 2020, https:// www.jta.org/2020/07/28/opinion/most-jews-dont-know-much-about-tisha-bav-that-gives -us-educators-a-huge-opportunity.

4. Hasia R. Diner, *We Remember with Reverence and Love: American Jews and the Myth of Silence after the Holocaust, 1945–1962* (New York: New York University Press, 2009), 53–54.

5. Tisha B'Av was observed at religious Jewish camps for urban youth as early as the 1920s, but the shift toward an emotional ceremony took place mainly in the aftermath of the Holocaust.

6. Eugene B. Borowitz, "Facing the Future of Jewish Education," *Jewish Education* 45, no. 2 (March 1, 1977), 37.

7. Diner, *We Remember*, 53.

8. Borowitz, "Facing the Future of Jewish Education," 37.

9. Rona Sheramy, "'Resistance and War': The Holocaust in American Jewish Education, 1945–1960," *American Jewish History* 91, no. 2 (June 2003): 287–288.

10. It is unclear from archival sources whether Yiddishist camps directly drew on Tisha B'Av in creating the concepts for their alternatives or decided separately that memorial days were needed. However, the fact that these alternate days tended to occur at the end of the summer, just as Tisha B'Av often does, helps make a case for a conscious decision on the part of Yiddishists to secularize Tisha B'Av.

11. "Evening Program," 1964, box 6, Olin-Sang-Ruby Union Institute (Oconomowoc, WI) Records 1941–2001, American Jewish Archives (AJA), Cincinnati.

12. "Tisha B'Av," File: DD15310, Habonim Labor Zionist Youth in New York, Central Zionist Archive, Jerusalem.

13. "The Commemoration of Tisha Be-Av: Remember and Rebuild," n.d., box 23, folder 25, Schoolman Family Papers, 1889–1994, American Jewish Historical Society (AJHS), New York.

14. "Tisha B'av," File: DD15310, Habonim Labor Zionist Youth in New York, Central Zionist Archive, Jerusalem.

15. "Tisha B'Av," in *Kovetz Elim* 1965, Camp Massad, F51–38, CZA. See also Massad, *Massad Reminiscences* (Jerusalem: Massad Hebrew Summer Camps Alumni Organization, 1996), 26.

16. "The Commemoration of Tisha Be-Av: Remember and Rebuild," n.d., box 23, folder 25, Schoolman Family Papers, 1889–1994.

17. Etan Levine, "Tisha Be-Av," 1962, box 23, folder 25, Schoolman Family Papers, 1889–1994. Jonathan Krasner also wrote about this moment in the history of Camp Cejwin and notes how it changed after the Adolf Eichmann trial in 1961, becoming more Zionist in character. See Jonathan Krasner, *The Benderly Boys and American Jewish Education* (Waltham, MA: Brandeis University Press, 2012), 308–309.

18. "Looking Back on the 1956 Season," Cejwin Newsletter, box 21, folder 17: Newsletters, 1956–1967, Schoolman Family Collection, AJHS; "Tisha B'Av," Camp Morasha 1966 Season Directors Report and Evaluation, "DCS Camp Morasha 1963–1966," Yeshiva University Archives; "Camp Hadas: Tisha B'Av," 1962, box 23, folder 25, Schoolman Family Papers; "Songbook of the Cejwin Camps," 1963, box 24, folder 11, Schoolman Family Papers, 1889–1994; Mistaken Identity: A Tisha Be'Ab Play," 1961, box 23, folder 25, Schoolman Family Papers, 1889–1994.

19. Eli Weber, "Games for Summer Camps," "Tisha B'Av," American Zionist Youth Foundation, n.d., box 3, Special Topics—Nearprint, AJA.

20. Ibid.

21. "Tisha B'Av," File: DD15310, Habonim Labor Zionist Youth in New York.

22. "Tisha B'Av Guide," n.d., box 10, folder 5, Records of the National Ramah Commission, JTSA.

23. Donald Splansky, "Creating a Prayer Experience in Reform Movement Camps and Beyond," in *A Place of Our Own: The Rise of Reform Jewish Camping: Essays Honoring the*

*Fiftieth Anniversary of Olin-Sang-Ruby Union Institute*, ed. Gary Phillip Zola (Tuscaloosa: University of Alabama Press, 2006), 160.

24. "Evening Program," 1964, box 6, Olin-Sang-Ruby Union Institute, AJA.

25. Splansky, "Creating a Prayer Experience," 160.

26. "Tisha B'Av Materials," 1951, box 10, folder 5, Records of the National Ramah Commission.

27. "Evening Program," 1964.

28. Leibush Lehrer, "Camp Boiberik: The Growth of an Idea" (37) 1959, YIVO Library.

29. See "Suggested Materials for Ghetto Memorials," published by the Workmen's Circle, box 4, folder 5, Camp Hemshekh Collection, YIVO Archives, YIVO Institute for Jewish Research, New York.

30. Lehrer, "Camp Boiberik," 37.

31. Ibid.

32. "Letter to Mr. Shaftel from Lion Rosenthal," 1962, Camp Boiberik in Camp Hemshekh Collection, RG 1468, box 4, YIVO Archives.

33. "Kinderring" in Camp Hemshekh Collection, box 5, n.d..

34. In a phone interview on June 10, 2017, Daniel Libeskind informed me that he designed the mosaic first, and then the campers who participated in his arts programming collectively placed the tiles in the appropriate places. "That is my first memorial—I've become so into memorials to the Holocaust—but this was my first," he added.

35. See Margie Newman, "Resistance: Camp Hemshekh and a Survivor's Daughter," *Jewish Currents* (March 2009), http://jewishcurrents.org/old-site/resistance/.

36. Ibid.

37. "Ghetto Nights Ceremony Scripts," 1960 and 1970s various, box 4, "Ghetto Nights" folder Camp Hemshekh Collection, YIVO.

38. Sore-Rukhl Schaechter, "Gedenk Der Umglik," 1968, Camp Hemshekh Collection, box 4, folder 5.

39. Melissa Biren, "Ghetto Night," in *The Hemshekh Weekly*, n.d., box 4, "Ghetto Nights," Camp Hemshekh Collection,

40. "Survival," Tisha B'Av Materials, SAFI Camp Boiberik Collection, folder 321, YIVO Archives.

41. Lehrer, "Camp Boiberik," 37.

42. Daniel Isaacman, "Jewish Education in Camping," *American Jewish Year Book* 67 (1966): 245–252.

43. Newman, "Resistance."

44. Splansky, "Creating a Prayer Experience," 160.

45. Lehrer, "Camp Boiberik," 37.

## Chapter Five

1. "Guide to the Records of Camp Massad," n.d., 1944–2015 [bulk 1949–1990]," 2013, Finding Aid at the American Jewish Historical Society, New York.

2. Sarah Bunin Benor, Jonathan Krasner, and Sharon Avni, *Hebrew Infusion: Language and Community at American Jewish Summer Camps* (New Brunswick, NJ: Rutgers University Press, 2020), 22.

3. In his book *Geshikhte fun der Yiddisher Shprakh* [History of the Yiddish language] (New York: YIVO Institute for Jewish Research, 1973), Max Weinreich included a section titled "inerlekhe tsvey-shprakhikeyt," essentially a Yiddish term for "diglossia," in which he described Ashkenazi Jews in Europe as diglossic. As linguist Yankl-Peretz Blum explained to me, Dovid Katz, in his book *Words on Fire: The Unfinished Story of Yiddish* (New York: Basic Books, 2007), "upped this to triglossia," including Aramaic as a third language (rather than discounting Aramaic or combining Hebrew and Aramaic into a single unit). For more on diglossia, see Joshua A. Fishman, *The Rise and Fall of the Ethnic Revival: Perspectives on Language and Ethnicity* (Berlin: De Gruyter Mouton, 1985), 39.

4. "Introduction: Hebrew Camps—Their Role and Place," translated from Hebrew, n.d., Camp Massad Collection, box 2, folder 7, American Jewish Historical Society (AJHS), New York.

5. Joshua Fishman, *Language and Nationalism: Two Integrative Essays* (Rowley, MA: Newbury House, 1973), 40. See also Benedict Anderson, *Imagined Communities: Reflections on the Origin and Spread of Nationalism*, rev. ed. (Brooklyn: Verso, 2016), 71.

6. Kenneth B. Moss, "Bringing Culture to the Nation: Hebraism, Yiddishism, and the Dilemmas of Jewish Cultural Formation in Russia and Ukraine, 1917–1919," *Jewish History* 22 (2008): 269, 263.

7. Ibid., 270.

8. See Benjamin Harshav, "Flowers Have No Names: The Revival of Hebrew as a Living Language after Two Thousand Years Was No Miracle," *Natural History* 118, no. 1 (February 2009): 24–29.

9. See Immanuel Etkes, "Haskalah," in *YIVO Encyclopedia of Jews in Eastern Europe* (2010), http://www.yivoencyclopedia.org/article.aspx/Haskalah.

10. Nokhem Shtif, "Essays on Yiddishism," trans. Maurice Wolfthal, *In geveb* (October 2015).

11. Mendele Mocher Sforim, "My Soul Desired Yiddish" (1862), in *The Jew in the Modern World: A Documentary History*, ed. Paul R. Mendes-Flohr and Jehuda Reinharz (New York: Oxford University Press, 1980), 404.

12. "Czernowitz Conference of the Yiddish Language (1908)," in *The Jew in the Modern World: A Documentary History*, ed. Paul R. Mendes-Flohr and Jehuda Reinharz (New York: Oxford University Press, 1980), 424–435.

13. On the subject of Hebraism and Hebrew revival, see Harshav, "Flowers Have No Names," and Benjamin Harshav, *Language in Time of Revolution* (Berkeley: University of California Press, 1993).

14. See Tudor Parfitt, "Ahad Ha-Am's Role in the Revival and Development of Hebrew," in *At the Crossroads: Essays on Ahad Ha-am*, ed. Jacque Kornberg (New York: State University of New York Press, 1983), 12–27.

15. For more, see Liora R. Halperin, *Babel in Zion: Jews, Nationalism, and Language Diversity in Palestine, 1920–1948* (New Haven, CT: Yale University Press, 2014).

16. See Daniel Blatman, "Bund," *YIVO Encyclopedia of Jews in Eastern Europe, 2010,* http://www.yivoencyclopedia.org/article.aspx/Bund.

17. "The Bund: Decisions on the Nationality Question (1899, 1901, 1905, 1910)," in *The Jew in the Modern World,* ed. Paul R. Mendes-Flohr and Jehuda Reinharz (New York: Oxford University Press, 1980), 421; "Frayland-lige," in *YIVO Encyclopedia of Jews in Eastern Europe,* https://yivoencyclopedia.org/article.aspx/Frayland-lige. For more on the territorialist movement, see Gur Alroey, *Zionism without Zion: The Jewish Territorial Organization and Its Conflict with the Zionist Organization* (Detroit: Wayne State University Press, 2016).

18. Hasia R. Diner, *The Jews of the United States, 1654 to 2000* (Berkeley: University of California Press, 2004), 88–89.

19. See Susan Tamasi and Lamont Antieau, *Language and Linguistic Diversity in the US: An Introduction* (New York: Routledge, 2014), 248.

20. See Fradle Freidenreich, *Passionate Pioneers: The Story of Yiddish Secular Education in North America, 1910–1960* (Teaneck, NJ: Holmes & Meier, 2010).

21. Chaim Zhitlowsky, "Our Future in America" (1915), in *The Jew in the Modern World,* ed. Paul R. Mendes-Flohr and Jehuda Reinharz (New York: Oxford University Press, 1980), 491.

22. Ibid., 241–242, 243.

23. For more on Yiddish and broader language politics in the Yishuv and the early years of the state, see Yael Chaver, "Outcasts Within: Zionist Yiddish Literature in Pre-State Palestine," *Jewish Social Studies* 7, no. 2 (2001): 39–66, and Halperin, *Babel in Zion.*

24. Diner, *Jews of the United States,* 243. See also Jonathan Sarna, *American Judaism: A History* (New Haven, CT: Yale University Press, 2004), 282.

25. For the subjects of Yiddish, humor, and nostalgia, see "Absolut Tchotchke," in Jeffrey Shandler, *Adventures in Yiddishland: Postvernacular Language and Culture* (Berkeley: University of California Press, 2008).

26. Mark A. Raider, *The Emergence of American Zionism* (New York: NYU Press, 1998), 8.

27. Alan Mintz, "The Erosion of the Tarbut Ivrit Ideology in America and the Consequences for the Teaching of Hebrew in the University," *Shofar* 9, no. 3 (1991): 52.

28. Ibid., 52–53.

29. For more on Hebrew in American Jewish summer camps, including deep dives into the history of Ramah and Massad Camps, see "Part 1: Past" in Benor et al., *Hebrew Infusion.*

30. "RE: Camp Ramah Formal Education," October 1971, box 2, folder 21, Records of the National Ramah Commission, Jewish Theological Seminary Archives (JTSA), New York.

31. Morris Freedman, "Camp Ramah: Where Hebrew Is the Key: A Full Jewish Education for a Full Jewish Life," *Commentary* (May 1955), https://www.commentarymagazine

.com/articles/camp-ramah-where-hebrew-is-the-key-a-full-jewish-education-for-a-full
-jewish-life/.

32. "Hebrew Usage Report," National Ramah Commission, "Camp Ramah Records 1951–1989," 1962, box 28, folder 15, JTSA.

33. Freedman, "Camp Ramah."

34. "Introduction to the Junior Training Program," box 8, Directors Files A: Wisconsin, Records of the National Ramah Commission.

35. "A Report of the Group Life of Aidah Aleph at Camp Ramah in Wisconsin," 1953, box 27, folder 23, Records of the National Ramah Commission.

36. Freedman, "Camp Ramah: Where Hebrew Is the Key."

37. "Introduction to the Junior Training Program," 1966, box 8, Directors Files A: Wisconsin, Records of the National Ramah Commission.

38. Neal Launder, "Essay Submitted to Mr. Haubrich, General Course in Curriculum Development," January 31,1966, box 8, Records of the National Ramah Commission.

39. "B'Yad HaLashon Advertisement," n.d., 1970s, box 2, folder 9, Records of the National Ramah Commission.

40. "Camp Ramah in the Poconos—B'Yad HaLashon," Steve Listfield, 1970, box 2, folder 5, Records of the National Ramah Commission.

41. "Cryptic Remarks," Joseph Lukinsky, 1970, box 2, folder 23, Records of the National Ramah Commission, JTSA.

42. Walter Ackerman, "A World Apart: Hebrew Teachers Colleges and Hebrew-Speaking Camps," in *Hebrew in America: Perspectives and Prospects*, ed. Alan L. Mintz (Detroit: Wayne State University Press, 1993), 118.

43. "HaMishbar," 1964, box 29, folder 12, Records of the National Ramah Commission.

44. "The Kallah Hebrew Immersion Program," n.d., box 8, folder 37, Records of the National Ramah Commission.

45. Ibid.

46. "Hebrew in Camp," box 8, folder 4, "Miscellaneous Papers," Records of the National Ramah Commission.

47. Shuly Rubin Schwartz, "Camp Ramah: The Early Years, 1947–1952," *Conservative Judaism* 40 (Fall 1987): 17, 22.

48. "Campaign to Improve Hebrew at Camp Massad," 1957, Camp Massad Records, box 3, folder 2, American Jewish Historical Society (AJHS), New York.

49. See the oral history with Lawrence Kobrin in *Massad Reminiscences*, vol. 3, ed. R. Shulsinger-Shear Yashuv (Jerusalem: Massad Alumni Organization and the Institute for Contemporary Jewry, 1996–2006), 26.

50. Author interview with Ira Spodek, February 2015, Camp Massad alumnus from 1962 to 1974, former camper and head counselor.

51. Leibush Lehrer, "Camp Boiberik: The Growth of an Idea," 2, 1959, YIVO Library, YIVO Institute for Jewish Research, New York.

52. Ibid.

53. Ibid., 69.

54. See "Jewish Hour Notebook" by Molly, 1951, box 5, folder 176, Sholem Aleichem Folk Institute Camp Boiberik Collection 1923–1978, YIVO.

55. Ibid.

56. Lehrer, "Camp Boiberik," 69.

57. Author interview with Marsha Kreizelman Singer, November 9, 2020.

58. Lehrer, "Camp Boiberik," 72.

59. "Camp Newsletter to Parents—Letter from Perry Millbauer," 1972, box 7, folder 315, SAFI Camp Boiberik Collection, YIVO.

60. "Letter to Rita Schwartz," 1972, box 7, folder 355, SAFI Camp Boiberik Collection.

61. Lehrer, "Camp Boiberik," 29.

62. This transition is apparent in Leibush Lehrer, "The Objectives of Camp Boiberik," 1962 pamphlet, YIVO Library.

63. "Educational Program," 1966, box 3, Camp Hemshekh Collection, YIVO.

64. Author interview with George Rothe, November 22, 2016.

65. Ibid.

66. Zory Lermer, "Etlekhe Bamerkungn," 1965, box 3, folder "Correspondence," Hemshekh Collection, YIVO.

67. Author interview with Rothe.

68. Sam Kazman, "Making It," 1973, box 1, folder 7, Camp Hemshekh Collection.

69. Sharon Cohn, "Me and Yiddish Culture," box 10, Camp Hemshekh Collection.

70. "Shavuos Play," 1967, box 4, Camp Hemshekh Collection.

71. Sam Kazman, "The Yiddish Pill" 1973, box 16—Duplicates, Camp Hemshekh Collection.

72. "RE: Camp Ramah Formal Education," October 26, 1971, box 2, folder "Formal Education, 1970–1972," Camp Ramah Records 1951–1989, JTSA.

73. "Letter to parents of Boiberik" from Camp Hemshekh, December 26, 1979, box 3, folder "Correspondence and Daily Activities," Camp Hemshekh Collection.

74. Author interview with Frank (pseudonym), November 8, 2020.

75. Sarah Bunin Benor, Jonathan Krasner, and Sharon Avni, "Survey of Hebrew at North American Jewish Summer Camps" (Waltham, MA: Jack, Joseph and Morton Mandel Center for Studies in Jewish Education, Brandeis University, 2016), 26.

## Chapter Six

1. "Some Freedom," 1967, box 13, Swig Camp Institute, American Jewish Archives (AJA).

2. For more on empathic inference, see William Ickes, ed., *Empathic Accuracy* (New York: Guilford Press, 1997).

3. Mona Gleason, "Avoiding the Agency Trap: Caveats for Historians of Children, Youth, and Education," *History of Education* 45, no. 4 (July 3, 2016): 452.

4. For more on youth and political activism in the 1960s, see Rebecca de Schweinitz, *If*

*We Could Change the World: Young People and America's Long Struggle for Racial Equality* (Chapel Hill: University of North Carolina Press, 2011), 5.

5. Leslie Paris, *Children's Nature: The Rise of the American Summer Camp* (New York: New York University Press, 2008), 245.

6. John L. Rury, *Education and Social Change: Contours in the History of American Schooling* (New York: Routledge, 2009), 156–165. For more on age relations in twentieth-century America, see Stephen Lassonde, "Age and Authority: Adult-Child Relations during the Twentieth Century in the United States," *Journal of the History of Childhood and Youth* 1, no. 1 (March 19, 2008): 95–105.

7. Randall R. Tillery, "Touring Arcadia: Elements of Discursive Simulation and Cultural Struggle at a Children's Summer Camp," *Cultural Anthropology* 7, no. 3 (1992): 377.

8. Xandra Ellin, "Encountering 'The Bubble' at Summer Camp," *JMORE* (blog), March 2, 2017, https://jmoreliving.com/2017/03/02/encountering-the-bubble/.

9. For references explaining Jewish camps as cult-like, see Lauren Waterman, "The Cult of the Jewish Summer Camp," *Town and Country*, July 26, 2017, https://www .townandcountrymag.com/leisure/arts-and-culture/a10352572/jewish-summer-camp/; Steven Davidson, "What It's Like to Be That Jew Who Didn't Do Summer Camp," *Forward*, July 10, 2017, https://forward.com/schmooze/376667/what-its-like-to-be-that-jew -who-didnt-do-summer-camp/; Ellin, "Encountering 'The Bubble' at Summer Camp."

10. Gleason, "Avoiding the Agency Trap," 448.

11. Paris, *Children's Nature*, 232.

12. Ibid., 234.

13. Ibid., 229–230.

14. John Dewey, *Democracy and Education: An Introduction to the Philosophy of Education* (New York: Macmillan, 1916), 99; Paris, *Children's Nature*, 237.

15. Paris, *Children's Nature*, 226–227.

16. Paul Mishler, *Raising Reds: The Young Pioneers, Radical Summer Camps, and Communist Political Culture in the United States* (New York: Columbia University Press, 1999), 56.

17. Paris, *Children's Nature*, 243. See Joshua Lieberman, *Creative Camping: A Coeducational Experiment in Personality Development and Social Living, Being the Record of Six Summers of the National Experimental Camp of Pioneer Youth of America* (New York: Association Press, 1931).

18. Paris, *Children's Nature*, 230. For more on group work, see Louis H. Blumenthal, *Group Work in Camping* (New York: Association Press, 1937).

19. Bernard Sterling Mason, *Democracy in the Summer Camp* (Washington, DC: US Government Printing Office, 1941). See also H. J. Boorman, H. S. Dimock, H. D. Edgren, R. E. Johns, and R. Sorensen, *Camping in a Democracy* (New York: Assoication Press, 1941), 1–2.

20. Mason, *Democracy in the Summer Camp*, 14, 15, 18.

21. See Elbert Fretwell, *Extra-curricular Activities in Secondary Schools* (Boston: Hough-

ton Mifflin, 1931), and Elbert Fretwell, "Delinquents Lack a Job to Do," *Clearing House* 18, no. 6 (1944).

22. Author interview with Judith Rosenbaum, former Kinderland camper, November 16, 2020.

23. Paris, *Children's Nature*, 12.

24. Ibid., 108–110.

25. Shuly Rubin Schwartz, "Camp Ramah: The Early Years, 1947–1952," *Conservative Judaism* 40 (Fall 1987): 101. See also Michael Brown, "It's Off to Camp We Go: Ramah, LTF, and the Seminary in the Finkelstein Era," in *Tradition Renewed: A History of the Jewish Theological Seminary*, ed. Jack Wertheimer (New York: Jewish Theological Seminary of America, 1997). See also "The Three Pillars of Ramah: Then and Now," in *Ramah at 60: Impact and Innovation,* ed. Mitchell Cohen, 93–104 (New York: National Ramah Commission, 2010).

26. Walter I. Ackerman, "Camp and School—Year-Round Education," *Jewish Education* 36, no. 2 (January 1, 1966): 94.

27. Solomon H. Green, "Serving the Jewish Teenager in the Camp," in *"Strengthening the Jewish Experiences of Children at Camp": Proceedings of the National Conference on Jewish Camping*, January 5–8, 1969, Hebrew Union College Library (HUC), Cincinnati.

28. Ibid.

29. "The Educational Principles of Camp Hemshekh," 1962, box 5, "Miscellaneous," Camp Hemshekh Collection, YIVO Institute for Jewish Research, New York.

30. "Bury the Old Hemshekh," *Di Hemshekh Vokh*, August 4, 1968, vol. 10, no. 5, Di Hemshekh Vokh, YIVO.

31. Green, "Serving the Jewish Teenager in the Camp."

32. Marshall Sklare, "The Greening of Judaism," *Commentary* 58, no. 6 (December 1, 1974): 51.

33. Author interview with Sarah (pseudonym), November 10, 2020.

34. "Imposed Leader," 1967, Camp Ramah, box 8, folder 1, "Miscellaneous Papers 1967–1994," MS-839, Louis Newman Papers, 1936–2006, AJA. See also "Machaneh Avodah in Ramah," n.d., box 9, folder 16, Ramah JTSA, box 9, folder 16, and "Machaneh Avodah," Records of the National Ramah Commission, 1951–1989, RG-28, Jewish Theological Seminary Archives (JTSA).

35. "Imposed Leader."

36. Janet Aviad, "Subculture or Counterculture: Camp Ramah," in *Studies in Jewish Education*, vol. 3, ed. Janet Aviad (Jerusalem: Magnes Press, 1988), 222.

37. Sklare, "Greening of Judaism."

38. Ibid.

39. "Don't Come Back," Camp Ramah in the Poconos, box 10, folder 15, National Ramah Commission Collection, New York.

40. Morris Freedman, "Camp Ramah: Where Hebrew Is the Key: A Full Jewish Education for a Full Jewish Life," *Commentary* (May 1955), https://www.commentarymagazine

.com/articles/camp-ramah-where-hebrew-is-the-key-a-full-jewish-education-for-a-full
-jewish-life/.

41. Sklare, "Greening of Judaism."

42. See "An Outline of Projections for the Compilation of a Course of Study for Ramah Camps," Alvin Mars, box 2, folder 8, Records of the National Ramah Commission; "1971 Season Information for Campers and Parents," 1971, box 8, Directors Files A: Wisconsin, Records of the National Ramah Commission; "Cryptic Remarks," Joseph Lukinsky, box 2, folder 8, "Educational Conference 1965–1966," Records of the National Ramah Commission, 1951–1989, RG-28.

43. Interview with Ethan (pseudonym), Ramah alumnus, November 10, 2020.

44. Sklare, "The Greening of Judaism."

45. Ackerman, "Camp and School," 94.

46. Author interview with Susan Jacobs Schaer, Tel Yehudah alumna, November 8, 2020.

47. "Director's Report," Tel Yehudah, 1948, gifted to me by Jamie Maxner, staff member at Camp Tel Yehudah, 12/7/12.

48. "Camp Kvutzah—Bulletin for Parents," n.d., DD1–53141, Central Zionist Archives, Jerusalem.

49. Avraham Schenker, "Zionist Camping in America," *Jewish Education* 36, no. 2 (January 1, 1966): 104–105.

50. Author interview with Dan Kaufman, November 12, 2020.

51. Author interview with Judith Lerner, November 11, 2020.

52. Author interview with Efrat Levy, November 15, 2020.

53. Author interview with Lerner.

54. Author interview with Kaufman.

55. Author interview with Katherine Lavine, November 9, 2020.

## Chapter Seven

1. Author interview with Josh (pseudonym), November 11, 2020.

2. Author interview with Sarah (pseudonym), November 18, 2020.

3. Author interview with Freydl (pseudonym), November 15, 2020.

4. See, for instance "Staff Manuals," box 4, Camp Kinderland Record, Tamiment Archives, New York University. At Kinderland, for instance, a folder of staff training materials recommended that counselors read several books with titles that suggested relevance to the issues, including *On Becoming a Woman* and *The Facts of Love and Life for Teenagers*, by Evelyn Duvall; *The Stork Didn't Bring You*, by Lois Pemberton; and *Pre-Adolescents: What Makes Them Tick*, by Fritz Redl.

5. Author interview with Sarah (pseudonym).

6. Multiple former campers mentioned such relationships, either between themselves and staff or between peers and staff, but have asked for anonymity.

7. See Adrienne Rich, "Compulsory Heterosexuality and Lesbian Existence," *Signs: Journal of Women in Culture and Society* 5, no. 4 (July 1, 1980): 631–660.

8. See Randall R. Tillery, "Touring Arcadia: Elements of Discursive Simulation and Cultural Struggle at a Children's Summer Camp," *Cultural Anthropology* 7, no. 3 (1992).

9. David Biale, *Eros and the Jews: From Biblical Israel to Contemporary America* (Berkeley: University of California Press, 1997), 176.

10. Leslie Paris, *Children's Nature: The Rise of the American Summer Camp* (New York: New York University Press, 2008), 48.

11. Ibid., 150–162.

12. Ibid., 161, 151.

13. Ibid., 151.

14. Abigail Van Slyck, *A Manufactured Wilderness: Summer Camps and the Shaping of American Youth, 1890–1960* (Minneapolis: University of Minnesota Press, 2006), xxvi.

15. Author interview with Jacob Sorensen, May 21, 2020.

16. Ivan Reitman et al., *Meatballs* (Dunning/Link/Reitman Productions, Mount Royal Productions, Haliburton Films, 1979); Trevor Eyster, Danny Cooksey, and Michael Bower, *Salute Your Shorts*, (Propaganda Films, 1991); Richard Shepard, "Hannah's Diary," *Girls*, May 6, 2012; Joseph Ruben et al., *Gorp* (Jeffrey Konvitz Productions, 1980); Andres Salaff, "The New Me," *Big Mouth*, December 4, 2020.

17. Author interview with Marsha Kreitzelman Singer, November 9, 2020.

18. Ibid.

19. Ibid.

20. Author interview with Judith Lerner, November 11, 2020.

21. Author interview with Susan Jacobs Schaer, November 8, 2020

22. Author interview with Judith Rosenbaum, November 16, 2020.

23. Author interview with Schaer.

24. Author interview with Steven (pseudonym), November 16, 2020.

25. Author interview with Dan Kaufman, November 12, 2020.

26. Author interview with Steven.

27. Beth L. Bailey, *From Front Porch to Back Seat: Courtship in Twentieth-Century America* (Baltimore: Johns Hopkins University Press, 1989), 80.

28. Alan Petigny, "Illegitimacy, Postwar Psychology, and the Reperiodization of the Sexual Revolution," *Journal of Social History* 38, no. 1 (2004): 63.

29. "Iton Moshava," 1970, 2968–60.1, Hashomer Hatzair Archives, Yad Yaari, Haifa.

30. See as examples "Iton Moshava," 1970, 2968–60.1, Hashomer Hatzair Archives, and Yad Yaari "Dear Trish" in *Di Hemshekh Vokh*, n.d., 1960s, 015009254, YIVO Institute for Jewish Research, New York.

31. "In Campers Words," Kol Yehudah 1961, Hadassah Archives, American Jewish Historical Society (AJHS), New York; RG 8: Young Judaea Records in the Hadassah Archives, 1911–2006, folder 18: TY newsletters 1960–1966, AJHS.

32. Ibid.

33. "Cejwin Dustpan," 1959–1960, box 21, folder 21: "CIT INK," P716, Schoolman Family Papers, 1889–1994, AJHS.

34. Author interview with Schaer.

35. See Matthew Ides, "'Dare to Free Yourself": The Red Tide, Feminism, and High School Activism in the Early 1970s," *Journal of the History of Childhood and Youth* 7, no. 2 (2014): 301.

36. Bailey, *From Front Porch to Back Seat*, 78.

37. "Proposals: Forum," July 24, 1965, box 3, folder "Correspondence and Daily Activities," Hemshekh Collection, YIVO.

38. "Letter to Staff," 1950s various, SAFI Camp Boiberik, YIVO.

39. "Counselor Guide," box 346, SAFI Camp Boiberik.

40. "Director's Report," Camp Ramah in Wisconsin, box 10, folder 22—"Director's Report 1961–62," Records of the National Ramah Commission, Jewish Theological Seminary Archives (JTSA), New York.

41. Bernard Gold, "General Report on Chalutzim: Director's Report 1961–62," Camp Ramah in Wisconsin, box 10, folder 22, Records of the National Ramah Commission.

42. "General Report on Adah Bet: Director's Report 1961–62," Camp Ramah in Wisconsin, box 10, folder 22.

43. Ibid.

44. "Boy-Girl Relationships—Div. III," M. Elovitz. Camp Ramah in Wisconsin, box 10, folder 22—"Director's Report 1961–62."

45. Ibid.

46. Ibid.

47. Federation of Jewish Philanthropies of New York Commission on Synagogue Relations, *Intermarriage and the Future of the American Jew: Proceedings of a Conference* (New York: 1965), Monographs (HQ1031.F27), AJHS.

48. Van Slyck, *A Manufactured Wilderness*, xxvi.

49. Lila Corwin Berman. "Sociology, Jews, and Intermarriage in Twentieth-Century America," *Jewish Social Studies*, new series, 14, no. 2 (2008): 32–60, http://www.jstor.org/stable/40207015, 311.

50. Lila Corwin Berman, Kate Rosenblatt, and Ronit Y. Stahl, "Continuity Crisis: The History and Sexual Politics of an American Jewish Communal Project," *American Jewish History* 104, no. 2 (2020): 170–171.

51. Milton Himmelfarb, "The Vanishing Jews," *Commentary* 36 (September 1963): 249–251.

52. Berman, "Sociology, Jews, and Intermarriage," 47. See Erich Rosenthal, "Studies of Jewish Intermarriage in the United States," *American Jewish Year Book* 64 (1963): 3–53.

53. Rosenthal, "Studies of Jewish Intermarriage," 53.

54. Marshall Sklare, "Intermarriage and the Jewish Future," *Commentary* 37(4): 1964, 46.

55. Thomas B. Morgan, "The Vanishing American Jew," *Look*, May 5, 1964.

56. Louis Shub, "The United States, Israel, and the Middle East," in *American Jewish Year Book*, ed. Morris Fine and Milton Himmelfarb 66 (1965): 299–312.

57. Lila Corwin Berman, *Speaking of Jews: Rabbis, Intellectuals, and the Creation of an American Public Identity* (Berkeley: University of California Press, 2009), 166.

58. Solomon H. Green, "Serving the Jewish Teenager in the Camp," in *Strengthening the Jewish Experiences of Children at Camp: Proceedings of the National Conference on Jewish Camping*, January 5–8, 1969, Hebrew Union College Library (HUC), Cincinnati.

59. "The Zionsville Platforms," 1972, box 5, folder 5, Myron S. Goldman Camp Institute Collection, American Jewish Archives (AJA), Cincinnati.

60. See "Junior Counselors Course: Judaism and Modern Problems," box 1, folder 1, Swig Camp Institute, 1964–1967, MC671, AJA; "Bnai Brith: A Study Guide to the BBYO," Judaism Pamphlet Series, "What Is a Jew? The Sabbath; Ritual in Jewish Life; Judaism and Ethics. Judaism and Christianity; A Jewish View of Love and Marriage," prepared by Harold Bleich, 1962, 000065398, AJHS.

61. "An Explanation of My Interests and Problems," Shalom Wall, National Ramah Commission, 1951–1989; n.d., box 5 "Mador—Program Material, 1965–1972," JTSA.

62. The term "hidden curriculum" was coined by Philip Jackson. See Philip W. Jackson, *Life in Classrooms*, rev. ed. (New York: Teachers College Press, 1990).

63. "Marriage Certificate," 1960s, box 3, folder "Correspondence and Daily Activities," Camp Hemshekh Collection, YIVO; "Marriage Contracts," box 4, folder 10: Activities, Myron S. Goldman Camp Institute; "CORE Carnival," Camp Kinderland Collection, Tam 439, folder 4: Cultural Program—General—1955–1969, Tamiment Archives, New York University.

64. Author interview with Josh (pseudonym).

65. Author interview with Debbie Lewis, November 15, 2020.

66. See Steven M. Cohen, "Building Jewish Identity: A Study of Young Judaea Alumni," Fall 1998, conducted for Hadassah, Hebrew University of Jerusalem and Alana Ganapol (Marketquest, Mohegan Lake, NY).

67. For more on Jewish masculinity and gender, see Daniel Boyarin, *Unheroic Conduct: The Rise of Heterosexuality and the Invention of the Jewish Man* (Berkeley: University of California Press, 1997).

68. Biale, *Eros and the Jews*, 177.

69. Ofer Nordheimer Nur, *Eros and Tragedy: Jewish Male Fantasies and the Masculine Revolution of Zionism* (Brighton, MA: Academic Studies Press, 2014), 50.

70. Ibid., 61.

71. Ibid., 140.

72. Ibid., xii.

73. Author interview with Efrat Levy, Hashomer Hatzair alumus, November 18, 2020.

74. Ibid.

75. Nordheimer Nur, *Eros and Tragedy*, 57.

76. Biale, *Eros and the Jews*, 283–284.

77. Interview with Levy.

78. Biale, *Eros and the Jews*, 177.

79. Author interview with Katherine Lavine, Habonim alumna, November 9, 2020.

80. Author interview with Kaufman.

81. Biale, *Eros and the Jews*, 177.

82. Ruth Katz and Yochanan Peres, "The Sociology of the Family in Israel: An Outline of Its Development from the 1950s to the 1980s," *European Sociological Review* 2, no. 2 (1986): 149. See also E. Kafkafi, "The Psycho-Intellectual Aspect of Gender Inequality in Israel's Labor Movement," *Israel Studies,* 4, no. 1 (1999):188–189.

83. Author interview with Naomi Segal, November 15, 2020.

84. Author interview with Lerner.

85. Author interview with Segal.

86. Ibid.

## Chapter Eight

1. Hasia R. Diner, *The Jews of the United States, 1654 to 2000* (Berkeley: University of California Press, 2004), 320, 306.

2. Sylvia Fishman, "Exploring Policy Implications of Data on Jewish Education from the 1990 National Jewish Population Survey and other Recent Studies," Brandeis University, March 1, 1994, 2. See Sidney Goldstein, "Profile of American Jewry: Insights from the 1990 National Jewish Population Survey," *American Jewish Year Book* (New York: American Jewish Committee, 1992), 77–173, and Barry Kosmin et. al., "Highlights of the CJF National Jewish Population Survey" (Council of Jewish Federations, 1991).

3. Jack Wertheimer, *A People Divided: Judaism in Contemporary America* (New York: Basic Books, 1993), xiii.

4. For more on the decline of Tarbut Ivrit, see Alan Mintz, "The Erosion of the Tarbut Ivrit Ideology in America and the Consequences for the Teaching of Hebrew in the University," *Shofar* 9, no. 3 (1991).

5. For more on this late 1960s transition, see Ari Y. Kelman and Janet Bordelon, "The Political Economy of Day Schools." *American Jewish History* 102, no. 1 (2018): 59–84.

6. Daniel Isaacman, "Jewish Education in Camping," *American Jewish Year Book* 67 (1966): 252.

7. Ibid., 251.

8. Correspondence from Arthur Brodkin to Emanuel Berlatsky, July 1, 1965, National Jewish Welfare Board Conference on Jewish Communal Camps I-337, National Jewish Welfare Board, Records, Subgroup II: Jewish Community Centers, Series A: Program Services, American Jewish Historical Society (AJHS).

9. Miriam R. Ephraim, "A Look at Jewish Communal Camping," *Journal of Jewish Education* (January 1, 1966): 97–102.

10. "The Future of Jewish Camping—What Directions and Emphases," Edward Robbins, Director of Camp Sabra, National Conference for Jewish Camping 1972, 16–18, BM 135.N2.85, Hebrew Union College Library (HUC), Cincinnati.

11. Jack Wertheimer," Jewish Education in the United States: Recent Trends and Issues,"

*American Jewish Year Book*, American Jewish Committee (AJC), Jewish Publication Society (JPS), January 1, 1999: 28. For more on Jewish education in this period, see Jonathan D. Sarna, "American Jewish Education in Historical Perspective," *Journal of Jewish Education* 64, no. 1–2 (Winter–Spring 1998): 8–21.

12. Jonathan Krasner, "American Jewry at Risk: 'A Time to Act' and the Prioritization of Jewish Education," *Contemporary Jewry* 36 (2016): 97.

13. Leslie Paris, *Children's Nature: The Rise of the American Summer Camp* (New York: New York University Press, 2008), 48.

14. Jacob Sorensen, "A Theological Playground: Christian Summer Camp in Theological Perspective" (PhD diss., Luther Seminary, (2016), 50.

15. Asher Melzer, "Camping in the 1980's: A Decade of Change," *Journal of Jewish Communal Service,* June 1, 1981, 354–536.

16. Ibid.

17. Fred Massarik, "A Report on Intermarriage," in National Jewish Population Survey 1971, Council of Jewish Federations, New York, 1.

18. Barry Chazan and Steven M. Cohen, "Assessing the Jewish Educational Effectiveness of the Jewish Community Centers—The 1994 Survey," Task Force on Reinforcing the Effectiveness of Jewish Education in JCCs, COMJEE II, October 1994, 1.

19. Krasner, "American Jewry at Risk," 85.

20. Ibid., 113.

21. Ibid., 114.

22. Lila Corwin Berman, Kate Rosenblatt, and Ronit Y. Stahl. "Continuity Crisis: The History and Sexual Politics of an American Jewish Communal Project," *American Jewish History* 104, no. 2 (2020): 181.

23. Chazan and Cohen, "Assessing the Jewish Educational Effectiveness," ii–iii.

24. Krasner, "American Jewry at Risk," 116.

25. "Jewish Summer Camp Vital to Maintaining Commitment," *Jewish Telegraphic Agency* (blog), June 29, 1998, https://www.jta.org/1998/06/29/lifestyle/focus-on-family -jewish-summer-camp-vital-to-maintaining-commitment-2. For more information on youth movement–commissioned studies, see "The Faithful Youth of NCSY: Quantifying the Dream," *Jewish Action*, March 25, 1999, https://jewishaction.com/religion/education /faithful-youth-ncsy-quantifying-drea/; "Between the Bunk Beds: Learning Jewish at Camp," *Jewish Telegraphic Agency* (blog), July 2, 1998, https://www.jta.org/1998/07/02/ lifestyle/focus-on-issues-between-the-bunk-beds-learning-jewish-at-camp.

26. Krasner, "American Jewry at Risk," 115.

27. For background on the concept of emerging adulthood, see Jeffrey Jensen Arnett, *Emerging Adulthood: The Winding Road from the Late Teens through the Twenties* (New York: Oxford University Press, 2004).

28. For more information about Trybal Gatherings, see Rachel Levin, "Jewish Summer Camp with Campfires, Crafts and No Lights Out," *New York Times*, September 18, 2019, https://www.nytimes.com/2019/09/18/travel/jewish-adult-summer-camp.html.

29. Sylvia Fishman and Steven M. Cohen. "Family, Engagement, and Jewish Continuity Among American Jews," Jerusalem, Jewish People Policy Institute (2017), 15.

30. Amir Blumenfeld, "The Truth about Jewish Summer Camps," MyJewishLearning .com, June 10, 2010, https://www.youtube.com/watch?v=rg9qLcjdU9s.

31. Emily Shire, "Hooking Up at Summer Camp," *Forward*, August 17, 2012, https://for ward.com/articles/161165/hooking-up-at-summer-camp/.

32. Jordan Dale, "Growing Jewishly at Surprise Lake Camp," in *Contact: The Journal of Jewish Life Network* 4, no. 3 (Summer 2002): 14–15.

33. "Ramah Marriages," Reshet Ramah, accessed April 15, 2021, http://reshetramah.org /marriages/; "Gazebo Zugot," accessed April 15, 2021, https://www.ramahpoconos.org/ giving/gazebo-zugot/; Elicia Brown, "JDate Partnership to Help Ramah Alumni Kindle Campfires of Romance," *Jewish Telegraphic Agency* (blog), January 16, 2015, https://www.jta .org/2015/01/16/lifestyle/camp-2015-jdate-partnership-to-help-ramah-alumni-kindle-camp fires-of-romance.

34. Liz Rose, "How Many More Orgasms Will Be Had for Zionism?," *Mondoweiss*, January 27, 2016, https://mondoweiss.net/2016/01/how-many-more-orgasms-will-be-had-for -zionism/.

35. See Penny Harvey, "'It's Camp': Summer Camp Culture, the Renegotiation of Social Norms and Regulation of Gender and Sexuality" (master's thesis, Georgia State University, 2017). On #MeToo issues in Jewish youth programs, see Elicia Brown. "Amid Increased Scrutiny and Risk, Camps Grapple with Teen Sexuality," Jewish Telegraphic Agency, September 26, 2017, accessed June 28, 2018, https://www.jta.org/2015/01/16/life-religion/amid-increased -scrutiny-and-risk-camps-grapple-with-teen-sexuality; Shire, "Hooking Up at Summer Camp."

36. Joshua Nathan-Kazis, "Are Jewish Youth Groups' Hookup Games about Romance—or Power?" *Forward*, December 18, 2017, https://forward.com/news/national/390 008/are-jewish-youth-groups-hookup-games-about-romance-or-power/.

37. Ibid.

38. Mitch Cohen, "'We Need More Ramah': An Interview with Professor Steven M. Cohen," Camp Ramah, December 10, 2015, https://www.campramah.org/news//we-need -more-ramah-an-interview-with-professor-steven-m-cohen. This link has since been removed from the Ramah website.

39. Sharon Otterman and Hannah Dreyfus, "Michael Steinhardt, a Leader in Jewish Philanthropy, Is Accused of a Pattern of Sexual Harassment," *New York Times*, March 21, 2019, https://www.nytimes.com/2019/03/21/nyregion/michael-steinhardt-sexual-harassment.html.

40. See Ben Sales, "The Fall of a Top Sociologist Could Change the Field of Counting Jews," *Jewish Telegraphic Agency*, August 3, 2018, https://www.jta.org/2018/08/03/united -states/the-fall-of-a-top-sociologist-could-change-the-field-of-counting-jews.

41. Kate Rosenblatt, Lila Corwin Berman, and Ronit Stahl, "How Jewish Academia Created a #MeToo Disaster," *Forward*, July 18, 2018, https://forward.com/opinion/406240 /how-jewish-academia-created-a-metoo-disaster/; See also "How a #MeToo Scandal Proved What We Already Know: 'Jewish Continuity' Is Sexist," *Forward*, accessed April 15, 2021,

https://forward.com/opinion/406271/how-a-metoo-scandal-proved-what-we-already-know-jewish-continuity-is-sexist/.

42. See Leonard Saxe, "Misogyny and the Continuity Crisis: Is Social Science Research Responsible?" *American Jewish History* 104, no. 2 (2020): 221–228; Hannah Dreyfus, "Steven M. Cohen, Shunned by Academy after Harassment Allegations, Makes Stealthy Comeback—and Provokes Uproar," *Forward*, March 23, 2021, accessed April 15, 2021, https://forward.com/news/466437/steven-cohen-shunned-after-harassment-accusations-trying-to-make-a-stealth/.

43. Madeline Canfield, Lila Goldstein, Ellanora Lerner, Lilah Peck, Maddy Pollack, and Dahlia Soussan, edited by Rebecca Long, "For Continuity's Sake? Addressing Hookup Culture in Jewish Youth Groups," *EJewish Philanthropy*, September 3, 2020, https://ejewishphilanthropy.com/for-continuitys-sake-addressing-hookup-culture-in-jewish-youth-groups/; see also JTEC on Instagram, https://www.instagram.com/jews4empoweredconsent/.

44. Josefin Dolsten, "How Jewish Summer Camps Are Talking about Consent in the Age of #MeToo," *Jewish Telegraphic Agency* (blog), March 18, 2019, https://www.jta.org/2019/03/18/lifestyle/how-jewish-summer-camps-are-talking-about-consent-in-the-age-of-metoo; The #MeToo Movement Goes to Summer Camp," *Jewish Telegraphic Agency* (blog), May 10, 2018, https://www.jta.org/2018/05/10/opinion/metoo-movement-goes-summer-camp.

45. See "Culture Shift," Moving Traditions, accessed February 2022, https://www.movingtraditions.org/cultureshift/.

46. Dolsten, "How Jewish Summer Camps Are Talking about Consent."

47. Sarah Miriam Seltzer, "When Jewish Transgender Teens Come Out, Many Leave Camp Behind," *Haaretz*, accessed March 15, 2021, https://www.haaretz.com/jewish/summer-camps-a-minefield-for-transgenders-1.5314224; Johanna Ginsberg, "Summer Camps Open Bunks to Transgender Jews," *Times of Israel*, accessed March 15, 2021, http://www.timesofisrael.com/summer-camps-open-bunks-to-transgender-jews/.

48. Julie Zauzmer, "A Camp Tries to Reinvent the Hebrew Language, so Transgender Kids Can Fit In," *Washington Post*, accessed March 15, 2021, https://www.washingtonpost.com/news/acts-of-faith/wp/2016/08/11/what-does-a-gender-neutral-kid-call-themself-in-a-gendered-language/.

49. Zev Eleff, *Living from Convention to Convention: A History of the NCSY, 1954–1980* (Jersey City, NJ: Ktav Pub. & Distributors, 2009), 4.

50. Etan Diamond, *And I Will Dwell in Their Midst: Orthodox Jews in Suburbia* (Chapel Hill: University of North Carolina Press, 2000), 14; Diner, *Jews of the United States*, 311.

51. Diamond, *And I Will Dwell in Their Midst*, 14–15.

52. For more on these transitions in Modern Orthodoxy, see Samuel C. Heilman and Steven M. Cohen, *Cosmopolitans and Parochials: Modern Orthodox Jews in America* (Chicago: University of Chicago Press, 1989).

53. "Agudath Israel Reports Record Summer Camp Enrollment," *Jewish Telegraphic*

*Agency* (blog), August 15, 1972, https://www.jta.org/1972/08/15/archive/agudath-israel-re ports-record-summer-camp-enrollment.

54. "History," *Camp Moshava I.O.* (blog), accessed March 16, 2021, https://moshava.org /history/.

55. "Our History: Sephardic Adventure Camp Seattle," accessed March 16, 2021, http:// www.sephardicadventurecamp.org/about/our-history/.

56. Diamond, *And I Will Dwell in Their Midst*, 137–138.

57. Some examples include Camp Nageela, Camp Chaya, and the Morristown Yeshiva Summer Program. See Joseph Berger, "At a Camp for Hasidic Boys, Studying Faith Is Their Daily Exercise," *New York Times*, August 6, 2014, https://www.nytimes.com/2014/08/07/ nyregion/at-new-york-camp-hasidic-boys-study-and-shun-sports.html.

58. Diner, *Jews of the United States*, 321.

59. The development of this trend can be seen in increasing press attention. See "Israeli Boy Scouts to Act As Young Judea Summer Camp Aides," *Jewish Telegraphic Agency* (blog), April 8, 1965, https://www.jta.org/1965/04/08/archive/israeli-boy-scouts-to-act-as-young -judea-summer-camp-aides; "250 Israeli Educators Start Work in Summer Camps," *Jewish Telegraphic Agency* (blog), July 9, 1970, https://www.jta.org/1970/07/09/archive/250-israeli -educators-start-work-in-summer-camps.

60. "About Israeli Scout Friendship Caravan—Boy Scouts of America, Dan Beard Coun- cil," accessed April 15, 2021, https://danbeard.org/about-israeli-scout-friendship-caravan/.

61. Nahum Guttman, "American Campers in Israel," *Journal of Jewish Education* (Jan- uary 1, 1966): 109.

62. Annette Hochstein, "'The Israel Experience': Educational Programs in Israel" (Jewish Education Committee, June 1986), 5.

63. Diner, *Jews of the United States*, 327–328.

64. Author interview with Dan Kaufman, Habonim alumus, November 12, 2020.

65. Author interview with Efrat Levy, Hashomer Hatzair alumus, November 18, 2020.

66. Aiden Pink, "What Jewish Camps Taught Your Kids about Israel This Summer," *Forward*, August 5, 2018, https://forward.com/news/406175/what-jewish-camps-taught -your-kids-about-israel-this-summer/.

67. Peter Beinart, "The Failure of the American Jewish Establishment," *New York Review of Books*, June 10, 2010, https://www.nybooks.com/articles/2010/06/10/failure-american -jewish-establishment/. On distancing, see also Esther Farber, Idon Natazon, "Are Young American Jews in the Diaspora Distancing from Israel?" colloquium report, American Jewish Committee, March 18, 2011.

68. Bethamie Horowitz, *Defining Israel Education*, iCenter, March 1, 2012, 2.

69. Ibid., 17.

70. Gil Troy, "Needed: Real Zionist Education, Not Hasbara," *Jewish Education News*, Coalition for the Advancement of Jewish Education, January 1, 2003, 1.

71. Peter Beinart, "The Failure of the American Jewish Establishment," *New York*

*Review of Books 57*, no. 10 (June 2020), https://www.nybooks.com/articles/2010/06/10/failure-american-jewish-establishment/.

72. Lisa Grant, "A Vision for Israel Education," paper presented at the Network for Research in Jewish Education Conference, June 2, 2008, 3–4, https://www.bjpa.org/search-results/publication/20968.

73. For information about the campaign, see "You Never Told Me," IfNotNow, accessed December 11, 2019, https://younevertoldme.org.

74. For information about Ramah's conflicts with IfNotNow, see Dina Kraft, "'Anti-Semitic, Anti-Zionist': Palestinian Issue Shakes up Most Famous U.S. Jewish Camp—U.S. News—Haaretz.Com," *Haaretz*, June 15, 2018, https://www.haaretz.com/us-news/.premium-camp-ramah-ifnotnow-1.6177197.

75. Ben Sales, "These Jewish Camp Counselors Want to Teach Their Kids about the Occupation," *Jewish Telegraphic Agency* (blog), May 31, 2018, https://www.jta.org/2018/05/31/united-states/jewish-camp-counselors-want-teach-kids-occupation.

76. "Seth Rogen Says Israel 'Doesn't Make Sense' and Opens Up about His Jewish Identity in Interview with Marc Maron," *Jewish Telegraphic Agency* (blog), July 29, 2020, https://www.jta.org/2020/07/28/culture/seth-rogen-says-israel-doesnt-make-sense-and-opens-up-about-his-jewish-identity-in-interview-with-marc-maron. See "Episode 1143: Seth Rogen," *WTF with Marc Maron,* July 27, 2020, http://www.wtfpod.com/podcast/episode-1143-seth-rogen.

77. For information on new Beit Midrash groups, see "Bringing a Piece of Jerusalem to North America: The Pardes Community Beit Midrash Initiative," *Times of Israel*, April 28, 2017.

78. Most notably, independent Jewish journals such as PRTCLS and the renewed *Jewish Currents*, as well as podcasts such as *Treyf, Unsettled*, and *Judaism Unbound*.

79. Jacob Plitman, "On an Emerging Diasporism," *Jewish Currents*, April 16, 2018, https://jewishcurrents.org/on-an-emerging-diasporism/.

80. See Jonathan Katz, "Learning to Undo 'Ashkenormativity,'" *Forward*, November 5, 2014, https://forward.com/opinion/208473/learning-to-undo-ashkenormativity/; Melanie Katz-Kantrowitz, *The Colors of Jews: Racial Politics and Radical Diasporism* (Bloomington: Indiana University Press, 2007).

81. On Yiddish youth activism, see Sandra Fox, "'The Passionate Few': Youth and Yiddishism in American Jewish Culture, 1964 to Present," *Jewish Social Studies* 26, no. 3 (2021): 1–34; Joshua Friedman, "Serious Jews: Cultural Intimacy and the Politics of Yiddish," *Cultural Dynamics* 32, no. 2 (August 2020).

82. Judi Ruderon, "Let There Be Camp—Please!" *Forward*, April 19, 2020, https://forward.com/opinion/444100/jewish-summer-camp-coronavirus/.

## Conclusion

1. "On Jewish Identity by Rabbi Greenberg, Remarks at a Shlichim Conference," in *Iggeret Lashaliach*, no. 22 (March–April 1972), 34, American Zionist Youth Foundation, file

2942: "Advertisements, Letters, and Educational Materials: 1963–1971," Hashomer Hatzair in North America Collection, Givat Haviva Archives, Israel.

2. Ibid.

3. Walter I. Ackerman, "Camp and School—Year-Round Education," *Jewish Education* 36, no. 2 (1966): 92.

4. For examples of articles and message boards that address summer camps as a "Jewish thing," see Jeri Zeder, "How Summer Camp Became a Jewish Thing," *My Jewish Learning* (blog), accessed March 3, 2022, https://www.myjewishlearning.com/article/summer-camps/; "TMF: What's Up with Jews and Summer Camps? / Jewish and Foolish," accessed March 3, 2022, https://boards.fool.com/whats-up-with-jews-and-summer-camps-22803234.aspx?sort=whole; Lauren Waterman, "The Cult of the Jewish Summer Camp," *Town and Country*, July 26, 2017, https://www.townandcountrymag.com/leisure/arts-and-culture/a10352572/jewish-summer-camp/; Chanan Tigay, "How Jewish Is Camp?," *Jewish Telegraphic Agency*, June 22, 2006, https://www.jta.org/2006/06/22/lifestyle/how-jewish-is-camp.

5. See "Find a Camp," American Camping Association, accessed March 3, 2022, https://find.acacamps.org/.

6. Tigay, "How Jewish Is Camp?"

7. Jacob Sorenson, "The Fundamental Characteristics and Unique Outcomes of Christian Summer Camp Experiences," *Journal of Youth Development* 13, no. 1–2 (April 20, 2018): 183.

8. Jacob Plitman, "On an Emerging Diasporism," *Jewish Currents*, April 16, 2018, https://jewishcurrents.org/on-an-emerging-diasporism/.

9. The Pew Research Center is a useful source for such information. In 2020, it found that in regard to Israel, "More broadly, young U.S. Jews are less emotionally attached to Israel than older ones. As of 2020, half of Jewish adults under age 30 describe themselves as very or somewhat emotionally attached to Israel (48%), compared with two-thirds of Jews ages 65 and older. . . . In addition, among Jews ages 50 and older, 51% say that caring about Israel is essential to what being Jewish means to them, and an additional 37% say it is important but not essential; just 10% say that caring about Israel is not important to them. By contrast, among Jewish adults under 30, one-third say that caring about Israel is essential (35%), and one-quarter (27%) say it's *not* important to what being Jewish means to them." In regard to intermarriage, it found that "among Jewish respondents who got married in the past decade, six-in-ten say they have a non-Jewish spouse. . . . By contrast, just 18% of Jews who got married before 1980 have a non-Jewish spouse." Jewish Americans in 2020," *Pew Research Center's Religion & Public Life Project* (blog), May 11, 2021, https://www.pewforum.org/2021/05/11/jewish-americans-in-2020/.

10. Many mainstream Jewish organizations and programs demonstrate a move in these directions. For example, in Young Judaea, a former national board explained that YJ's value of social action has already eclipsed Zionism in the Zionist youth movement's programming, in large part due to the discomfort members feel about the movement's Zionism

("What Does It Mean to Be a Zionist Youth Movement in 2022?," Mel Reisfield Day of Learning, Zoom Panel, March 2022). The national organization Repair the World, which "mobilizes Jews and their communities to take action to pursue a just world, igniting a life-long commitment to service," holds youth programs centered on these goals, which place exclusive emphasis on local American issues. A Jewish camp, Eden Village, founded in 2006, has gained popularity in part for its lack of emphasis on conventional Jewish concerns like Israel and intermarriage and the greater values it places on sustainability, Jewish diversity, and a "culture of kindness." See "Our Values," Eden Village Camp, accessed March 2022, https://edenvillagecamp.org/our-values/.

# Index

## STANFORD STUDIES IN JEWISH HISTORY AND CULTURE

David Biale and Sarah Abrevaya Stein, Editors

This series features novel approaches to examining the Jewish past in the form of innovative work that brings the field into productive dialogue with the newest scholarly concepts and methods. Open to a range of disciplinary and interdisciplinary approaches, from history to cultural studies, this series publishes exceptional scholarship balanced by an accessible tone, illustrating histories of difference and addressing issues of current urgency. Books in this list push the boundaries of Jewish Studies and speak compellingly to a wide audience of scholars and students.

David Biale, *Jewish Culture Between Canon and Heresy*
2023

Alan Verskin, *Diary of a Black Jewish Messiah: The Sixteenth-Century Journey of David Reubeni through Africa, the Middle East, and Europe*
2023

Aomar Boum, Illustrated by Nadjib Berber, *Undesirables: A Holocaust Journey to North Africa*
2023

Dina Porat, *Nakam: The Holocaust Survivors Who Sought Full-Scale Revenge*
2023

Christian Bailey, *German Jews in Love: A History*
2023

Matthias B. Lehmann, *The Baron: Maurice de Hirsch and the Jewish Nineteenth Century*
2022

Liora R. Halperin, *The Oldest Guard: Forging the Zionist Settler Past*
2021

Samuel J. Spinner, *Jewish Primitivism*
2021

Sonia Gollance, *It Could Lead to Dancing: Mixed-Sex Dancing and Jewish Modernity*
2021

Julia Elsky, *Writing Occupation: Jewish Émigré Voices in Wartime France*
2020

Alma Rachel Heckman, *The Sultan's Communists:
Moroccan Jews and the Politics of Belonging*
2020

Golan Y. Moskowitz, *Queer Jewish Sendak: A Wild Visionary in Context*
2020

Devi Mays, *Forging Ties, Forging Passports: Migration and the Modern Sephardi Diaspora*
2020

Clémence Boulouque, *Another Modernity: Elia Benamozegh's Jewish Universalism*
2020

Dalia Kandiyoti, *The Converso's Return: Conversion and Sephardi
History in Contemporary Literature and Culture*
2020

Natan M. Meir, *Stepchildren of the Shtetl: The Destitute, Disabled,
and Mad of Jewish Eastern Europe, 1800-1939*
2020

Marc Volovici, *German as a Jewish Problem: The Language Politics of Jewish Nationalism*
2020

Dina Danon, *The Jews of Ottoman Izmir: A Modern History*
2019

Omri Asscher, *Reading Israel, Reading America: The Politics of Translation Between Jews*
2019

Yael Zerubavel, *Desert in the Promised Land*
2018

Sunny S. Yudkoff, *Tubercular Capital: Illness and the Conditions of Modern Jewish Writing*
2018

Sarah Wobick-Segev, *Homes Away from Home: Jewish Belonging
in Twentieth-Century Paris, Berlin, and St. Petersburg*
2018

Eddy Portnoy, *Bad Rabbi: And Other Strange but True Stories from the Yiddish Press*
2017


For a complete listing of titles in this series, visit the
Stanford University Press website, www.sup.org.